DIPLOMACY
OF ASYMMETRY

Diplomacy
of Asymmetry

KOREAN-
AMERICAN
RELATIONS
TO 1910

JONGSUK CHAY

University of
Hawaii Press

Honolulu

90 91 92 93 94 95   5 4 3 2 1

A Study from the Center for Korean Studies, University of Hawaii

The Center for Korean Studies was established in 1972 to coordinate and develop the resources for the study of Korea at the University of Hawaii. Its goals are to enhance faculty quality and performance in Korean studies; to develop comprehensive, balanced academic programs; to stimulate research and publications; and to coordinate the resources of the University of Hawaii with those of other institutions, organizations, and individual scholars engaged in the study of Korea. Reflecting the diversity of the academic disciplines represented by affiliated members of the University faculty, the Center seeks especially to promote interdisciplinary and intercultural studies.

Library of Congress Cataloging-in-Publication Data

Chay, Jongsuk.
    Diplomacy of asymmetry : Korean-American relations to 1910 / Jongsuk Chay.
        p.   cm.
    Includes bibliographical references (p.)
    ISBN 0-8248-1236-0 (alk. paper)
    1. United States—Relations—Korea.   2. Korea—Relations— United States.   3. United States—Foreign relations—1865-1921. I. Title.
E183.8.K6C44   1990
327.730519—dc20   89-20502
                                                                 CIP

University of Hawaii Press books are printed on acid-free paper and meet the guidelines for permanence and durability of the Council on Library Resources.

TO MY WIFE JUNGPIL

AND OUR CHILDREN—

MARY, SYLVIA, AND CHRIS

CONTENTS

PREFACE

Almost half a century has elapsed since the publication of *God, Mammon and the Japanese: Dr. Horace N. Allen and Korean-American Relations, 1884–1905* toward the end of World War II. This book, written by Fred Harvey Harrington, among the most capable of American diplomatic historians, is a fascinating account of Korean-American relations. As its subtitle indicates, however, the book is limited, covering only partially the relations between the two nations before 1910 and centering on one man, Horace N. Allen (admittedly the most important individual for the topic). Yet the book is the most comprehensive to date, and the ensuing neglect is difficult to explain. It would seem natural that the task of filling this gap with a full-scale, formal Korean-American diplomatic history would fall to one of the Korean students who came to the United States in the post–Korean War years. Accordingly, I gave myself the assignment when I began work in the 1960s.

I am grateful to the University of Michigan Graduate School Research Fund, the Earhart Foundation, and the Piedmont Foundation for financial support that helped defray research expenses. I am also thankful for the many services provided by staff members at numerous libraries and archives—the Michigan Historical Collections, the Houghton Library, Harvard University, the New York Public Library, the National Archives, the Library of Congress, and the Hoover Institution Library.

Among the many to whom I owe so much for this book, two of my mentors come first. Alexander DeConde, under whose direction I began my graduate study in history, has been generous with much-needed encouragement. Bradford Perkins, under whose very capable supervision I finished an early version of three chapters, taught me the skill and discipline I needed to complete this book. I am also grateful to two fine scholars, the leading specialists on the early period of Korean-American relations, Fred Harvey Harrington and Robert R. Swartout, Jr.; both read the entire manuscript and gave me numerous suggestions for its improvement. The encouragement and support I received from Dr. Harrington for this book and other related works have been invaluable. Michael H. Hunt, Raymond A. Esthus, and Akira Iriye kindly read the chapters relating to China and Japan, and their advice was helpful. I am also grateful to two people without whose assistance this book could not have been completed at this time. Robert W. Brown, one of my colleagues at Pembroke State University, generously gave his time and read the entire manuscript with care. And to Shirley Deese, who more than once typed the whole manuscript, I extend thanks for her dedication. I am also grateful to Patricia Crosby, University of Hawaii Press editor, for her thoughtful and efficient management of the publication process. Above all, I am thankful to my wife Jungpil and our three children—Mary, Sylvia, and Chris—for their understanding and support, which enabled me to bring this long-overdue work to completion.

INTRODUCTION

The relationship between Korea and the United States was "peculiar" from the beginning.[1] The United States opened the door of the "hermit kingdom" in 1882 without sufficient national need and interests. Once the door was open, however, Korea expected the distant American republic to help save the old kingdom from the two contending neighboring powers, Japan and China. Since American interests remained small, the United States provided little assistance during the nearly three decades of the formal relationship. This basic asymmetry—the imbalance between Korean expectations and American interests—caused an estrangement between the two nations. Then, when the Korean door was closed during the first decade of the twentieth century, the United States was the first nation to pack up and depart the country.

What were the causes of the "peculiar relationship"? Seven factors help to explain the nature of the American-Korean relationship during the first three decades: economics, missionary interests, security interests, historical circumstances, geographical considerations, cultural influences, and the image factor.

Of the seven factors under consideration, the first three—economics, missionary interests, and security interests—belong to the category of national interests. In view of the American need for additional overseas markets and the Korean need for Western goods and technology, the economic factor—which may be divided into trade and investment—was significant.

One of the problems in examining the trade between Korea and the United States is statistical. There are at least three sets of figures, and obtaining accurate figures from these three sets is not an easy task. Only by using fully all available figures together with careful inferences and judgments can one hope to reach an approximation of the real figures. The U.S. Treasury Department and Department of Commerce and Labor provide us with a set of figures based on goods going through American ports. The first year for which the Treasury Department publication listed trade with Korea was 1892, when a total trade of $608 was recorded; in the following year it dropped to $79; it then gradually rose to $1,566,158 in 1908—the maximum for the period covered by this study.[2] The Department of State provides another set of figures, based on American products coming into Korea through the treaty ports as reported by the consular officials in Korea. According to these figures, the trade between the United States and Korea was a little over $200,000 in 1895 and about $800,000 in 1901.[3] Overall, the State Department's figures are at least three times as large as those provided by Treasury and Commerce and Labor. The figures supplied by the Japanese Residency General for the years between 1905 and 1910 are very similar to those of the State Department: the Japanese source listed $4,239,635 for 1908.[4] Certainly, both sets of figures are reliable, but the figures of the State Department and the Residency General can be said to be more inclusive and thus closer to the real amount of the trade.

But even these figures are undoubtedly lower than the actual amount of trade. According to the American Consul General Horace N. Allen, the figures he obtained for the State Department through interviews with American merchants were far lower than the actual amount of trade because large amounts of American goods were brought into nontreaty ports by Japanese and Chinese merchants and there was no way to do more than estimate the amount. Allen estimated that only a third of all foreign goods came through the treaty ports; however, because the situation varied from year to year, it is hard to generalize with confidence.[5] Nevertheless, based on all available information, an estimate of American-Korean trade can be made: between 1892, the first year of the Treasury Department's record, and 1908, the year of the maximum amount of trade for the period, trade ranged between $700 and a little over $4,500,000—certainly a large increase in sixteen years.

Such measurements are always relative, and when examined against the total trade of the United States and its trade with the East Asian countries, the figures become more significant. Total American foreign trade in the critical interwar years, 1894–1904, was between $1,539,508,130 and $2,636,074,737; the Korean average annual share of this trade was 0.01 percent—certainly a small figure. The Korean share of American exports was only slightly larger, 0.02 percent, still a negligible amount. A comparison between American trade with Korea and American trade with two other East Asian countries—China and Japan—shows an equally important picture: during the fiscal year 1904/1905, American trade with Korea was $1,014,086; trade with China was $81,331,913; trade with Japan was $103,541,086.[6] These figures represent shares of 0.35 percent, 43.95 percent, and 55.70 percent, respectively, of American–East Asian trade. Thus despite the great rate of increase in American trade with

Korea, the trade volume was low, and trade interest therefore negligible.

When we turn to American capital investment in Korea, however, the picture is somewhat different. The Korean share of American investment in East Asia in the peak year (1908) during the period under this study was at least $6,000,000 out of $23,000,000, or 27 percent.[7] The largest and most important American enterprise in Korea in 1909 was the Unsan gold mine, one of twenty-two mines owned by Americans. This mine, which was situated near the Yalu River, was a $5,000,000 enterprise, the most profitable owned by a Western businessman in the Far East. James R. Morse, head of the American Trading Company and one of the earliest American businessmen active in Korea, obtained the concession in the spring of 1896, and the Americans operated it profitably throughout the period. In 1908 the mine employed 75 Americans and Europeans and 2,960 Asians, including 2,300 Koreans. By the summer of 1908, the total production of the mine from the beginning of the operation reached over $10,000,000. The net profit in the year was about $750,000, and at the end of the year the owners estimated about 1,000,000 tons of ore in sight.[8] The Unsan gold mine was the best American mining enterprise in Korea, but it was not the only successful one; on the eve of the Japanese take-over of Korea, the Americans dominated the mining.

Another area of American business enterprise in Korea was railway building. In the spring of 1896, Allen obtained the concession of the Seoul-Chemulpo railway for Morse. This twenty-five-mile-long railway, the first to be constructed in Korea, was built by American businessmen and engineers with materials brought from the United States. (Morse sold it to the Japanese in 1898 because of financial difficulties.)[9] There were several other American enterprises; most of them were initiated in the latter part of the 1890s. Henry Collbran and Harry Bostwick, two prominent American businessmen in Korea, built an electric plant, the largest of its kind in the Far East, to supply electricity to Seoul.[10] They also built an extensive electric railway between Seoul and its environs.[11] Other American businessmen obtained concessions for the Seoul waterworks and sugar industry, and they operated the largest rice mill in the country.[12] In addition to these large undertakings, they had many minor business enterprises in Korea. Allen proudly wrote to William W. Rockhill in early 1898: "I am glad to say that all the considerable financial undertakings known in Korea are our own."[13] Three years later he seriously worried about the American monopoly of business in the peninsula, which he thought might cause trouble with other powers in Korea.[14] The $6 million American financial investment in Korea at the turn of the century seemed considerable to the Koreans, even if it did not seem so impressive to the Americans.

From the American viewpoint the 0.01 percent trade with Korea was no doubt negligible and insignificant. But from the Korean side, the picture appears quite different. Korean trade was small—between $6 million and $17 million during the interwar period.[15] While Korea's two neighbors took a majority of this small trade (the Japanese share in 1910 was 68.2 percent), the American share of Korean foreign trade was not a small one from the Korean viewpoint: it ran between 10 and 20 percent during the interwar years (it declined in later years, particularly after 1905). For certain consumer goods, especially kerosene, the United States was the only supplier. Machinery and other materials from the United States were necessary for the construction of railways, mills, electric plants, and other facilities that made an important contribution to the Korean economy and society as a whole.

American capital investment in Korea was even more significant in the eyes of the Koreans. The Americans were certainly the leaders in foreign enterprises in Korea: the Koreans saw that those who owned the most profitable gold mines in the country, those who constructed the first railway in the country, those who supplied electricity to the capital, and those who operated railways in Seoul were all Americans. It is not difficult to imagine the kind of image the Koreans must have formed of the magnitude of American business enterprise in Korea—an image of domination of business in Korea.

An important point regarding the economic factor in the American-Korean relationship is that the American share of Korean foreign trade and the American financial investment in Korea were relatively large and very significant, while the Korean share of American trade was extremely small, and there was no Korean investment in the United States. This asymmetry influenced the development of American relations throughout the whole period.

But even more important than the economic factor in the American-Korean relationship was the religious one, the missionary interests. American missionary work in Korea played an important role in the cultural dimension of the relationship. This role was not confined simply to the proselytizing, which was certainly important in the long run; it also had a role in "civilizing" the Koreans. In addition to their general influence, American missionaries and others in related fields such as education and medicine acted as an interest group, promoting such benefits among the Koreans. Even more important, some of them acted as agents of Korean diplomacy, as will be shown later.

For the missionaries, undoubtedly, proselytizing was the most important part of their work in Korea. The roots of American mission work were deep; soon after the beginning of official diplomatic transactions in 1883, the first American missionary, Horace N. Allen, the same man who served later as the secretary for the American legation and the minister for the American government, arrived in Korea. The missionaries arrived one after another from the United States, mostly from the Presbyterian and Methodist churches in the north and the south. The Korean government still took a negative attitude toward the mission work in the 1880s, and the missionaries were rather cautious in their evangelical work. They produced the first convert in Korea in 1886 and saw the establishment of the first church in the following year. The growth and degree of enthusiasm of the Koreans in accepting the new religion was unusual, and many who were involved directly in the work or knew it well thought that Korea was a "miracle" in the missionary field.[16] The Korean churches grew quickly in the 1890s when the missionary work was carried out openly, and the *Missionary Review of the World* recorded 5,000 members of the Korean churches in 1898.[17] The membership of the Korean Protestant churches reached 40,000 in 1905, and even greater increases came after that year; 113,499 adherents with 24,025 regular memberships were listed for 1908.[18]

As with the economic factor, a comparative investigation shows an interesting picture in the missionary field. According to the *Missionary Review of the World*, the United States in 1898 had a total of a little more than two million converts throughout the world.[19] The Korean share, therefore, was only 0.25 percent. If we rely on the figures given by E. E. Strong, secretary of the American Board of Protestant Missions, to the *Boston Transcript* in 1905, the United States had a total of 2,126,977 converts; Korea's 40,000 in the same year amounted to 1.9 percent, a great increase, but still a small share.[20] The Korean share of American missionaries, however, was larger: Korea had about 0.9 percent of the total number of missionaries of the United States in 1900.[21] If we compare this work with the works accomplished in two other countries in the Far East, American mission work in Korea shows clearly its success. American mission work started early in China and Japan, and China already had more than 30,000 Christians and Japan almost 20,000 in 1887, when Korea counted about twenty of them.[22] But the growth of mission work in Korea showed a startling speed: in 1898, there were 41,000 Protestants in Japan and 5,000 in Korea; seven years later, the numbers had risen to 50,000 in Japan and 41,000 in Korea[23]—a sevenfold increase in the latter, only a 22 percent increase in the former.

As in other parts of the world, the nonevangelical side of American missionary work in Korea was important, and it had a significant impact upon the political, social, and cultural aspects of the nation. One of the important areas for nonevangelical work was education. In 1886, American Methodist missionaries established Pai Chai School (for boys) and Ewha Girls' School, two of the most prominent missionary educational institutions in Korea. There were a total of 1,623 schools of all categories operated by American missionaries in Korea in 1910—about 93 percent of all missionary schools in Korea in that year—with a little more than 120,000 students.[24] These missionary schools amounted to a little more than one-third of the total number of schools in Korea.[25] These schools, which ranged from primary schools to colleges, not only introduced Western culture to the Koreans, but also produced young patriots who later played an important role in every field of Korean society. Many of the missionary schools were for girls, and the role played by the American missionaries in bringing about equality of the sexes in Korea was also significant.

Another area of nonevangelical work by the American missionaries in Korea was medicine. Allen, the first American missionary, was a medical missionary, and he laid the ground for future American missionary work on the peninsula. Allen and many other missionary doctors served in the governmental hospital, which was opened in 1885 with the support of the king; control of it was transferred to the missionaries ten years later.[26] Another important medical institution was Severance Hospital, now a part of Yonsei University. This hospital was established by the Methodists with funds given by Louis H. Severance of Ohio, and it became the only general hospital for the capital, a city with a population of 300,000.[27] Beside these two major hospitals, there were smaller ones in major Korean cities; in 1910, a total of six hospitals and nine dispensaries were under the control of American missionaries.[28] The missionary doctors working at the hospitals also bore the burden of medical education for Korea.[29]

Publication was another important area of missionary activities. In addition to the translation and distribution of the Bible, the missionaries published several periodicals in English and Korean. *The Korean Repository*, one of the most important journals ever published in Korea, was edited and published by Methodist missionaries, who also published the *Christian News*, the *Methodist Chris-*

tian Advocate, and tracts, books, and leaflets through their own publishing house, Trilingual Press. They maintained a book store, later called the Methodist Book Corner, and wrote numerous books and articles on Korea and the Koreans for the English-speaking public.[30] Most of the materials were published for the Americans in Korea and at home, and they became an important source of information on Korea.

Thus as preachers, teachers, doctors, authors, and publishers, the American missionaries were very active and influential in Korea, and as Allen noted in 1903, they regarded Korea as their most successful missionary field.[31] Certainly their role as savers of souls was important; but even more important, from the perspective of this study, was the role they played in bringing Western culture to the Korean youths who later made very important contributions in politics, education, and many other areas. As agents of cultural transmission, the missionaries probably played the most important role of any group of Americans involved in Korean affairs.

The third important factor in the American-Korean relationship concerned American security interests in Asia. It is fair to say that the United States did not have much, if any, direct security interests in Asia before 1898, when it acquired the Philippine Islands after the Spanish-American War. Once it became an Asian power with a considerable stake in the power configurations of the region, policy makers, especially Theodore Roosevelt and his aides, began to be sensitive to the changing nature of the international system in the area, which was a balance-of-power system[32] in which Korea was not a full-fledged member and independent player, but a victim, a small power squeezed between the two great powers in the region—China and Japan. Russia, with a short common border with Korea, was involved in the system sometimes as a full-fledged player, sometimes as a balancer with a secondary interest.

Korea's independence depended upon the balance of power in the region, and American-Korean relations were also affected by it. From the 1880s to the end of the Sino-Japanese War, China and Japan competed over Korea; in this competition, Russia acted as a balancer. China had the upper hand, but because the Russians sided in most cases with Japan, the balance was successfully maintained until the Sino-Japanese War. When the war between China and Japan eliminated, at least temporarily, the former as a major power in the system in the fall of 1895, it looked as if the system was breaking down and a change taking place. But, rather fortunately for the maintenance of the system, Russian stepped in and, taking over the former position of China, sustained the system, at least for another decade. For the satisfactory functioning of the system, a balancer was desirable, but none of the Western powers, including the United States, had enough interest in playing that role in Korea, and the precarious decade ended with another war, the Russo-Japanese War. When the war eliminated one of the two players, the system faced its demise. Since Korean independence depended upon the maintenance of the balance-of-power system, the Koreans sought a new player to replace Russia as a counter to Japan—United States. But to the policy makers of the United States, the Russian menace was still formidable; they did not see any need for a nation to counter Japan. Thus, the international system in Korea was a very important factor in American-Korean relations.

The historical, geographical, cultural, and image factors seem to have been less important than the preceding three major factors, but they were still significant in American-Korean relations and cannot be neglected. As is the case in an individual life, the past is an important factor in national life. For both Americans and Koreans, and especially for the latter, the fact that the Americans opened the Korean door to the Western world in 1882 was very important and was remembered throughout the whole period under this study. If those Americans who were involved in dealing with the Koreans in one way or another in the past felt some sense of obligation toward the Koreans, it came mainly from this factor. For the Koreans this was even more important; they turned first to the Americans, who had sponsored their entrance into a new world, whenever they needed outside help.

Like other factors, the geographical factor played an interesting role in American-Korean relations. The two countries are separated by more than six thousand miles of ocean; under normal circumstances, this geographical distance would tend to lessen the chance of contact between them. And in one sense, this physical distance was a negative factor in the relationship: to the Americans, Korea was a distant and insignificant power; to the Koreans, the United States was a giant lying beyond an ocean. But distance often lends enchantment, and in this case it made the United States attractive to the Koreans. Combined with the good nature, wealth, strength, and nonimperialistic general outlook of the United States, its distance and location made the Koreans feel secure in associating with and relying on the Americans. Thus the same factor—great physical distance—had opposite effects on the two nations: the physical distance created a psychological distance for the Americans, but it attracted the Koreans even more to the United States.

The cultural dimension of international relations is a subject still to be explored; at this point it should be said that it is an extremely important factor in international relations, even though its weight varies from case to case in a real situation. In American-Korean relations, it seems that it was fairly important, and the importance came from two aspects: the differences in the nature of the two cultures to which the two nations belonged and the degree of advancement in certain areas of the cultures, particularly the material area. American culture was a product of Judeo-Christian and Greco-Roman heritages, with a highly rationalistic and materially oriented value system, while Korean culture was deeply rooted in the Confucian ideology, with a highly moralistic and humanistic value orientation. Admittedly, the two cultures shared certain common elements. The cultural differences, however, like differences in any other aspects of life, were more repelling than attracting in international relations. The degree of advancement of the two countries must also be considered. Not everyone would be convinced that American culture at the turn of the century was more advanced than Korean culture. Culture cannot be quantified, and unidimensional measurements of cultural advancement often raise more questions than one can answer. In this case, however, everyone would agree that the United States was becoming rapidly industrialized in the latter part of the nineteenth century and was definitely advanced in the material aspect of culture while Korea was still in a premodern stage based on agriculture. Here, the important point is that when these two aspects—the difference in the nature of the two cultures and the differences in the degree of advancement of the material side of the two cultures—are combined, they produced an interesting tendency in the two nations: the Koreans were more attracted to the modern American culture than the Americans were to the backward Korean culture, and this became an important factor in American-Korean relations.

The cultural factor had an effect upon almost every case of American-Korean diplomatic relations. One of the most prominent cases was the interpretation of the "good offices" clause in the first article of the 1882 treaty. As will be discussed later in detail, the two countries promised to help each other by offering their good offices whenever the other treaty power was in distress. The term had a meaning well established in Western international legal practice, and it had a precise meaning for the Americans. However, the Koreans, who must have soon learned the technical meaning of the term, took the term in only a quasi-legal sense and often read moral implications into it, equating the term with "assistance" or even "intervention." Throughout the whole period, but especially during the

Russo-Japanese War, the term became a key issue because of these two different views.

The last, but not the least significant, factor in the American-Korean relationship was the "image" factor. Sometimes expressed in such slightly different but similar terms as "perception," "opinion," or "attitude," "image" is now an almost essential part of all serious studies of the foreign policy-making process and histories of international relations. There are three related questions to be answered here regarding the image problem. First, was there a mutual image in the United States and Korea during the period covered by this study? Second, if there were images, what were their natures? Third, how did they affect the policies of each nation toward the other?

Kenneth E. Boulding, Gabriel A. Almond, James N. Rosenau, and others have provided a framework for examining the subject. In studying the foreign policy-making process, we must divide the public into two major categories: the mass public and the attentive public.[33] The mass public includes a large portion of the general public—75 to 90 percent—and is uninformed about and apathetic toward foreign policy issues, except for brief periods during a crisis when it becomes temporarily an attentive group. The attentive public is a small segment of the public—10 to 25 percent—well-educated and well-informed about foreign policy issues and willing to be involved in the foreign policy-making process. Both of these groups have images—not necessarily the same or even similar ones—of the foreign countries with which their government deals. Even though not explicitly pointed out by the scholars who undertake image studies, there is another group of people whose image of a foreign country is important in the foreign policy-making process—the policy makers. It is clear that policy makers have to have an image of or views on other powers in the foreign policy-making process and they have to translate those views into policies. A key assumption is that there is a linkage between the images of the policy makers and the images of the two other groups.

If we approach the problem from a utilitarian point of view, the third question, that of the linkage between the image and policy, should be taken up first; if there is no impact of the image upon policies, then there is no need to take up the subject. Logically, however, it seems that the question of whether or not images exist should come first. An important question to decide is at what point, or with what percentage of a particular group having an opinion on the subject, to declare that there is an image. Since there are no definite guidelines, we may posit that, when a substantial portion of the group—at least a majority—possesses views on a certain subject, an image exists. With regard to this preliminary consideration, if we first approach the American side of the image problem, we find the *New York Times Index, Poole's Index,* and the *Readers' Guide* available as crude indicators. Between 1866 and 1881, the *New York Times* published a total of 39 articles about Korea, an annual average of 2.4 articles; for the same period, *Poole's Index* listed only 9 articles, an average of not quite two articles a year.[34] Korea attracted a little more attention from American newspapers and magazines during the period between 1882 and 1893. The same New York paper published 129 articles, an annual average of nearly 11, while magazine publication saw a much greater increase—a total of 42 articles were listed by *Poole's Index,* for an annual average of 3.5 articles.[35] When the war between China and Japan came to Korea, the American mass media exploded on the subject: 235 articles were published in the *New York Times* during the first year and 195 articles in the following year.[36] *Poole's Index* listed 32 articles for the two war years.[37] As soon as the war was over, the exposure of Korea to the American public through the publication media returned to more normal levels, with an annual average of 23 articles in the *New York Times* during the eight interwar years and 7 magazine articles during the same period as indexed by *Poole's Index* and the *Readers' Guide.*[38] Then, another war came—this time between Russian and Japan—but the major battleground was in Manchuria, not Korea, and, although Korea drew more attention than it did in peacetime, it did not draw as much as during the previous war: 87 articles in the *New York Times* and 45 magazine articles as indexed by the *Readers' Guide.*[39] Between 1906 and 1910, the number of articles in the *New York Times* on Korea and the Koreans remained about the same as the preceding eight-year period (an annual average of 23 articles); the publication of magazine articles on the same topics maintained a steady increase, with an annual average of 14.5 articles.[40]

Of course, the *New York Times* was only one of the many newspapers in the United States, and *Poole's Index* and the *Readers' Guide* are far from being comprehensive, but it may be said that these figures at least indicate an American image of Korea and a uniformity and stability of data. What else do they tell us about the existence of an American image of Korea for the period covered? Was the American public able to formulate some kind of picture about Korea and the Koreans based on such media coverage? It may be said that a relatively small number of Americans—probably no more than a few hundred—paid some attention to the subject, and they belonged to the category of the attentive public or to an even smaller special interest group who read some of the magazine articles in addition to the newspaper articles. As far as the mass public was concerned, Korea did not exist except in the time of a crisis—such as the Sino-Japanese War—and it is difficult to say that an American public image of Korea in a general sense existed throughout the whole period through 1910.

If there is an indication that at least a small segment of the attentive public in the United States had some kind of image of Korea during the nearly half century between 1866 and 1910, what was the nature of that image, and did it change or remain stable throughout the years? A trend can be discerned through which the three components of the image—cognitive, affective, and evaluative—dominated the American image of Korea.[41] Probably this is not an exceptional case; it seems that the image matured through this process, which took place through three stages over the course of the three periods. The period of about three decades to 1894, the year of the outbreak of the Sino-Japanese War, forms the first period, and in it the cognitive aspect of the image was dominant: most of the magazine articles were factually oriented and gave some detailed information of the "land and people" type. Some of the best examples are the articles that appeared in *Galaxy* (1872), *Cosmopolitan* (1888–1889, 1890–1891), and the *National Geographic Magazine* (1890), all of which gave straightforward information about the people, government, life, and culture of the country—the most needed elements for image formation in this early stage.[42]

Then came the second period, 1894 to 1905—the twelve years that included two wars in the Far East—during which the affective element was added and played an important role. This added element came mainly from American feelings toward the Japanese and their view of the Japanese role in the two wars: a large number of Americans thought that the Japanese were the champions of Western civilization and were fighting against the Chinese, the leader and symbol of Oriental civilization, and the Russians, the leader and symbol of tyrannical power in the region, and they had affectionate feelings toward underdog Japan, which had been a good learner from the West. Korea was not only the target of Japanese aggression but was considered a part of the decadent Oriental civilization, and the Americans began to pick up a negative feeling toward it. Such well-known experts on Oriental culture as William E. Griffis, Arthur J. Brown, and James S. Gale wrote articles in *Outlook, Harper's Weekly,* and other important magazines pointing out the laziness of the Korean people, the filthiness of the countryside, the corrupt, autocratic government, and the hopeless future of the nation.[43] The author who was most eloquent and influential in painting the Korean picture at its darkest was George Kennan, the correspondent for *Outlook* during the Russo-Japanese War.[44]

When the war between Japan and Russia ended, the emotional fervor died down; and, when Japanese policies and actions in Korea began to show their ugly side, the American image of Korea went into the third stage, in which the evaluative dimension was added. Detailed and specialized factual information that was pro-Japanese and anti-Korean appeared repeatedly in the American magazines, especially in articles by such prominent authors as Itō Hirobumi and Ōkuma Shigenobu in addition to Kennan, Griffis, and Willard Straight.[45] But in 1906 and 1907, soon after the Japanese took control of Korea, some new authors began to notice the darker side of Japanese activities in Korea, and such magazines as *Outlook* and *Harper's Weekly*, which had devoted numerous pages to give a bright picture of what the Japanese were doing in Korea, began to use critical words about the Korean situation.[46] An even more remarkable phenomenon was that the very same authors who had been so optimistic about the Japanese for a long time, writers such as George Kennan and Arthur J. Brown, began to be skeptical about what the Japanese were doing in Korea.[47]

The general trend of the American image of Korea and the characteristics of the image in each of the three periods are certainly important; another equally or even more important point is that the image gradually deteriorated, with 1894 as the turning point. The combination of curiosity about a different culture and an increase in the amount of information about Korea must have increased the affective image. But because of the prevailing pro-Japanese feeling among Americans, the image of Korea gradually deteriorated between 1894 and 1905. As the more evaluative dimension became prominent, the deterioration must have slowed down during the last five-year period; but even at this point more sources for a bad image than for a good were available. If image has any meaning at all for policy making, the trend of deterioration must have considerable meaning.

The last, and the most important, question regarding image is its role in policy making. Unfortunately, this is the weakest link in the study of the foreign policy-making process; and it is still not clear how important image is in policy making. The idea that image plays a significant role in the foreign policy-making process is still a hypothesis, albeit an important one. As we have noted, policy makers have to have some kind of image, and it has to be formulated one way or another. Unless they create it by pure imagination, they have to get the material from somewhere, and that source must be one or a combination of the mass public image, the attentive public image, the views of their aides and friends, and their own sources of information. The linkage between the image and a policy is rarely found, except in exceptional cases; usually, we can only infer the image behind the policy. In this particular case, however, a linkage can be found between President Theodore Roosevelt's Korea policy and his images; even the sources of his images can be located. As we will see later, Roosevelt's view of Korea was clearly expressed in a statement he made in the spring of 1905; the two main sources of his image of Korea and the Koreans were his own very favorable feelings toward the Japanese and George Kennan's very unfavorable image of Korea.[48] With regard to other policy makers, it must be stated that the image of the small segment of the attentive public, or the same sources that led to the image formation of this group, must have been at least one of the sources of these policy makers' images.[49]

Because less material is available, less can be said about the development of the Korean image of America. It was, however, a similar development, spanning the same three stages and three periods. During the first period, which lasted from the mid-nineteenth century through 1881, little or no differentiation was made between the Americans and the Europeans, and the image of the United States was very unfavorable because of the imperialistic activities of the Westerners in China, Japan, and on the coast of Korea. Toward the end of this period, some Koreans began to learn about the United States, and the cognitive process at least got underway. A period of more learning and favorable image formation followed and lasted to the outbreak of the Russo-Japanese War in 1904; during this time the king and his family showed very warm feelings toward all Americans who came to Korea. Because of the benevolent outlook and activities of Commodore Shufeldt, who came to Korea to sign the treaty of 1882 and about whom the king heard much from the Chinese sources, especially from Li Hung-chang; the American representatives in Seoul, Lucius H. Foote and George C. Foulk; and the American advisers, missionaries, and educators, men like Homer B. Hulbert, the image of the king and his advisers toward the American was very favorable.[50] The image was somewhat tarnished during the last six years of this period, between 1897 and 1903, when Minister Allen in Seoul had a difficult time in dealing with the cool attitude of the Republican presidents and their assistants in Washington. This period was also the stage on which the cognitive and affective dimensions were prominent in the Korean image structure. The last five-and-a-half-year period began with a great disappointment for the Korean leaders when the American government turned its back on them and collaborated with the Japanese, who were trying to absorb the peninsula. It is not difficult to imagine that the Korean image of America, which had been overly favorable until this time, underwent a severe deterioration during this period. Thus, even though the periodization was not exactly the same, the development of the image each nation had of the other was more or less parallel. However, one very important point is that overall the Korean image of America was much more favorable than the American image of Korea, with the possible exception of the years prior to the treaty making. This difference was an important one for the whole period.

Both the issues of the existence of the image and its impact upon the policy-making process are simple and clear on the Korean side. Because Korea was a highly centralized autocratic system, the most important image in Korea belonged to the king, and whatever image he had had a direct impact upon his policy making. Parenthetically it should be pointed out that, when a good portion of the Confucian literati, the Korean version of the attentive public, showed a definite view on the issue of making a treaty with the United States, even the autocratic monarch could not ignore it. When the Confucian scholars rose up against the opening of the nation to the Western world throughout the year 1881, the king had to respond firmly: while taking stern punitive measures against these people, he took the route of relying on the Chinese to carry out the negotiations in their country.[51]

Thus seven basic factors determined American-Korean relations. The Korean share of American trade was negligible, while the American share of Korean trade was considerable and American investment in Korea was great. Although the American missionary interest in Korea was small in relative terms, it was both special and significant. For the United States the continuation of the balance-of-power system in the Far East was fairly important, but the survival of the Korean empire would have to be subordinated to overall American security interest in the region; meanwhile, Korea's independence depended upon continuation of the system, and the Koreans wished that the Americans would play a role in maintaining the system on the peninsula. For the Americans the Shufeldt treaty was a relatively minor event, but for the Koreans the opening of the nation to the Western world through the treaty was an important historical event and has been remembered as such. The more than 6,000-mile distance between the two nations made Korea seem a tiny, distant, and insignificant power to the United States, whereas the United States was even more attractive to the Koreans because the physical distance meant less danger of invasion or conquest; to the Americans, Korea was simply another small Oriental nation, separated by great psychological and cultural distance, but the Koreans were attracted by the culturally distant United States, the representative of modern civilization. The American image of Korea was negative and became more so, while the Korean image of the United States was much more favorable despite some fluctuations. These factors made the relationship asymmetrical: to the Americans, Korea was insignificant; but to the Koreans, the United States was very important in every respect.

We will see how American-Korean relations developed during their first half-century by taking account of these seven asymmetrical factors.

PRELUDE

Early, informal contact between the United States and Korea began in the mid-eighteenth century. When Korean tributary missions brought ginseng to Peking, they found themselves in competition with British and Dutch merchants who supplied the Chinese market with similar medicinal herbs from the banks of the Hudson River in Connecticut and Massachusetts.[1]

The first direct contact between the two nations, however, did not occur until nearly a century later. Because of its geographical location and other factors, Korea was not fortunate enough to be opened up by the Western powers during the two decades between 1840 and 1860. But the developments that followed the opening of the two other East Asian nations, especially China, did not leave Korea undisturbed for long. As American trade with China grew and as more American ships passed through the Yellow Sea between China and Korea, the chance of shipwrecks and other incidents in Korean waters increased. Thus, direct contact between the United States and Korea began in the mid-nineteenth century with a series of incidents.

The first American ship to appear in Korean waters was a whaling boat, which reached the tip of the southeast coast of the peninsula in the winter of 1852–1853. The local magistrate tried to obtain information on the nature of the boat through his interpreter, but because of a language difficulty, the effort failed.[2] Three years after this inconsequential incident, a group of American seamen, apparently survivors from a shipwreck, arrived on the east coast of Korea in Kan'gwŏn Province. The Korean authorities escorted these four seamen to Peking, where it was learned they were Americans.[3] Ten years later a similar incident took place: in the summer of 1865, a ship with three American seamen reached the east coast of Korea; the men were well treated and sent on to Peking.[4] In early spring of the following year, an American boat from San Francisco, which had been engaged in trade with Nagasaki, Japan, was returning from that port and was blown by wind to the southern coast of Korea, near Pusan. The Korean authorities denied the trade requested by the

Americans but provided them with necessary supplies.[5] Surprisingly, none of these cases was brought to the attention of the American authorities.

Then, in the later spring of 1866, the case of the *Surprise* drew for the first time the official notice of the American government. The *Surprise*, an American schooner sailing from Chefoo to Ryūkyū with merchandise, was blown by unfavorable winds to the northwestern coast of Korea and sank in late June. Five American seamen and two Chinese crewmen left the sinking ship on June 24 and, after stopping by a small island, reached Ch'ŏlsan district. The Koreans greeted them with curiosity and caution but without hostility. During a twenty-four-day stay in the village, the natives provided the unfortunate men with an "abundance of good food, tobacco, and even medicines, for the sick." The Ch'ŏlsan district magistrate, Paek Nak-yŏn, and other Korean officials interrogated the men. Finally, a special courier arrived from Seoul to escort the party to the border town between Korea and China; the group traveled partly on foot but mostly on horseback. The Koreans treated the foreigners with uniform courtesy and generosity; in addition to good food and comfortable lodging, they gave the American seamen new clothes and even some gifts. The humane treatment the Americans received from the Koreans contrasts sharply with the treatment they received from the Chinese. The Koreans treated the foreigners as guests in distress, although not without some caution; the Chinese treated them almost like prisoners. The long journey of the shipwrecked American seamen finally ended when they were delivered to the American consul in Peking nearly two months after the disaster.[6]

In more than one sense, the *Surprise* case was important for American-Korean relations. First of all, this was the first shipwreck on Korean shores that was reported to Washington. Although no immediate reaction by the State Department was documented, the detailed story of the treatment the American seamen received at the hands of the Koreans and the Chinese must have left some impression on the minds of the American policy makers. Later, the *Surprise* case became an excellent point of comparison and contrast with the *General Sherman* case.[7] Another equally important point is that the American government extravagantly thanked Father Gillie, the French missionary who made an "energetic remonstrance and intervention" when the American seamen were thrown into the Chinese jail in Mukden, but no American official expressed even one word of thanks for the Korean hospitality.[8] Two years after the incident, George F. Seward, American consul general in Shanghai, suggested that Secretary of State William H. Seward do justice to the Koreans for their kindness in the *Surprise* case.[9]

For American-Korean relations, the *General Sherman* case of the summer of 1866 was without doubt one of the most important of a number of incidents that took place on the Korean coast in the mid-nineteenth century. Not a shipwreck or a natural disaster, like preceding cases, this was a case in which Koreans took the lives of a number of Americans and other nationalities and destroyed an American ship. The impact of this first violent contact between Americans and Koreans was great and lasting; it contributed to the eventual opening of Korea in 1882. Because neither side was sure that the story told by the other side was accurate, the exact nature of the *General Sherman* affair remained clouded for a long time after the incident.[10]

The *General Sherman*, an American schooner of about eighty tons, was engaged in trade in East Asian waters. Chartered by Messrs. Meadows and Company, a British firm in Tientsin, the ship left Chefoo for Korea in early July with cotton goods, glassware, tin plates, and other merchandise. On board the ship were three Americans (W. B. Preston, the owner of the ship; Captain Page; and the chief mate, Wilson), two British citizens (the supercargo and the interpreter), and nineteen Malays and Chinese. Judging from the fact that the ship was "heavily armed" and from the behavior of the crew in Korean territory, suspicion existed that at least part of the objective of the voyage was piracy. It cannot be disputed, however, that the main objective of the venture was trade. Shortly before the middle of July, the ship arrived in Korean waters and began to ascend the Taedong River near P'yŏngyang. When the ship stopped in the Hwangchu district, the local magistrate, Chŏng Tae-sik, approached the *General Sherman* to inquire about the nationality of the ship and the objectives of the voyage. The crew answered that they were British, Americans, and Chinese, and that they had come to barter their goods for Korean paper, rice, gold, ginseng, hides, and other native products. They told the Koreans that they had no intention of harming the natives and would depart P'yŏngyang as soon as the trade was over. The Korean magistrates told the crew that entering inland waterways and trading with the natives were acts prohibited by Korean national policy. The crew was not deterred by this remonstration. In response to the query of another local magistrate, Yu Cho-hwan of Yongkang-hyŏn, the Americans and British on the ship went beyond the subject of trade to ask questions about the terrain of the P'yŏngyang area, the existence of treasure in the city, the execution of French missionaries, and the arrival of a number of American and European ships in Korean waters. Since many of these questions touched on delicate subjects, the Koreans became even more anxious concerning the real objective of the voyage. Then, on the twentieth of July, the ship moved up the Taedong River and anchored near P'yŏngyang, where it enjoyed about a week of tense but still quiet rest. The governor of P'yŏngan Province, Pak Kyu-su, took up the matter and sent the mayor of P'yŏngyang and other officers to the ship to make inquiries. The conversation between the two sides was similar to the previous ones: the interpreter, Reverend Robert J. Thomas, explained that the objective of the voyage was trade. He also asked the reason for the persecution of Christians in Korea and explained the virtues of Christianity. The Korean officials repeated the statement that the trade they sought was illegal; but the crew, especially the owners of the ship and the supercargo, insisted on completing various commercial activities. Still amicable, the Koreans provided the crew on request with rice, meat, chicken, eggs, and other necessary supplies. This quiet period ended six days later when the crew of the *General Sherman* captured a small Korean boat and kidnapped Colonel Yi Hyŏng-ik and two other officials.[11]

On the following day, July 27, the citizens of P'yŏngyang exhibited, for the first time, hostility toward the crew of the *General Sherman* by demanding the return of the colonel who had been kidnapped by the ship's crew. The crew retorted with ill-chosen words, escalating the crisis. The Koreans demonstrated their feelings by throwing stones and shooting arrows at a boat dispatched from the *General Sherman* to acquire drinking water up the river. Soon the violence worsened. According to the Korean records, the crew members stole rice and other necessary supplies from the natives. During this struggle, seven Koreans were killed and five others wounded. Pak, the governor of the province, after realizing that "good words" would not make the foreigners retreat, decided to order the destruction of the ship. Under the governor's direction the Koreans, both soldiers and civilians, united in an assault against the ship, which soon ran out of ammunition and went aground. The Koreans then devised fire-rafts and ultimately succeeded in setting the *General Sherman* on fire. The schooner was completely destroyed and the entire crew killed by the Koreans. Thus, after four days of violence, the *General Sherman* ended her venturesome voyage on the Taedong River, leaving behind many puzzles and problems that were not easily solved.[12]

The *General Sherman* case was the first unfortunate incident in American-Korean relations, and the Koreans definitely had to share the blame for the incident. Even after Colonel Yi was captured by the crew of the *General Sherman*, had the Koreans controlled their emotion and extended further their generosity to their uninvited and insolent visitors, loss of life could have been avoided. But such action was probably too much to demand of a crowd influenced by mob psychology. Governor Pak, the official most responsible for the Korean side of the incident, not only failed to restrain the P'yŏngyang citizenry, he also allowed the soldiers to join the crowd, first in the demonstration and later in the attack on the ship, instead of using them to protect the foreigners from the mob. Once the situation had escalated to the stage of the death of seven Koreans, there was no way to effect a peaceful solution to the problem. (It is important to note that since all Westerners seemed the same to the Koreans, who hardly distinguished among the different nationalities, the Korean authorities recognized and recorded the ship as British and the merchants also of the same nationality, not even mentioning the Americans.)[13]

But even though the Koreans must share the blame for the incident, its tragic end lies with the *General Sherman*'s crew. First, the heavily armed *General Sherman* did not have a legal right to enter Korean waters, especially into the vicinity of P'yŏngyang, an ancient capital, still the center of the northern part of the peninsula, and second in importance only to Seoul. Second, the time for the venture was ill-chosen. In early spring of the same year, a large-scale religious persecution had been carried out in Korea. French missionaries and many Korean Christians had been executed, and the Koreans on the west coast were in a state of fear and excitement about the expected French punitive expedition when the *General Sherman* arrived on the Korean coast. Third, since the voyage was illegal, knowledge that the crew certainly must have had, the crew of the ship should have exercised much caution and modesty in handling the ship and especially in dealing with the natives to reduce the chance of an undesirable incident. But the Westerners on the ship completely ignored the warnings of the local officials not to proceed further up the river. And, through their later words and actions, they built up more and more suspicion, irritation, and fear in the minds of the Koreans. The recklessness and arrogance of the crew, more than anything else, was responsible for the unfortunate disaster.[14]

The physical impact of the *General Sherman* incident upon Korea was small. The Koreans salvaged three cannons with some shells, two loads of iron, 1,300 pounds of tin, 2,250 pounds of wire, and 2,145 pounds of miscellaneous metal from the wreckage of the ship.[15] They then constructed a steamboat similar to the *General Sherman* with the materials from the destroyed vessel, but the steam generated by charcoal was not adequate and pushed the boat only a few knots an hour. The psychological impact of the incident on the Koreans, however, was great. The successful destruction of the ship gave a sense of victory to the Koreans and boosted their morale, which helped them to face the forthcoming French expedition of the same year and the American expedition of 1871. But this temporary morale boost was not a blessing to the Koreans in the long run; it strengthened the hands of the advocates of the exclusion policy of the government, delaying the opening of the nation to the Western world.

The impact of the *General Sherman* case upon the American side was also great: two fact-finding missions, one in 1867 and the other in 1868, followed, and the incident was at least partly responsible for the Low-Rodgers expedition of 1871 and the first American-Korean treaty of 1882. The Department of State first learned of the *General Sherman* case about three months after the incident. The report from Peking was short, informing the department that the American schooner had been burned and the crew killed by the Koreans.[16] Two months after the first report, diplomatic and consular despatches from China brought more information to Washington; they identified as responsible for the "murder" the Korean king or his father, the regent, without giving the details of the circumstances leading up to the unfortunate incident.[17] The American consul in Chefoo even conjectured that the crew might have been kept as prisoners for possible future use. These reports must have made Secretary of State Seward anxious, for on February 23 he instructed Minister Anson Burlingame in Peking to make a "diligent inquiry" into the truth of the case, and on March 4 he indicated to the secretary of the Navy the desirability of finding the "whole truth" of the matter.[18]

While communications took place between the State Department and its representatives in China regarding the *General Sherman* incident, a separate and independent investigation was begun by an American naval officer. Rear Admiral Henry H. Bell, who was commanding the Asiatic Squadron, showed an unusual zeal in responding to the event on the Korean coast. In his first two letters to the secretary of the Navy, dated November 30 and December 12, 1866,[19] he reported the shipwreck case, based on a British source, and stated his plan to send the *Wachusett*, one of the ships under his command, to Korea to investigate. In his two following letters, dated December 14 and 27, he expressed his willingness to launch a punitive expedition against Korea. He wanted to have a force of 1,500 to

2,000 troops from the Pacific coast of the United States to occupy Seoul, the capital of Korea, and then quickly withdraw, the objective being to redress the wrongs the Koreans committed, to demonstrate to the Asiatic powers and the world the capacity of the United States Navy, and to show them who was "the master of the Pacific."[20] Bell's ambitious project was not carried out until some years later and then on a smaller scale and under his successor's command. The milder portion of his project—the fact-finding mission—was carried out immediately.

The person Admiral Bell picked for the first fact-finding mission was Captain Robert W. Shufeldt, later to play an important role in opening the Korean door to the Western world in 1882. This was certainly a good choice, even though the admiral's main consideration when making the choice was not the person but the ship.[21] After a painstaking collection of information on the *General Sherman* case and the careful selection of a Chinese pilot and an interpreter, Shufeldt finally left for Korea on January 22, 1867, arriving in Korean waters on the following day.[22] Purposely avoiding the Han River area where the French punitive expedition had been launched and being unable because of winter ice to reach the Taedong River near P'yŏngyang where the *General Sherman* incident had occurred, Shufeldt chose to anchor his ship between the two rivers, near Wŏlnae Island of Oupo in Hwanghae Province. He persuaded a local official to take his letter to the chief official of Changyŏn prefecture with an enclosure, a letter addressed to the Korean monarch.[23] In the letter addressed to the king, Shufeldt first clearly stated that he did not come to the Korean shore "to engage in war, nor any unlawful business." Then he thanked the king for the kind treatment of the crew of the *Surprise* by the Koreans and asked why, in contrast, the people of the *General Sherman* had suffered such a "cruel treatment." While waiting for the return of the messenger with answers to his letters, Shufeldt cultivated the friendship of the natives and learned from them that the people of the American ship were killed by the mob, not by order of the Korean government. On January 29 Shufeldt had an unsatisfactory interview with an official who came from Haeju, the capital city of Hwanghae Province. Because the Korean official from Haeju was arrogant and beyond the reach of reason or argument, Shufeldt decided he would not be able to carry on conversations with the Korean government through the local officials. Shufeldt left Oupo that same day, before the arrival of the reply from Changyŏn, and, after stopping by Port Hamilton (Kŏmundo), returned to Shanghai on February 5.[24] When the Korean reply reached Oupo, the *Wachusett* had already departed the area;

the letter was finally delivered, to Captain John C. Febiger, the following spring.

Admiral Bell praised Shufeldt's "intelligence" in the execution of his mission.[25] Certainly, the captain was cautious and considerate in carrying out his mission, but because of his lack of experience in dealing with the Koreans, he found it difficult to trust the people and often misjudged what the Koreans did. Had he been a little more patient, he would have been able to conclude at least the communication he commenced with the Korean officials. To complete the inconclusive Shufeldt mission, Admiral Bell planned another mission after the winter was over.[26]

However, before that mission—the Febiger mission of 1868—could commence, a lively action took place on the Korean coast that drew the attention of all the Westerners in the Far East, of Washington, and of some European capitals. In the spring of 1866, nine French missionaries and a large number of native Christians in Korea had been executed by order of the Taewŏn'gun, the regent and father of the young Korean king. As a result, the French squadron in the Far East carried out two punitive expeditions in the fall of 1867. Secretary of State Seward showed great concern and interest in the developments on the Korean coast when he was informed about the incidents. Moreover, when the French expeditionary force of six ships and the 600-man force under Admiral Pierre Gustave Roze's command returned to China after failing to complete its campaign on Kanghwa Island, both Europeans and Americans involved in Far Eastern affairs became concerned about its impact on the Western powers' prestige in the region; a rumor circulated that there would be another French expedition or a joint international expedition the following spring. In his despatch of January 31, 1867, Anson Burlingame, the American minister in Peking, reported to Secretary of State Seward that the British and Russian ministers in Peking would take action to protect their countries' interests during the anticipated French demonstration against Korea in the spring or early summer and requested "full power to act as may be best" for American interests.[27] Not knowing that the French government had repudiated Admiral Roze's expedition, which had been carried out without the approval of his government, Secretary of State Seward, who hastily assumed that another French expedition would soon take place, proposed in the course of a conversation with the French minister in Washington on March 2, 1867, a joint expedition to Korea to conclude a treaty with the Koreans similar to those concluded with the Chinese and the Japanese and to obtain satisfaction for the murder of the French missionaries. The French government declined the Seward proposal.[28] As Tyler Dennett has pointed out, it was fortunate for the United States that Seward's idea miscarried, even though the plan was not out of place when viewed in the context of the two major policies of the United States in the Far East in the latter part of the nineteenth century: gunboat diplomacy and the cooperative policy.[29]

Even though the Shufeldt mission established that the crew of the *General Sherman* was killed by a mob because of their own misbehavior, officials in the State Department and the Navy remained suspicious and apprehensive.[30] Then, a new factor was thrown into an already tense situation: at the end of 1866 a rumor appeared in China that four members of the *General Sherman*'s crew might be being held captive in Korea.[31] Having as its dual objectives the delivery of the captives (if they existed) and the acquisition of more information on the *General Sherman* case, the Febiger mission was undertaken in the spring of 1868.[32]

Captain John C. Febiger arrived in Korean waters on April 8 and stayed in the area more than forty days, until the eighteenth of the following month. His ship, the *Shenandoah*, anchored in the Taedong River where the *General Sherman* had been destroyed, then traveled upriver until Febiger commenced communication with the Korean officials. Within a month, Febiger had extensive communication with two Korean officials, Yi Ki-cho, the magistrate of Samhwa, and Pak Chong-hwa, the prefect of Changyŏn. From them he heard an account of the incident and learned that there were no captives alive in Korean hands. He also made an effort to send a letter to the Korean king, but it was returned with a notation that it could not be forwarded to the king because it was not from the American government. However, he did receive an answer from a high Korean government official to the Shufeldt letter, which had not been delivered earlier because of Shufeldt's departure. Febiger also carried out a thorough survey of the river, during which one of the cutters was fired upon from a Korean military installation. The cutter did not return the shot. Febiger later protested the incident to Korean officials, stating that the American boat was fired upon without warning, and if such an event happened again, the shots would be returned. The last act of the mission was an interview with Kim Cha-p'yŏng, an old Korean who was the source of the baseless story that the Koreans were holding the Americans captive.[33]

American naval authorities considered the Febiger mission a failure,[34] primarily because the government did not believe the Korean testimony.[35] If the mission is evaluated in terms of its original objectives, however, the official assessment was unfair. Captain Febiger achieved both objectives: finding out that there were no survivors from the *General Sherman* incident and hearing the first Korean official's explanation of the incident. Furthermore, the Korean government recorded (probably also learned) for the first time the involvement of the Americans in the incident.[36]

While the *Shenandoah* was still in Korean waters, an unusual international tomb robbery took place on the coast of the Korean peninsula. As an event, it was not more than a brief episode, and American involvement in it was slight. However, because it created a strong impression in Korean minds about Westerners in general, it deserves a short description. Ernest J. Oppert, a resourceful Prussian merchant adventurer who made three voyages to the west coast of Korea in 1866, was the leading spirit of this expedition. The *China*, a heavily armed ship of 648 tons under the German flag, arrived on the coast of Ch'ungch'ŏng Province, south of Chemulpo (Inchŏn), on May 10, 1868; she carried a crew of twenty Manilans and about a hundred Chinese, as well as three major figures—Ernest J. Oppert; a French priest; and an American citizen, Henry B. Jenkins.[37] The expeditionary force soon landed and, after assaulting the Tŏksan-gun office building, it marched to Ka-dong, to the tomb of Namyŏn-gun, the father of the Taewŏn'gun, where they began exhuming the bones with tools they obtained in the vicinity. When they reached the rock coffin, they were unable to do more work with the tools they possessed and had to abandon the project and retreat to their ship. After the expeditionary force moved northward and anchored near Yŏngchong Island in Kyŏnggi Province, Oppert sent a letter to the Taewŏn'gun explaining that the leader of the group was a Prussian admiral and that, if the Korean government did not send a high official to negotiate, Korea would soon be endangered by a foreign invasion. The Korean government refused to receive the letter and reproached the Prussian admiral for his impiety in invading the tomb at Tŏksan. Later, on May 17, Oppert's group landed on Yŏng-chong Island and tried to enter the city forcefully, but they were attacked by the guard of the castle and forced to withdraw to the ship, leaving behind two killed in the action. This infamous expedition soon became a subject of much talk among the Westerners in China. Jenkins was tried in Shanghai by the American consul general for "his act against the peace and dignity of the United States of America"; he was acquitted on inadequate evidence.[38] The incident had a great impact upon Koreans, already culturally prejudiced against the Westerners; their firm exclusion policy became even firmer.

The last and most important act in American-Korean relations before the treaty making of 1882 was the Low-Rodgers mission of 1871. In more than one sense, it was significant: it was the first official mission of the United States to Korea; it was the last of the series of incidents on the Korean coast that troubled American-Korean relations before 1882; and it was the first and only military clash between the two nations before 1950. As early as mid-December of 1866, Admiral Bell suggested a large-scale American expedition against the Koreans as a punitive and demonstrative action.[39] Later, the idea was proposed as a cooperative venture, but the idea was dropped because the French were not interested. The idea of a punitive expedition to Korea never died, however; it continued to live in a mystic cloud surrounding the *General Sherman* case, for which no explanation that satisfied the Americans, especially those offered by the Koreans, was ever given. Another motivating force, probably the most powerful one, for the 1871 action came from George F. Seward. Even more vigorous and energetic than his uncle, Secretary of State William H. Seward, the young consul general had showed much concern about the *General Sherman* affair from the beginning. More than anyone else, he was responsible for linking the idea of making a treaty with Korea with the 1866 shipwreck incident. Not only did he first conceive the idea, but he also communicated it effectively to those officials responsible for American foreign policy. On April 24, 1866, while the Febiger mission was still on the Korean coast, the young consul general in Shanghai asked the secretary of state for authority to go to Korea to get an official explanation of the *General Sherman* affair from the Korean government and to negotiate, if possible, with the Koreans to make a treaty of amity and commerce similar to the ones made with the Chinese and the Japanese.[40] When the Febiger mission returned to China, Seward considered the mission a failure and, in the same fall, he proposed a mission in which the objectives were clearly spelled out: the acquisition of information on the destruction of the *General Sherman*, the collection of reparations if appropriate, and the making of a commercial treaty. This proposal led Hamilton Fish, the new secretary of state, to instruct Minister Frederick Low in Peking in April 1870 "to secure the presence and cooperation" of the consul general in his mission (these instructions were not carried out because of Seward's absence in China at the time of the 1871 expedition).[41]

All these forces culminated in Fish's instruction of April 20, 1870, in which the secretary of state authorized Minister Low to negotiate with the Korean authorities to conclude a treaty to protect shipwrecked seamen and, if favorable, to open trade. He advised Low to ʌin, in advance, the good will, or even the good offices, of the ʌese government in approaching the Koreans. He also suggested that the minister secure the cooperation of George F. Seward and the full support of Admiral John Rodgers, the commander of the Asiatic fleet, who would be instructed to accompany the minister and make his flagship available for an adequate display of force.[42] To carry out these instructions, Low left Shanghai on the *Colorado*, the flagship of the Asiatic fleet, and after a brief stop at Nagasaki arrived in Korean waters on May 19. Admiral Rodgers brought four more ships —the *Alaska*, the *Benecia*, the *Monocacy*, and the *Palos*—to add "dignity" to the mission.[43] With a total tonnage of 10,015, these five main ships carried 85 guns and 1,135 men.[44] After moving anchor to the area near Eugenie Island (P'ungdo), the admiral dispatched the *Palos* and four steam launches under Commander H. C. Blake to examine the channel up to the Isle Boisee (Mulyudo). Commander Blake carried out the five-day survey mission without any difficulty, returning safely to the anchorage on May 28. Meanwhile, the party from the ships remaining near Eugenie Island conducted a survey of the vicinity and made initial contact with the Koreans. Although the Koreans first fled to the hills, they gradually overcame their fear and approached the boats. Shin Ch'ŏl-gu, the magistrate of Namyang-pu, and others made an inquiry to learn the origin and the objective of the mission. Edward B. Drew, the minister's acting secretary, and Captain Edward T. Nichols, the admiral's chief of staff, delivered written words assuring the Koreans of the peaceful intention of the mission. On May 30, soon after the ships moved their anchorage to Isle Boisee, four minor Korean officials came in a boat and exchanged letters with the Americans. The Koreans made another inquiry about the objective of the mission; the Americans informed the Korean officials that a "high envoy" had come to transact important business with the Korean government; that, while waiting for the appointment by the Korean government of a high official to confer with the American minister, further exploration would be made up the Han River; that the people need not to be afraid of the ships; and that the admiral and the minister hoped an instruction would be given to the people so that no trouble would occur. This American assurance of peaceful intentions seemed to be accepted by the Korean officials with great satisfaction. On the following day, May 31, three third-grade officials from the Korean government arrived to greet the Americans and to inquire about the objective of the voyage. Because they appeared to be low-ranking officials and were without official credentials, the minister decided to have his subordinates meet them. The Koreans were again informed that surveying ships would go up on the following day toward Kanghwa and were assured of the American desire to avoid trouble. The Korean officials not only did not make any objection, but even "gave tacit assurance that the expedition would meet with nothing but civility and kindness from the natives."[45]

Then, the day most momentous for the mission dawned. Again Commander Blake led the expedition with the *Monocacy* and the *Palos*, the two smaller ships, and four small steam launches to survey the Han River. The American ships did not encounter any show of hostility on the Korean side until they reached the lower end of Kanghwa Island, Sondolmok. When the expeditionary force had passed Sondolmok and reached the Korean forts—Kwangsŏng, Tŏkpo, and Tŏkchin—the forts suddenly opened heavy fire and shelled the ships and boats for about fifteen minutes. The American vessels promptly returned the fire and drove the Koreans from their guns to the ravines. As the ships steamed back to the anchorage, they fired again upon the forts; their shots were unanswered.

The Korean fire had been ill-directed and caused almost no damage to the American side. However, the *Monocacy* struck rocks and began to leak badly and the *Palos* was disabled from some damage to the bulwarks. Nevertheless, all ships returned safely to the anchorage near Isle Boisee on that day. The Korean side lost one artillery man.[46]

During the following nine days, the local Korean officials and the Americans exchanged a number of letters in which each side accused the other of causing the "unfortunate mistake." The Koreans criticized the Americans for their penetration of Korean territory through an "important pass"; the Americans blamed the Koreans for their "unprovoked and wanton attack" on their "peaceful overtures."[47] Further, in these communications the Koreans tried to convince the Americans that since the Korean government treated humanely all foreigners shipwrecked along the Korean coast as a matter of a national policy, there was no need to make a treaty regarding the treatment of shipwrecked seamen. Because Korea was a small, poor country with a meager amount of products to sell and limited natural resources, the Koreans reasoned that neither side would benefit from trade relations. Moreover, the Koreans would not be able easily to change their five-centuries-old exclusion policy.[48] The Americans, however, saw the situation in a different light after the incident. Minister Low was afraid that, even though the June 1 exchange of fire could be considered a "complete victory" for the American side, the Koreans would undoubtedly construe the incident as their victory and, unless the wrongs and the "insults on the American flag" were redressed, the laxity would have an injurious effect upon the future of American interests in Korea and China. The navy was more direct. After the return of the survey expeditionary force, Admiral Rodgers decided that a landing force would return at once to the spot and "attack and destroy the fortifications." After some thought, however, the Americans decided to allow the Korean king time to learn about the incident and to send an apology for the outrage, if it was unauthorized by him, and appoint a high official to meet the American envoy.[49] Other than some words of accusation and some overblown rhetoric, no apology seemed to be forthcoming from the Koreans, and American patience was quickly exhausted. Even before the date given as a mild ultimatum was reached, an American punitive expedition was underway, and the Low-Rodgers mission moved into its last stage.

The expeditionary force was composed of two ships—the *Monocacy*, an iron sidewheel, double-ended steamer with 747 tons and six guns; and the *Palos*, a screw tug of 350 tons, carrying six howitzers—and four steam launches, with 759 men, including a landing force of 651, of which 105 were marines. Under Commander Blake, the expeditionary force left the Isle Boisee anchorage at 10 A.M. on June 10 with the admiral's instruction to take and destroy the forts that had fired on the American vessels and hold them long enough to demonstrate American capability to punish such offenders.[50] As soon as the expeditionary force reached the first fort, Fort De Conde (Ch'ojin), the *Monocacy* began to shell it, driving out the Korean defenders. A successful landing was made early in the afternoon despite the difficult terrain; the Americans met no resistance and soon occupied the fort. Two more forts were occupied without any difficulty, and destruction of the first two was completed by late afternoon. The guns were dismounted and thrown into the river. The American force finished the day's work early and bivouacked on a favorable spot. Early the next morning the expeditionary force advanced toward the next target, Fort Monocacy (Tŏkjin). The stone fort upon a bluff was easily occupied after being shelled by the *Monocacy*. The expeditionary force moved on toward the last and most important target of the expedition, Fort McKee (Kwangsŏngjin), which was named after a lieutenant killed in the fighting. This attack was the most difficult one; the expeditionary force had to march over steep hills separated by deep ravines. A bombardment from the ships upon the citadel began and continued for an hour. At 11:15 the final assault began; 350 sailors and marines set out through a deep ravine, eighty feet deep, and then marched up a steep hill against the enemy's fire. When the Americans reached the top of the hill, they leaped into hand-to-hand fighting. Lieutenant Hugh W. McKee, the first to mount the parapet, fell at the head of his men. Desperate fighting continued until the last Korean fell. The expeditionary force stayed that night on the island; the next morning the men returned to their ships and sailed back to the Isle Boisee anchorage, arriving at 10:30 A.M. Thus, the three-day American expedition to Kanghwa Island was over. American forces took five forts, fifty flags, and 481 guns, including some 32-pounders and fourteen 24-pounders, in the campaign. In this conflict as many as 350 Koreans were killed or wounded, including Ŏ Chae-yŏn, the commander in chief of the defending force, and nine were captured. The casualties on the American side were small: three men, including Lieutenant McKee, were killed, and nine were wounded.[51]

After the destruction of the forts, the American fleet remained in Korean waters for three weeks "to induce" the Korean government to enter into negotiations, but this was a futile endeavor. It became much more difficult to communicate with the Koreans, who were furious over their humiliating defeat. When Drew proposed to Chŏng the return of the Korean prisoners, Yi, the prefect of Pup'yŏng, responded indignantly by saying that the Americans were free to decide.[52] In a letter written on June 11, which was delivered to the American side on the following day, Yi used severe language concerning the aggressive action of the Americans: "Looking at it now," he said, "one can know this much for certain: Under outward profession of friendship you cherish false and deceitful desires. To come to your landing, and thoroughly displaying your force of committing public buildings to the flames, burning cottages, stealing property, sweeping up everything to the veriest trifle. These are the actions of thieves and spies." Then he went on to say that the Americans brought Korean outlaws as guides and asked, "Where was such unsparing the implacable savagery ever exceeded?"[53] Drew calmly stated that he regretted the necessity that compelled the American action and requested the delivery of a letter from the minister to the king.[54] Two days later Yi returned the letter addressed to the king with the statement that he would not dare deliver it. Drew wrote back to Yi that the latter's action would not be sanctioned by the king and made a mild threat, saying that the mission would stay in Korean waters until it could find a man capable of delivering the communication to the King.[55] After nearly two weeks Drew sent another letter, the last of the series of communications, announcing that the "friendly overture" of the Americans had failed. On the following day, the fleet left the Korean coast, ending the nearly two-month-long expedition.[56]

The Low-Rodgers mission was a military victory for the Americans, but it was definitely a failure in a political sense, since the mission failed to achieve its original objective of concluding a treaty with the Koreans. Low himself admitted the failure.[57] A part of the responsibility for this failure should be attributed to the ignorance and rigidity of the Koreans. As Secretary of State Fish acknowledged later, the Koreans did not have a duty to conclude a treaty and open their country to the United States. But if their leaders had known the condition of the world at that time and the meaning of isolation, and if they had been flexible enough to adjust to the rapidly changing situation in the region, they could have turned disaster into an opportunity by opening the nation to the Western world in 1871 instead of 1882. By so doing, the Koreans would have gained a decade, a decade that could have made a great difference in the rapidly changing world of the latter part of the nineteenth century. In view of the general ignorance of the people and the conservatism of the ruling class at that time, the degree of enlightenment and flexibility needed for such a treaty was probably too much to ask of the Koreans. Nonetheless, the Koreans could have avoided disaster at the hands of the American expeditionary force in 1871 if they had chosen to do so. The Korean records show that the Korean court and the government knew before the incident that the American survey mission was coming toward Kanghwa Island and that the Americans wished to avoid trouble.[58]

But the Americans were even more responsible for the failure of the mission. In both encounters they won military victories and demonstrated successfully to the Oriental nations the capacity of the American military force. However, because of this military success, they failed to achieve the objective of the mission—making a treaty with the Koreans. The Americans made a costly mistake in carrying out the first surveying expedition. They did well in giving notice of the mission to the Korean officials, but they were too optimistic or even too careless in placing much value on the seeming assurance of minor officials for cordial treatment. No Korean official document reported such approval.[59] Moreover, an attempt to go through Sondolmok, the same spot at which the French expeditionary force had had a similar difficulty with the Koreans five years earlier, amounted to inviting trouble.[60] The Americans did not realize that passing the Sondolmok area was about the same as passing through Chesapeake Bay toward Washington. As some Americans themselves pointed out, the punitive action was also out of proportion and too harsh on Korea,[61] which in the latter part of the nineteenth century was a nation almost without any defense force and hardly a major military threat to any nation. Even though the course of action was approved by Secretary of State Fish,[62] it is regrettable that the Low-Rodgers mission failed to achieve its original objective because it was carried away by a military show of force.

The Low-Rodgers expedition had a considerable impact upon the Koreans. Unfortunately, it was not the kind of effect the mission wished to bring about; instead of becoming conciliatory, as the Japanese had as a result of the Perry mission to Japan, the Koreans made even firmer their anti-Western and belligerent policy. The government sent more troops and military supplies to reinforce the Kanghwa defense force. Moreover, it disseminated its declaration throughout the peninsula, showing its determination to continue the struggle against the invading forces and to treat those who urged peace with the foreign invaders as traitors. Antipeace inscriptions began to appear in Seoul and other major cities in Korea.[63] Nearly a decade later, Commodore Shufeldt put in succinct terms the effect of the forceful actions of the mission on American-Korean relations: "The attempt however gallant was fruitless, except in embittering Koreans and deferring the prospect of a friendly treaty."[64] The actions of the expeditionary mission were too forceful for acts of a peaceful mission, but not forceful enough to coerce the Koreans into granting what the mission sought.

Thus, American-Korean relations during the twenty-years after 1852, the year in which the first American ship appeared on the Korean coast, were turbulent. In a sense, this turbulent era resulted from the clash between the gunboat diplomacy of the United States and the seclusion policy of Korea. Some important factors can be discerned under the surface of this clash: among them, leadership, power, and culture may be considered as the most significant ones.

On the American side, the Department of State was headed by William H. Seward and Hamilton Fish, both very capable and dynamic, during the five years of the post–Civil War period, the most crucial period for pre-1882 American-Korean relations. During the years between 1866 and 1869, American diplomacy toward Korea was handled by three extremely energetic and almost too vigorous men—Secretary of State Seward, Consul General George F. Seward, and Rear Admiral Henry H. Bell. Secretary Seward did not particularly desire an extensive American involvement in Asia, but when an American action was required in the area he did not hesitate to show his usual vigor. George F. Seward, nephew of the secretary and one of the two men who, together with Commodore Shufeldt, most persistently pushed the American government toward more action in Korea, played the most important role for an active American policy in Korea during the six-year period. Admiral Bell, on the other hand, was the person who first conceived the idea of the punitive expedition of 1871 soon after he had learned of the *General Sherman* case. His idea was most vigorous to the extent of being reckless. The same spirit of vigorous American policy toward Korea was shared by several others during the period of two decades: Secretary of State Fish, Minister Burlingame, Minister Low, and Admiral Rodgers. The vigor and zeal of these Americans for an active American policy was a very important contributing factor to post–Civil War American policy in Korea.

On the Korean side, the ruling circle still held fast to the exclusion policy. The most dominant spirit in formulating Korean policies, both domestic and foreign, was the Taewŏn'gun, the young king's father. His will, intelligence, and stubbornness were unmatched by any of the Korean ruling class. Unfortunately, his mind was closed to the outside world, and he carried out mercilessly his antiforeign policy.[65] With such actors on the two sides of the Pacific Ocean, incidents such as the *General Sherman*, the 1871 conflict, and other events during the twenty-year period were almost inevitable.

The power discrepancy among nations is always an important factor in international relations. This is especially true in American-Korean relations in the early period because of the large degree of discrepancy. The United States in the post–Civil War years was not a great power. The army was quickly scaled down to the peacetime level of 40,000, and the premodern navy was by no means impressive. However, the nation had a great potential, with large territorial, population, and resource bases. The economy was recovering quickly from the war, and industry was anticipating bright decades. In contrast, Korea was a small nation still untouched by the industrial revolution. It lacked almost completely a power base, and its defense forces were practically nonexistent. Faced with a modern army, as well demonstrated in the Low-Rodgers expedition, the Korean army, with its obsolete weapons and without any proper military training, was helpless.

Above all, it seems that the most powerful factor affecting American-Korean relations during the early years was cultural. The Americans involved in the follow-up of the *General Sherman* case considered the Koreans "savage" or "barbarous people," while the Koreans considered the Americans arrogant and haughty.[66] The cultural barrier created a mutual distrust and became the single most formidable inhibiting factor preventing satisfactory communication between the two people. Even Commodore Shufeldt, who had some understanding of and sympathy toward the Koreans, fell into this trap.[67] Low's lack of trust toward the Koreans, whom he considered a "semi-barbarous and hostile" people, became the most basic factor in determining his actions in the 1871 expedition. Before any contact with them, he had already anticipated meeting with Oriental "cunning and sophistry," and he had decided to consider it a mistake in policy in dealing with the Korean government and people "to allow insults and injuries to go unredressed."[68] Low's distrust of Oriental culture was best revealed in the different attitudes he showed toward the stories about the *General Sherman* incident as told by Korean officials and by Korean Christians. When a Korean Christian approached the American ship and told his version of the *General Sherman* case, which was actually incorrect, Low immediately thought he obtained "the most important intelligence" and an "apparently trustworthy" account of the incident. In contrast, he refused to trust the version of the story that was repeatedly told by the Korean officials as "scarcely worthy of credence."[69]

The Korean view of the American people was equally ugly; since the Oppert bone-robbery expedition incident, Koreans thought all Westerners were "barbarians" and that many of them were thieves and robbers. After the June 1 exchange of fire, the king demonstrated his determination to resist the American invasion and declared to his ministers that a civilized nation with millennia of history behind it could not make peace with a nation of barbarians (a nation of "dogs and sheep").[70] Thus the two nations, with different cultural backgrounds and each considering itself highly civilized according to its own value systems and looking down on the other as barbarous and uncivilized, could not find a plane on which they could meet on equal terms.

Although different nations do not always have to meet in conflict, they often do so. The Koreans and the Americans met first in a conflict, as two groups of equally proud and stubborn people. The result was a clash between a rising, great Western power and an old, decaying Oriental kingdom—a war between two groups of "barbarians." There was little chance for a meeting of the two nations at this stage to be peaceful.

2 SHUFELDT
OPENS KOREA

Korea was the only closed nation in East Asia
after its neighbors—China and Japan—were
opened in the mid-nineteenth century, and the opening of its doors
has been considered significant by many historians. Tyler Dennett,
one of the most prominent historians of American–East Asian relations, declared it to be the most important political action undertaken by the United States in Asia before the occupation of the Philippines in 1898.[1] Charles Oscar Paullin, a specialist in naval history,
thought that Shufeldt's act was "the most important work of the
American navy in the Far East" during the period between the Civil
War and the Spanish-American War.[2] Without risk of exaggeration,
it can be said that the signing of the first treaty between the United
States and Korea on May 22, 1882, was one of the most important
events in American-Korean relations during the entire pre-1910
period, or even during the whole period of the two-nation relationship since 1866.

If the opening of Korea by the United States in 1882 was an important act, it was an important purposive act, an action with definite
purposes, and thereby quite different from the series of episodic or
incidental events that took place before 1871. This is not to claim
that episodic or incidental acts in history lack meaning; they certainly have meaning, sometimes even more meaning than purposive acts when viewed from a large or long historical perspective.
But because human beings are more interested in their own history,
or human history, purposive acts become more important and
demand more of our attention. The particular objectives of the participants will be discussed in the following pages as the story devel-
ops. The present concern is to ascertain what forces lay behind the
particular purposes and objectives. Of the number of forces influ-
encing the opening of the Korean door by the Americans toward the
end of the nineteenth century, political and economic forces were
the most significant.

Ever since the beginning of the modern era, the nation-state system has dominated the political scene of the world; it is hardly an
exaggeration to say that the formulation and development of this

system has been the most significant political phenomenon in the modern world. Its origin may be traced back to the tenth century, when England first became a unified nation and when France consolidated its territorial nucleus around Paris; the formation of the system was well under way by the time of the Treaty of Westphalia in 1648. In the nineteenth and twentieth centuries a large number of countries, first in Europe and then in the non-Western world, developed into nation-states. This organizational system is the single most important political organizing principle in the modern world. Modern international society, which was based on the principle of the equal sovereignty of nations, was formulated as a necessary part of the nation-state system and, energetic and aggressive, demanded that nations lying outside the society—including those in East Asia —join the system.

Another formidable dynamic that helped force open the Korean door in the later nineteenth century was economic. From the time when farming began on the eastern hills of Mesopotamia, this revolutionary food-getting technique spread all over the globe, eventually reaching the Korean peninsula. By the eighteenth century Korea, like China and Japan and most of the Western world, was an agricultural society. But a new economic system was developing, and Korea, like the two other nations in the area, was not able to escape from the impact of the industrial revolution. Emerging first in England in the latter part of the eighteenth century, the revolution spread, first to Europe in the nineteenth century and later to the non-Western world in the following century. Like the nation-state system, though much larger in scale and degree, the new economic system brought with it vast changes. Newly created industries began searching for outlets, for new markets and sources of raw material. Industrialization created a volume of products and an accumulation of wealth never before seen; traditional agricultural societies gave way before the great thrust of the new economic force. Social and cultural forces in Korea certainly affected outcomes, but it was political and economic forces that sent the Americans to the doorstep of Korea in the late nineteenth century.[3]

Even though great forces worked to open the Korean door in the nineteenth century, the door to the "Hermit Kingdom," which had been kept closed for more than two hundred years for self-protection, was not to be cracked easily; half a century was needed to prepare for its opening. At least six attempts were made before the 1871 Low-Rodgers expedition. The first abortive attempt occurred in 1830. Edmund Roberts, a merchant from New Hampshire who had played an important role in American expansionist policy in Asia by concluding treaties with Siam and Muscat and who had initiated an action that eventually had led to the opening of these East Asian countries, included Korea in his 1834 report to Secretary of State Louis McLane concerning targets of American trade interest. Two years later, while journeying to Japan to negotiate a treaty, he died in Macao. In view of Roberts' unusually wide and intensive interests in Asian countries, it is highly possible that, had he lived, he would have extended his attention to Korea.[4]

Roberts' death, along with Korea's remote location and small size, among other reasons, kept Korea closed during the important two decades around mid-century. During this twenty-year period two moves, not important in terms of the consequences yet not insignificant, occurred; they were the first official actions with regard to Korea of the American government. In the spring of 1845, soon after the conclusion of the first treaty between the United States and China, Congressman Zadoc Pratt of New York, the chairman of the House Naval Affairs Committee, introduced before the House of Representatives a resolution calling for immediate steps to open commercial relations with Korea as well as Japan; it failed to go through the Congress.[5] The second action came about a decade later. By this time enough need was felt in Washington for an action to open Japan, and the Perry mission was well under way. Secretary of State William L. Marcy told Robert M. McLane, the new commissioner to China, that he would be empowered to make, if possible, treaties with Korea and other Asian countries. The secretary added if the Perry mission failed, McLane should renew the effort to make a treaty with Japan. It should be noted that in both of these cases, Korea drew, along with Japan, the attention of the American government. But apparently it was still too early for the Korean peninsula to draw enough attention that the Americans would send a mission; both proposals died without any follow-up.

Then came the two busy decades of the 1860s and the 1870s. Korea drew much more attention from Washington, and the Americans made some serious efforts to open the Korean door. In addition to the 1871 Low-Rodgers expedition, three more incidents occurred during these two decades. The first one came in 1868 in the wake of the *General Sherman* case. In the spring of 1868, when the facts of the *General Sherman* incident were still uncertain, George F. Seward, consul general in Shanghai, sent a request to Secretary of State William H. Seward asking for the authority to go to Korea with the dual objectives of acquiring from the Koreans a satisfactory explanation of the 1866 disaster and of making a treaty with the Korean government. The consul general's request was based on information from

Frederick B. Jenkins, an American merchant-adventurer in China.[6] Secretary Seward responded quickly, giving his nephew the requested authority.[7] Meanwhile, George F. Seward discovered that Jenkins' information about the three-man Korean mission in China and Korea's desire for a treaty with the United States, on which the request to the secretary of state had been based, was not true, and he reported the discovery to the secretary.[8] Secretary Seward immediately withdrew the permission he had given to the consul in Shanghai, thus ending the episode.[9] It is interesting to note just how casually an important national policy decision was handled; it seems also to indicate that by the late 1860s at least some American policy makers wanted to conclude a treaty with the Koreans.

The ill-fated Low-Rodgers expedition derailed efforts to conclude such a treaty. In 1882 the importance of Low's mismanagement in carrying out his mission became even more obvious when one of the major reasons given by the Korean public in objecting to a treaty with the United States was the very incident at Kanghwa in 1871. The Korean public insisted that Korea should not make a treaty with the nation involved in the 1871 incident.

The third incident during this period took place in 1878, two years after the conclusion of the Kanghwa Treaty, which opened Korea to Japan. Apparently, the United States and other Western powers did not consider this treaty as opening the Korean door to the outside world. Nevertheless, it had an impact upon the Western powers, which appeared in the form of the Sargent Bill in the United States Senate. On April 8, 1878, Senator Aaron A. Sargent of California, the chairman of the Senate Naval Affairs Committee, introduced a bill before the Senate authorizing the president to appoint a commission to make a commercial treaty with Korea. Referred to the Senate Foreign Relations Committee on April 17, the bill never emerged. An identical bill, introduced before the House by Representative Henry B. Banning of Ohio, met with the same fate.[10] Americans were apparently still pessimistic about the prospect of making a treaty with Korea.

The last abortive attempt was the Shufeldt mission of 1880. Definitely an abortive incident, it was certainly the most important, not only because it was the last of the series but also because a link was established during the incident that led to the successful conclusion of a treaty with Korea. The *Ticonderoga* mission of 1878–1880 was an unusual opportunity for both Shufeldt and the United States for naval diplomacy. After stating the overall objective of the mission, which was "to visit the unfrequented ports of Africa, Asia, the islands of the Indian Ocean with a view to the encouragement and extension of American commercial activities," Richard Wigginton Thompson, the navy secretary, told Shufeldt, in his instructions of October 29, 1878, regarding Korea, "to visit some parts of Korea with the endeavor to reopen by peaceful means negotiations with that government."[11] No evidence indicates the degree of importance of Korea in Shufeldt's nearly two-year mission, but, in view of his first visit to the country ten years before and the degree of seriousness, and even determination, he showed later, it may be that Korea held a special interest for him when the USS *Ticonderoga* departed the navy yard of Norfolk on December 7, 1878.[12]

When the *Ticonderoga* reached Asiatic waters early in 1880 after more than a year's voyage along the African coast and through the Asian islands, Shufeldt sent a telegram from Singapore to John A. Bingham, American minister in Tokyo, on February 14 to ask his assistance for the Korean overture.[13] Shufeldt explained to Bingham the objective for his Korean visit, referring to Evarts' November 9, 1878, communication to Secretary Thompson, which indicated the secretary's sending of instructions to Bingham to render assistance to Shufeldt.[14] Although the November 9 instruction had not been sent to Bingham at that time through some "inadvertance," Bingham immediately acted to obtain the Japanese government's good offices.[15] Bingham wrote to Inouye Kaoru, the Japanese foreign minister, on March 12, explaining Shufeldt's plan for a friendly visit to Korea and requesting Inouye to assist the mission by writing a letter to the Japanese official in Korea and one to Korean officials asking for a "favorable consideration."[16] A reply came from Inouye on April 7, nearly a month later, in which he explained candidly that because only a few years had elapsed since the treaty had been concluded between his country and Korea, because the treaty was not yet fully implemented, and because the Korean government was still "disinclined" to open the country to other powers, he feared his introduction of Shufeldt to the Korean officials might cause some "complications" for Japanese-Korean diplomacy. However, he promised that he would be happy to instruct the Japanese officials in Korea "to do their best in their power in facilitating the said mission."[17] On April 9 Bingham had a conversation with the vice minister for foreign affairs about the prospect for assistance for Shufeldt, and the next day he received a copy of a letter from Inouye to Kondo Masuki, the Japanese consul at Pusan. The short letter simply instructed the consul to give "every possible assistance" that might be required.[18] In his letter of April 20, Bingham suggested to Shufeldt, who had been in Nagasaki since the fifteenth of the month, to go to Pusan because it was the only Korean port open to the Japanese. Equipped with the letter from Inouye to Kondo, Shufeldt left Nagasaki on the *Ticonderoga* in the early morning of May 3 for a four-day visit to Korea. The next day Shufeldt explained to Kondo at Pusan the purpose of his visit and asked him to transmit his letter to the Korean king through the local official. Kondo immediately took the steps necessary to carry out his duty. Early in the morning of the sixth he returned the letter to Shufeldt with the explanation that he had failed to convince the local magistrate, Shim Tong-shin, who had been firm in his assertion that he would not transmit a communication from a foreigner to his government and that, further, it was inappropriate for the Japanese government to act as a channel of communication with the United States, the nation of the 1871 Kanghwa expedition.[19] Disappointed, but not discouraged, Shufeldt went directly to Yokohama and then to Tokyo to undertake the second round of activities of his 1880 Korean mission.

In Tokyo Shufeldt found Bingham still willing to help. After meeting with Shufeldt on May 12 and 15, Bingham arranged for Shufeldt to meet with Inouye on May 20. At this important conference, in which Bingham also participated, Shufeldt read a portion of his letter to the Korean monarch to show Inouye the purpose and the friendly nature of the letter; he explained to Inouye that he only wanted the Japanese government to enclose his letter in a letter of its own to the Korean authority.[20] Inouye indicated that he would have to get the approval of the cabinet to communicate directly with the Korean government, and he promised the Americans that he would take up the proposition with the cabinet, which was scheduled to meet four days later. On the day of the cabinet meeting, Bingham informed Shufeldt that he had received a communication from Inouye stating that the Japanese government had decided to forward the letter.[21] How the letter would be delivered to the Korean authority was a question that yet remained. Shufeldt and Bingham held candid discussions with two Japanese officials, the minister to Korea, Hanabusa Yoshichika, who happened to be in Tokyo, and Vice-Minister Uyeno. After some consideration, Shufeldt decided to leave the delivery of the letter in the hands of the Japanese and to wait at Nagasaki for sixty days to hear from Korea.[22] Soon Inouye informed Bingham that the letter would be sent by mail steamer to Kondo at Pusan, and he enclosed a copy of his covering letter to the Korean minister of ceremony, Yun Cha-sŭng. Inouye wrote a fine letter to the Korean official: after stating the objective of the Shufeldt mission, he told Yun that since the general state of the world had changed much in recent years it was no longer possible for any nation to reject foreign intercourse, and he advised him to comply with the request of the United States government in a friendly spirit. Inouye also wrote a detailed letter to Kondo instructing him not to reveal the enclosure of Shufeldt's letter to Yun and counseling him in a note to use his own discretion about this matter.[23] Kondo saw the importance of his duty, and on June 10 he prevailed on Sim Tong-sim, the Tongnae prefect, to deliver the Shufeldt letter to Seoul. He even suggested to Sim that if the letter were not delivered, the American envoy would surely return to the Korean port to open negotiations with the Korean government, a statement that amounted to a mild threat to the local official.[24] Shufeldt's letter was finally delivered in the middle of June; no one was sure how the Korean government would respond.

The Korean government spent a month pondering a response to the Shufeldt overture and then returned the letter unopened to Kondo on July 21, eight days before the due date.[25] Uyeno informed Bingham of the Korean response on August 4, and Bingham sent the information to Shufeldt two days later; the latter did not receive it until the seventeenth of the month, nearly a month after the date of Kondo's receipt of the Korean communication in Pusan.[26] Yun explained that he was returning the Shufeldt letter because first, Korea was addressed as "Great Corai," the title of the former dynasty, instead of "Great Chosen"; and second, the letter from the American envoy was addressed to the king instead of the minister of ceremony.[27] When Shufeldt finally received the long-waited Korean reply, he was furious and his reaction was immediate; he wrote on the same day to Bingham pointing out that the Korean reply was evasive, that addressing the king was not inappropriate because the organization of the Korean government was not clear to the outside world, that if the change of name from "Great Corea" to "Great Chosen" was that important it should have been pointed out by the Japanese Foreign Office, and that the Japanese official in Pusan should not have received back the communication.[28] In agreement with him, Bingham initiated the second round of action on September 11.[29] Bingham, not only sympathetic with Shufeldt's effort but also irritated by the outcome, used strong words in his last effort to employ the Japanese good offices: he pointed out to Inouye that the Korean act of returning the letter amounted to an indignity to both the United States and Japan; he said that if the Japanese consul at Pusan had known the meaning of receiving the returned letter he should have refused it as an offense to both countries; and he requested Inouye to again submit the Shufeldt letter to the Korean government through the Japanese minister in Seoul.[30] On the same day, September 11, Shufeldt left Yokohama for San Francisco; Bingham was sorry to see him leave before the completion of the mission and promised to send the results of his own further action directly to the State Department.[31] However, not much resulted from his further action; on September 18 Bingham received a negative answer from Inouye. In his letter, the tone of which more than matched that of Bingham, Inouye pointed out that when he agreed to transmit Shufeldt's letter to the Korean government, he was not accepting responsibility for its acceptance by the Korean government, that if it was refused by the Korean government his government was not in the position to force its acceptance, that the acceptance or rejection of the communication depended solely upon the decision of the Korean government, that in view of the state of affairs in Korea the refusal was understandable, and that, therefore, he was declining to comply with the new American request. He added, however, that he would be glad to try once more through Kondo in Pusan.[32] Thus ended Shufeldt's efforts in the summer of 1880 to reach the Koreans through Japanese assistance.

Even though Shufeldt had some hope that his second round of efforts to communicate with the Korean king might prove successful, he grew impatient as July progressed, and when the end of the sixty days approached, his irritation was almost unbearable.[33] Fortunately, however, a new development emerged in the meantime, and when he left Asian waters on September 11, he was again hopeful about the future prospects of his Korean project. While he was in Nagasaki waiting for the Korean reply, he made the acquaintance of the Chinese consul in the city, U Tsing, a protégé of Li Hung-chang, the most powerful Chinese statesman. Because of its traditional relations with Korea, China was in a position to know everything that transpired in Korea. Because of the rising influence of Japan in Korea after the Kanghwa Treaty of 1876 and because of other concerns in international relations in East Asia, Li was kept informed about the Shufeldt mission in the summer of 1880. When he learned from U of Shufeldt's predicament, he jumped at the opportunity and invited Shufeldt to come to Tientsin.[34] Willingly accepting the invitation, Shufeldt visited Li in Tientsin and had an important three-hour interview with him on August 26. After Li heard Shufeldt's views on the likelihood of war between the Chinese and the Russian fleets and on other international matters, he promised his assistance for the commodore's Korean project, saying he would advise the Korean government to respond favorably and suggesting a possibility of using the commodore's services for the Chinese navy. Li was sincere with Shufeldt and parted from him with a word that he would keep the American minister in Peking informed about the follow-up of his advice to the Korean government. Thus, with the promise of Li, Shufeldt left Asian waters in the summer of 1880 optimistic about the future prospects of his Korean project. It remains for us to determine why Shufeldt's Korean mission of 1880 failed.

Shufeldt was happy with the dedicated cooperation of Bingham; he was well-satisfied with the minister's "very efficient aid."[35] However, he was not satisfied with the assistance he received from the Japanese, and at the conclusion of his mission, he openly questioned the good faith of the Japanese officials involved in the service and attributed the failure of his Korean mission to the shortcomings of the Japanese aid.[36] Specialists on Korean diplomacy readily accepted Shufeldt's view; one thought the Japanese were "acting with duplicity," and another thought the act of secretly urging the Koreans to refuse Shufeldt's proposition while openly introducing it was a "tricky method."[37] There is, of course, the possibility of duplicity on the part of the Japanese; but judging from Inouye's openness and sincerity and his straightforward attitude toward Shufeldt and Bingham and the distance that separated him and his subordinates from the Korean officials, it is doubtful that there was lack of sincerity on the part of the Japanese. Their real problems were the restraints that hindered them as they tried to help the Americans at this point. The Japanese occupation of the Ryūkyū, which had taken place in the previous year, displeased both the Koreans and the Chinese; the Japanese were also trying to open two more ports in Korea, Wŏnsan and Inchŏn, at this time (through Hanabusa, their representative in the Korean capital) as well as trying to impose high tariffs on Korean imports while also trying to reduce their own with the Western nations. This is not to deny that they also wanted to acquire as large a share as possible of the foreign trade of Korea and they probably also did not want to show the foreigners how badly they treated Korea. Actually, Inouye was brutally frank in confessing in his early communication that the help given Shufeldt might give rise to some complications with regard to the execution of the Japanese treaty with Korea, and at the end of the whole episode he seemed to have mobilized all the courage he had in bluntly turning down the request of a friendly power for use of its good offices.[38]

Shufeldt thought that the denial of permission to use force in any form in carrying out his mission in Korea also hindered its successful conclusion. At the conclusion of the mission, he wrote to the navy secretary: "While I consider that the Korean matter is not entirely concluded I think that I am authorized to predict an unfavorable result. Without some exhibit of force upon the Korean coast it will be difficult to convince that government of the earnestness of our purpose."[39] At one point he even suggested occupying Port Hamilton.[40] The exhibit of force might have given a sense of inevitability to some Koreans, especially those among the ruling cirle in Seoul, and might have induced them to receive Shufeldt's letter. But a more likely outcome is that such an act would have delayed the final conclusion of the treaty by at least a few more years. The Confucian leaders effectively used the 1871 incident when they spoke out against the Inchŏn treaty of 1882 and almost blocked it at the last moment. If Shufeldt had used force in 1880, especially if he had lost control, the action would almost certainly have been used by the noisy reactionaries in the later years to block the treaty.

The fundamental reason for the failure of the Shufeldt mission of 1880 must be sought in the domestic condition of Korea. As will be explained in the following pages, the year 1880 was the decisive year of education for the Korean ruling circle; they did not yet realize the need to conclude a treaty with the United States. The education of the Korean elite circle did not begin until the Kim Hong-jip mission to Japan took place, the first meeting between Kim and Ha Ju-chang, the Chinese minister in Tokyo, occurring on August 20. During the conference of the king's advisers and in the presence of the king himself, Prime Minister Yi Ch'ae-ung openly regretted that the government had not entertained Shufeldt's wish when he had come to Pusan the previous spring.[41] Inouye revealed an understanding of the Korean situation when he said in his September 18 communication to Bingham: "Considering the present state of affairs in Korea it is to be inferred that in thus refusing to accept that commodore's communication the Korean government have judged themselves fully justified in the course pursued and have intended no insult toward the government of the United States."[42] In the middle of October the king debated actively with his advisers about the desirability of opening the nation to the United States; by the end of the month he had built enough support to take necessary actions. Thus, if Shufeldt's letter had reached Seoul three months later than it did, the response of the Korean government might have been quite different.

In the final analysis, it must be said that the Koreans were not yet ready to respond positively to Commodore Shufeldt's knocking at their door in the summer of 1880 and that if the effort had to be made with the assistance of a foreign power in the region, Japan was a wrong choice. The choice was made by the State Department on the basis of an insufficient understanding of the relationship between Korea and Japan, which the department incorrectly described as a "state of intimacy."[43] (John Hay, assistant secretary of state, probably surmised correctly when he thought that even if Inouye had yielded to the American entreaty of September 11, that effort too, would have failed.) China had much more influence over Korea and was, in fact, probably the only nation at that point with some power to persuade; its leaders had already begun to educate the Korean leaders about the need to open the nation to the outside world through a treaty with the United States. China was the power Shufeldt could rely on for his project, and happily the connection was made before his departure. Nevertheless, the Koreans needed at least two more years before their education was complete. The *New York Times* published an interesting editorial while Shufeldt was agonizing over his mission in Asian waters.

> The only forbidden land on the surface of the globe is the Kingdom of Korea. Loosely speaking, there are not many men in the world who care whether the country is open or shut. But there are enough who care to make it very uncomfortable for the Koreans, who would much rather live in a land forbidden to strangers than to be liable to constant interruptions of foreigners, with their proposals for trade, their outlandish notions, the strange influences on the domestic manners, speech, and religion.[44]

In a sense, Shufeldt's meeting on August 26, 1880, with Li Hung-chang was the most important step taken during his Korean mission; his actions in 1881 and the following year were little more than a follow-up to that first important step. No policy maker in Washington could ignore the attractive possibility of opening Korea through Li's assistance; and with his unusual ability for the task, his fine background, and his connections with important people in the policy-making circle in Washington, Shufeldt was easily able to obtain the instruction from Secretary of State James G. Blaine in the spring of 1881 to pursue his incomplete mission in the Far East.[45] Still, however attractive the proposition, the American government was not sure about the outcome in view of its past experience in Far Eastern affairs, and Shufeldt's mission in the spring of 1881 was of an exploratory and preliminary nature to find out whether conditions would be favorable for the proposed act. Blaine gave very detailed and cautious instructions for Shufeldt to follow in China.[46] The commodore left San Francisco on May 19, reaching China on June 21. He immediately went to see Viceroy Li in Tientsin and obtained much information in an interview on July 1.[47] Li told the commodore that a Korean official visiting in Peking, Yi Yong-suk, had informed the viceroy that the Korean government was favorably inclined to make a treaty with the United States. Shufeldt learned also that Koreans were divided on this issue: the king and most of his ministers favored making a treaty while most of the minor officials and the people did not. Having perceived that the danger of war between China and Russia had passed, Shufeldt realized that there was no feeling of urgency in China or Korea for treaty making. From this interview and from a follow-up interview with Li that took place on July 18, Shufeldt emerged feeling positive about successfully completing his mission. Li told Shufeldt that he was sending a letter to the Korean officials urging them to support the treaty making, and he asked the commodore to be patient and to wait for about ninety days. Thus, another trying period of waiting began for Shufeldt.

This time the commodore's daughter and son were with him in China, but it was still another difficult summer for him. Waiting idly for half a year, not ninety days, as it turned out, was hard enough, but there was an added vexation. The previous summer Li had made a vague promise of trying to find an important position for Shufeldt in the Chinese navy, probably as the commanding officer of the entire fleet. But because the threat of naval warfare between Russia and China had subsided, Li no longer showed much interest in hiring Shufeldt for his navy; in addition, Shufeldt found the jealous and suspicious eyes of the foreigners in China, who had all heard something about his possible employment in the Chinese navy, almost unbearable.[48] By the middle of October, toward the end of the ninety-day period, even James B. Angell, the American minister in Peking, began to prod the commodore, saying that it was hardly becoming for an officer of his rank and reputation to remain too long at Tientsin when his continued presence there was misunderstood.[49] October and November passed, and still Shufeldt heard nothing from Li regarding the Korean answer. By early December Shufeldt probably lacked the patience to appreciate the humor of his son, who wrote: "I was of course delighted to hear from you, but felt sorry you had not your appointment a fixed fact. You don't say whether the Chinese government pay you a salary or not. What is the use of living among the barbarian unless they do?"[50] December was approaching its midpoint when Shufeldt's patience and persistence was rewarded. Li's telegram of December 15 informing him that the Korean government was willing to make the treaty with the United States reached him through the American minister's office.[51] The onerous period had ended; from this point on, good fortune was Shufeldt's.

To understand why Shufeldt was kept waiting so long, the Korean side of the story needs to be recounted. According to the Chinese sources, the idea of opening Korea to the Western powers as a counter to the Russian pressure from the north originated simultaneously and independently in the fall of 1878 with two men, Governor Ting Jih-ch'ang and the British minister Thomas F. Wade.[52] In 1878 and 1879 these two convinced Li Hung-chang. Li then began the long process of convincing the Koreans, a task that took about a year (from the summer of 1879 to the fall of the following year). His efforts, however, did not reach beyond the ruling elite in the capital. Meantime, Ho Ju-chang, the Chinese minister in Tokyo, joined Li in this formidable task. Ho attempted to enlighten the Koreans in the six conferences he had with Kim Hong-jip, who was heading the Korean learning mission in Japan. The small booklet called *Chao-hsien ts'e-lueh* (The policy for Korea), authored by Huang Tsun-hsien, the consul in the Chinese legation in Tokyo, for the very purpose of educating the Koreans, was handed to Kim, and it became the most important source of inspiration for the Koreans in the formulation of the open-nation policy. Interestingly enough, the Korean ruling elites readily accepted the ideas set forth. Especially surprising was the speed and the eagerness of the young king toward the ideas. In October, as soon as the king found a near consensus among his advisers supporting the idea of an open-nation policy, he began to dispatch his secret missions in all directions. A most formidable, and indeed nearly impossible, task faced by the leaders of the nation during the next year and a half was to educate the rest of the population. The Confucian literati's opposition to opening the nation to the West had begun in 1879. Most fierce in the spring of 1881, the opposition movement continued to late May of 1882, when Shufeldt was at Inchŏn getting ready for the last act of treaty making. Fortunately, the king, who was notorious for his weakness, used very strong measures against the opposition while carrying out a secret diplomacy to buy time for the education of the general public. In the fall of 1881, when the opposition was still strong, Li's message was brought to the king, urging him to seize the excellent opportunity to make a treaty with the American delegate. The king immediately despatched his messenger, Ŏ Yun-jung, who delivered to Li on December 1 the king's message of willingness to conclude a treaty with the United States, a message that eventually reached Shufeldt two weeks later. The American delegates in both Tokyo and Peking were aware of the situation in Korea,[53] but Shufeldt did not seem to know, at least at this point, why the Korean leaders failed to move faster. In the fall of 1881, Korea was still not ready, as a nation, to open itself to the outside world. Nevertheless, its leaders had decided to act by that time, and Shufeldt received the news on December 15.[54]

After a month of quiet, Shufeldt began to be bombarded by important messages originating in Washington. On January 19, 1882, he received from the new secretary of state, Frederick T. Frelinghuysen, a congratulatory telegram on his good prospect for treaty making with the Koreans.[55] The next day, he received Blaine's instruction of November 15 of the previous year.[56] It is interesting to note that it was a gloomy moment when Blaine drafted this important document in Washington; he had not received any promising information from either Shufeldt or Angell about the prospect of concluding a treaty. All he knew was that the Korean communication was overdue by about a month and a half and that Shufeldt was still waiting for it in China. Blaine was seemingly guided by a political concern—Shufeldt was his appointee, if not his protégé, and, after the death of President James A. Garfield, he was anticipating leaving his position within a month or so—and probably by the bureaucratic necessity of trying to conclude the business he had initiated. Whatever reason he may have had for writing the instruction at this time, he wrote a lengthy and thoughtful one. After listing a number of procedural precautions, he clearly set down the major objectives of the proposed Korean treaty—the relief and protection of American vessels and crews who might be shipwrecked on the Korean coast. Should conditions be favorable, he continued, Shufeldt should also acquire trading rights from the Koreans. A list of particulars followed: tariff rates were not to be fixed by the treaty; import duties should be levied only once; American citizens should have the right to travel into the interior; extraterritoriality and consular rights to communicate with the Korean government should be acquired; and a political representative should be established in due time. In comparison with this detailed instruction, a similar document from the new secretary of state, which Shufeldt did not receive until March 11, was short and simple.[57] After indicating that the shipwreck provision was the "first necessity," the new secretary of state left the commercial part to the commodore's discretion. He remarked that the treaty was a "mere first step" and the gains should be "simple and few." Three days later, Shufeldt learned from Admiral John M. B. Clitz, the commander of the Asiatic Squadron, about the assignment of the USS *Swatara* to his mission. This was the result of Blaine's action of November 17 of the previous year.[58] Now, with Blaine's instruction in his hand and a naval vessel at his service, Shufeldt was ready to take action in China. He immediately notified

Li that he had received the authority to conclude a treaty with Korea and requested an interview with him.[59] At this point, the viceroy was almost ready to go to Paoting-fu, his winter resort, and he suggested that Shufeldt come to the place incognito. Shufeldt declined this offer to avoid giving any feeling to the Westerners in China that he was making a secret deal with the viceroy, preferring to wait until Li's return to Tientsin. His first meeting with Li took place on March 25.

While Shufeldt was idle in Tientsin during February, the Chinese side was not; Li and the Korean envoy were taking preliminary actions. In the fall of the previous year, when the king was responding to Li's pressure for treaty making, he sent to China a special envoy, Kim Yun-sik, whose formal duty was supervising a group of Korean students who were sent to China to study various types of technology but whose much more important mission was to participate in the treaty-making process in China. Kim arrived in early January of 1882; the first of his six meetings with Li took place on the seventeenth. After exchanging information each had for the other side and after dealing with matters of general concern in the first three meetings, which took place on January 17 and 19 and February 7, Li and Kim took up the substance of the treaty in their fourth meeting on February 14.[60] Kim had brought three different drafts of the treaty—one prepared by Yi Tong-in, a Korean monk who was one of the king's trusted advisers and who drew his inspiration from the Chinese representatives in Japan and the Japanese leaders; a second drafted by Li's assistants in Tientsin, sent to Korea in 1881 through Yi Yong-suk, and now brought back to China; and a third drafted by Consul Huang in the Chinese legation in Tokyo. After some general comments on Yi's draft, the viceroy pointed out some particulars: Li indicated to Kim that the five-year delay in the establishment of diplomatic representation and in the drafting of trade regulations and a clause prohibiting missionary activities would not easily be accepted by the American envoy.[61] His main concern, however, was the dependency clause, which soon became the center of controversy in the negotiations between Li and Shufeldt. The viceroy suggested to Kim the desirability of inserting a clause in the treaty indicating the dependent relationship of Korea to China but stressing the former power's autonomy in its domestic and foreign affairs. Kim agreed with Li, a fact that Li used effectively in his discussion with Shufeldt. Kim also learned from Li that Shufeldt was contemplating a personal visit to Korea on May 1 if the Korean delegates had not arrived in China by that date; Li was therefore anxious to see the coming of the Korean delegates. Kim dispatched Pyŏn

Wŏn-kyu, one of his assistants, to Korea, from which the Ŏ Yun-jung mission to Peking resulted. Thus, while Shufeldt was idle, preparations were made on the Chinese and the Korean sides in January and February, and the ground was prepared, without his noticing it, for his March and April actions.

Shufeldt's long-awaited negotiations began first with two of Li's assistants—Ma Chien-chung, Li's foreign affairs adviser who had been trained in international law and politics in France, and Chou Fu, customs *tao-tai* of Tientsin—on March 9; during the course of these talks, the Chinese revealed that the dependency clause and several other clauses were to be included in the treaty.[62] Somewhat disappointed, Shufeldt decided to wait until Li's return to Tientsin. Shufeldt's first meeting with Li took place at his yamen on March 25, the day after Li's return. At this fruitful meeting, the two sides showed what they intended to accomplish through the treaty. They exchanged their drafts, and Li shared with Shufeldt some new information regarding the Korean involvement. Shufeldt's draft, which was prepared with assistance from Chester Holcombe, the secretary of the U.S. legation in Peking, contained all the essentials in the instructions of the two secretaries of state—the shipwreck clause, trade rights, extraterritoriality, the most-favored-nation clause, and the appointment of diplomatic representatives. In the first draft, it should be noted, there appeared clauses prohibiting the opium trade and calling for a ten percent tariff rate. The draft handed by Li to Shufeldt was called a revised version of the Korean draft but it actually was the work of his two assistants—Ma and Chen Chao-lu; it had been sent to Korea the previous year and brought back, along with two other drafts, by Kim Yun-sik.[63] The Chinese draft also included the clauses relating to shipwrecks, trade, extraterritoriality, and diplomatic representation, but with some variations. The most conspicuous feature of the Chinese draft was the inclusion of both the good offices clause and the dependency clause, as had already been indicated by Li's aides. The dependency clause read: "Chosen, being a dependent state of the Chinese Empire, has nevertheless hitherto exercised its own sovereignty in all matters of internal administration and foreign relation." This clause, which remained the center of a controversy even after a treaty was concluded, did not appear in Li's original version but emerged for the first time in Ha's version, probably at the behest of the Chinese minister in Tokyo. Nevertheless, once Li adopted the idea he pushed it persistently. Shufeldt also learned from Li during this conference that the opposition in Korea was still powerful, that the Korean government had arranged to send its delegate to China for the purpose of treaty making, and that if the envoy did not arrive within a month, by April 25, Li would send his delegate or a letter to accompany Shufeldt to Korea.[64]

From the beginning, Shufeldt felt that the most difficult single issue was the dependency clause; it remained critical until early May and still lingered at Chemulpo. The Chinese held firm on the issue in the April 1 meeting between Shufeldt and Li's assistants. On April 4, in a systematically reasoned written argument against the dependency clause, Shufeldt contended with both clarity and force that the United States had no complaint about Korea's freedom to take advice or whatever else from China, and that, as long as Korea had sovereign power in handling its own domestic and foreign affairs, the United States had the "right" to make a treaty with it. Moreover, he continued, the insertion of the clause would cause "complications" through the establishment by implication of a "joint protectorate over Korea."[65] However, the commodore's reasoned statement seemed to have no effect upon the Chinese; on the following day, during the April 5 meeting, Li said that the Koreans also wanted the clause and that he would not give any further assistance if the clause was deleted. Shufeldt was equally adamant, and he insisted that he would not go to Korea under Chinese auspices.

The breakthrough came from the Chinese side in the following meeting, on April 10, when Li suggested that the dependency clause might be omitted if the Korean king would write a letter to the president explaining that Korea, being a dependent state of China, concluded the treaty with the approval of the Chinese emperor and if Shufeldt would also write a letter to the Chinese indicating that he had sought Chinese assistance because of the special relationship between China and Korea. While Shufeldt had no objection to Li's idea, he said that he needed the approval of his government.[66] Two days later Shufeldt sent a telegram to the State Department asking for its decision on the dependency issue. The entire telegram read: "May I insert in a treaty with Korea an article admitting dependence of Korea upon China. China conceding sovereign power of Korea. They desire it. I have objected. Ans. Shufeldt."[67] No answer came from Washington.

With the dependency issue still unresolved, one last meeting on April 19 completed the treaty. Shufeldt and Holcombe produced the fourth draft by revising the third (a modification of the first American draft) and incorporating certain items from the first Chinese draft. The fourth draft, fourteen articles in length, became with a minor revision at Inchŏn the final version.[68] In this fourth draft the missionary clause was omitted; the rice issue, which was not brought up until two days later by Kim in his last meeting with Li, did not appear. By April 19 the treaty was complete except for the dependency clause, and Shufeldt eagerly waited for instructions from the State Department. That same day he sent another telegram to the department about the dependency issue. The department ignored this communication also. On April 28 Shufeldt, utterly frustrated and exhausted, wrote to the State Department: "When not hearing, and no further action being taken on the part of the Chinese government, I shall apply by telegram to be relieved from the duty assigned me."[69] The problem seems to have been more than a simple communication difficulty; it has been a cause for conjecture among scholars. Some imagined that the new secretary of state thought the silence would help Shufeldt bring his dealings with the Chinese to a successful conclusion;[70] others have surmised that Frelinghuysen might have wished for Shufeldt's failure because he was an appointee of the former administration.[71] Whatever the reason, the department left Shufeldt to make his best of the situation, which he did. Not able to abandon the project at this point, he went ahead and completed it; he proceeded to Chefoo on May 4 and left the port three days later aboard the USS *Swatara* for Korea. On May 6 Shufeldt confided to Holcombe: "I confess myself somewhat surprised at the evident desire of the Chinese government to act upon this treaty without imposing any conditions whatever and under these circumstances and in the absence of answers to the telegrams I feel it my duty to carry out my original instruction."[72]

Immediately after his meeting with Li on April 21, Kim sent the final version of the treaty through a messenger, Yi Ŭng-jun, to the Korean government; Li even volunteered to send a Chinese naval vessel to the Chinese border for the Yi mission.[73] (It is interesting to note that the Korean delegates failed to arrive in time to participate in the negotiations. The two Korean envoys, Ŏ Yun-jung and Yi Jo-yŏn, who both lacked the power of formal representation, did not leave Korea until April 4; they reached Tientsin on May 15, eleven days after Shufeldt left China and three days after the American envoy arrived in Korean waters.)[74]

Shufeldt's final act in Korea was largely ceremonial. When the commodore arrived in Korean waters on the *Swatara*, the two Chinese gunboats, which had arrived two days before, were there, and Ma and Admiral Ting Jih-ch'ang awaited his arrival. The Korean government extended its utmost courtesy to their important visitor. It had appointed as the chief delegate Sin Hŏn, the chief minister of the royal cabinet, and as his deputy, Kim Hong-jip, a member of the cabinet and an experienced diplomat. There were courteous greetings and exchanges of visits. Behind the pleasant formal protocol, however, two business transactions took place. The Koreans took up once more, this time much more seriously, the rice issue with Ma. Not considering it a serious matter for the Americans in the future, Shufeldt allowed the prohibition of the export of rice from Inchŏn in the eighth article.[75] The Chinese had also had the more serious business of dealing with the Koreans on the dependency issue. On May 14 Ma had sounded out Kim's view on the letter to be written by the king to the president explaining the dependency relationship, and even presented his prepared draft. Kim saw the importance of the matter and indicated that he would get the king's approval. The king did not have any choice on the issue, and Ma was able to hand the approved copy of the letter to Shufeldt on May 22 during the pleasant occasion of the celebration party given by the Chinese after the signing of the treaty.

The signing, of course, had been a ceremonial affair. Escorted by fifteen officers in full dress and the marine guard, Shufeldt left the *Swatara* on the morning of May 22 and went directly to the shore near Chemulpo and into the tent that the Koreans had prepared. As the final signature was appended to the six copies of the treaty, the *Swatara* honored the Korean monarch with a twenty-one-gun salute. Thus, the last hermit kingdom in East Asia was opened to the Western world on a fine spring day in 1882. Two days later Shufeldt left Korea for Shanghai, where his daughter was waiting for him.[76]

The treaty-making process was concluded within a year from the date of the signing by the exchange of the ratifications of the treaty. The Arthur administration presented the treaty with Korea to Congress for its approval on July 29, 1882.[77] No real difficulty in obtaining approval was anticipated, but because of unsatisfactory developments in ratification of treaties between Korea and three European countries—Great Britain, France, and Germany—concluded soon after the American-Korean treaty, there was some anxiety. The Koreans were eager to see the treaty ratified;[78] the Americans, especially the U.S. diplomatic representatives in the two East Asian countries, also thought the treaty should be ratified.[79] Congress adjourned without taking action on the Korean treaty, but the Senate approved it early in the following year, on January 9.[80] President Chester Alan Arthur signed the document on February 13; the exchange of documents took place at Inchŏn on May 19 between Lucius H. Foote, the first American minister to Korea, and Min Yŏng-mok, the Korean foreign minister.[81] Thus, the Treaty of Peace, Amity and Navigation between the United States and Korea became effective in the spring of 1883, opening a new era for the small Oriental kingdom.

What did the treaty provide? There were four open door or nonequal treaty clauses: the second through the fourth and the fourteenth articles. The second article stipulated the appointment of diplomatic and consular representatives; the third was the shipwreck clause; the fourth dealt with extraterritoriality; and the fourteenth was the most-favored-nation clause.[82] Commercial relations were covered in the fifth through ninth articles. The fifth article fixed the maximum tariff rate at 10 percent for ordinary goods and 30 percent for luxury goods; the sixth article prohibited the importation of opium into Korea; the eighth prohibited the export of rice from the open port of Inchŏn; the next article restricted the importation of ammunition by requiring a license from the Korean government. In addition to these two groups, which were common among all nonequal treaties, there was a third extraordinary group. This group had three articles: the first article contained the famous good offices clause; the tenth article gave Americans the right to employ Koreans (a similar provision can be found in the China treaty of 1844 with the additional right of the local police to arrest them);[83] and the eleventh article gave special protection to the students of the contracting parties studying in the other country. The fourth and last group had two procedural clauses: the twelveth article gave a five-year time for supplementary regulations, while the thirteenth article designated Chinese and English as the official languages for future correspondence.

Containing fourteen articles, the Korean treaty was longer and more detailed than the Japanese treaties, that of 1854 having nine and that of 1867 having twelve articles, but it was shorter and more concise than the two Chinese treaties, that of 1844 having thirty-four articles and that of 1860 having thirty articles.[84] The Korean-American treaty also lacked the clarity and organization of the Korean-British treaty to be concluded the following year.[85] Nevertheless, Shufeldt and Holcombe did an excellent job in preparing a detailed but not complicated treaty.

When making a comparative analysis of the Korean-American treaty of 1882, one should not forget that it was one of the nonequal treaties concluded between the Western powers and the East Asian nations in the nineteenth century. However, there was more of a sense of mutuality, equality, and fairness in this treaty than in any of the other nonequal treaties: these qualities prevailed in the stipulations for mutual diplomatic representation, the temporary nature of the extraterritorial rights, and the generous trade regulations and restrictions, including the prohibition of the opium and the rice trades. It demonstrated good will in the good offices and the student clauses. None of these favorable conditions, with the exception of the good offices clauses, which was in the treaty with China of 1858, can be found in the treaties the United States made with other East Asian countries or the treaties Korea later made with other Western countries. As noted by some scholars, of course, Korea's gain was America's loss.[86] But the United States could afford to be generous, and moreover, the loss was only temporary, because the Americans were to take advantage of the much more favorable conditions the British obtained from the Koreans through their treaty of 1883. This generosity and fairness probably had, to a certain extent, to do with the times—the 1880s were much different from the 1840s and the 1850s when the U.S.-China and the U.S.-Japan treaties were concluded—and the American national character. But it seems that the role of Shufeldt was also important; he was very firm when it was necessary—for example, on the dependency issue—but was also graceful in yielding minor points to the Koreans.

One point should be made concerning the translation of a phrase in the treaty. The misinterpretation or the misunderstanding of the good offices clause, which came not only from cultural differences but also from the wording in the Chinese text, caused much difficulty. The term "good offices" was a perfectly clear legal term to the Americans; but the phrase, when translated in the Chinese text as *p'ilsu sangjo* (literally, "must help each other"), could imply, especially to someone from an Oriental culture, an imperative.

Like an assessment of any piece of diplomacy, an evaluation of the treaty making of 1882 must be done within the framework of national objectives and circumstances or conditions. First, the interests and objectives of the participants in the treaty making must be determined. Because the United States initiated the action and pursued it to completion, its objectives were the most important force. The American objectives were clearly spelled out in the two instructions of the secretaries of state of November 14, 1881, and January 6, 1882. As had been noted, Frelinghuysen's instruction was relatively short and Blaine's much more detailed and specific, but both were clear about the two major objectives of the treaty: to resolve questions concerning shipwrecks and trade. Because of past experiences on the Korean coast, the first was more important than the second. With regard to trade, Frelinghuysen had modest hopes: he asked Shufeldt to use his discretion and stated that he should not seek too many gains. Blaine asked for more and was more specific: he demanded no fixed rates of tariff, one time payment of tariff, the right of American citizens to travel to the interior, and the right to establish consuls. The third objective, less explicit than those in the two other categories, was the attaining of special privileges, like extraterritoriality and most-favored-nation treatment. Although a few minor items came out somewhat differently from what Blaine wished, Shufeldt achieved all three objectives and more. On the issue of the exchange of representatives, he went directly to the level of an exchange of diplomatic representatives and obtained much more than Blaine had asked.[87] In addition to the national objectives, there was a personal objective on the American side, which was an equally dynamic force for the completion of the task. This was Shufeldt's personal motive. At least from 1867, when he first visited Korea, he never lost his interest in Korea. He was conscious about the magnitude of his task, calling his mission "the one unaccomplished event of final importance to Western nations" in the Far East.[88] There is no question that if Shufeldt had not opened Korea in 1882 another American would have done it; but it is also true that Shufeldt, with his high degree of intelligence, experience, maturity, grace, understanding of Oriental ways, fair amount of vanity, and above all plenty of patience was peculiarly fitted for the role.

The Chinese motives were equally clear. They desired, first, to counter both the Russian and the Japanese threats by enlisting the aid of the United States and other powers through the treaty-making process. Second, they wanted to bring the vague, traditional dependency relationship between the two Oriental countries—China and Korea—into the Western legal framework. The former objective was clear from the beginning;[89] the latter became evident in early 1882 and was definite by the time of Shufeldt's first meeting with Li's aides on March 9. Frederick Foo Chien lists another motive, which sounds almost too altruistic to be true: the introduction of Korea into the family of nations for its own welfare.[90] The inclusion of the good offices clause, the student clause, the limitation on extraterritoriality, and the many favorable conditions in the trade regulations seem to support this motive.

The most neglected actor in the 1882 treaty-making process has been Korea. While the Americans considered Korea the object of an action, to the Chinese it was always a passive follower. In fact, Korea was hardly an actor, even in this event in which its interest was most in stake. But although as a nation the country was still asleep, the young king and most of his advisers were awake about their national interest in the treaty making from at least the fall of 1880. They readily perceived the value of the power factor in the Chinese argument that had been presented by Li, Ha, and others.[91]

Another, not yet clearly defined but equally powerful, reason for the treaty making was the sociocultural consequences of learning from the Western nations. Korea had just begun to learn from both the Japanese and the Chinese through various special missions led by Kim Yun-sik, Kim Hong-jip, Ŏ Yun-jung, and others who played key roles in the treaty making. The Korean leaders, at least, were now eager to learn directly from the United States and the other Western nations from whom the Japanese and the Chinese had been learning since mid-century. Shufeldt himself saw clearly the necessity for the Koreans to make the treaty with the United States.[92]

The zeitgeist was also an important factor for the treaty making of 1881–1882. The pressure for the opening of Korea had built up, and the door had been opened in 1876 to one of the powers—Japan. Since that time, Japanese influence on the peninsula had increased. Russia had long been interested in the Korean peninsula, and its threat from the north was also mounting. China felt threatened, and its apprehension was translated into Li's move to persuade the Koreans to negotiate the treaty with the United States. Thus did other nations' interests and objectives influence Korea's actions. But the Koreans also used for their own national purpose the peculiar relationship with China and its pressure for the treaty to solve an internal problem; to a certain extent, this external pressure was effective in calming the conservative scholars and the general public. For his valuable service, Li demanded as a high price the insertion of the dependency clause in the treaty; it was, however, a necessary condition for the whole process.

In view of the nature of the treaty, the objectives of the nations involved, and the conditions, it should be said that the treaty making was very successful. The benefits received by the United States from Korea, as had been anticipated, were not large, but the treaty nevertheless did a good service for Korea and other Western nations. It is true that China failed to legalize the dependency relationship with Korea;[93] but as it turned out later, this failure was but a temporary setback, and Li did achieve his two other important objectives. For the Koreans, the treaty making was the greatest event in the nineteenth century. The treaty became a model for the treaties Korea concluded in the following years with the European powers; it provided a legal framework to combat Chinese encroachments in the following decades; and it opened the way to modernization.

Some would argue that the United States did a disservice to Korea by disturbing the delicate balance of power in East Asia, a disruption that eventually led to the downfall of the Korean kingdom in the early twentieth century.[94] A point to be made here is that the opening of Korea in 1882 through the treaty was not the cause of the downfall of the kingdom; there were many graver reasons for that event. If the treaty making was involved in any way in the demise of the kingdom, the fact is that the lateness of the event hurt the nation. If the nation had been opened three decades earlier, in the 1850s, or even a decade earlier, in the early 1870s, the course of history not only for Korea but also for the whole of East Asia might have been quite different in the twentieth century.

Shufeldt was naturally happy to see the successful conclusion of his important mission. But, other than his personal satisfaction, he received little reward.[95] He never received from his government the recognition and appreciation he well deserved for his service. Although promoted to rear admiral, he was disappointed at not being chosen to succeed Admiral Clitz as the commander of the Asiatic Squadron. President Arthur did not even mention his name when he reported the conclusion of the treaty making to Congress.[96] The Koreans, however, were extremely grateful to him for his service, and the king invited him to be an adviser, an invitation he was not able to accept. Even while he was still in Chemulpo, he complained about his bad health;[97] after resting some time in California, he returned to naval service, but retired in early spring of 1884.

3

THE FIRST
TWELVE YEARS

The twelve-year period from 1882, the year of the signing of the Shufeldt treaty, to 1894, the year in which the Sino-Japanese War broke out, was of considerable importance for American-Korean relations. During this formative era, the direction of American policy toward the peninsula kingdom was firmly established. The Koreans were also able to ascertain how much the distant, friendly nation was willing and able to do to help them in their struggle for independence against a powerful and rapacious neighbor and in their efforts toward modernization. An accurate assessment of the policies of the two nations toward each other is, therefore, the most important concern of this chapter. A correct treatment of the dependency issue, the most important problem faced by Korea during this period, is the second major task of this chapter. For convenience and ease of comprehension, this complex twelve-year period is divided into three subperiods: the three years from the spring of 1882 to the spring of 1885; the two years from the spring of 1885 to the spring of 1887; and the seven years from 1887 to the outbreak in 1894 of the Sino-Japanese War.

The first three years following the conclusion of the Shufeldt treaty were eventful years in Korea. Even before the first American minister reached Seoul, the first test case for American diplomacy appeared with the military rebellion of December 1882, in which Americans were involved. Then, Minister Lucius H. Foote arrived in Seoul, itself an important event for the bilateral relationship. The sending of the ten-month Korean mission to the United States followed. The period ended with the dramatic coup of December 1884, in which the Americans were inevitably involved. In the course of these events, the policies of the two nations toward each other were formulated and executed, and the dependency issue made its initial appearance.

On July 23, 1882, exactly two months after the signing of the Shufeldt treaty, violence broke out in Seoul, and when American officials in Washington and Peking recognized the possibility of a clash between two contending powers in Korea—China and Japan—they despatched a gunboat to Chemulpo. Initiated by a group of Korean soldiers who hated both the corrupt and oppressive Min family who controlled the government and the Japanese who were behind the recent reorganization of the Korean military system, the violence also attracted many common people equally unhappy about the chronic misgovernment of the nation and the arrogance of the Japanese, whose power had grown rapidly in the peninsula since the Kanghwa Treaty of 1876. By evening the wrath of the people had focused on the Japanese legation; and on the following morning, when the pressure from the mob on the legation building was too much to bear, the Japanese minister decided to abandon it and make his way to Chemulpo with twenty-seven others. Fortunately, they were picked up by the British survey boat *Flying Fish* and arrived safely in Nagasaki on July 29. Nevertheless, Japanese casualties in the incident were considerable: thirteen were killed, many others were wounded, and the legation building was burned down.[1]

The American reaction to the crisis was prompt. As soon as he learned of the disturbance in Seoul, Minister John R. Young in Peking acted immediately: he sent a telegram to the Department of State on July 30: "Mob attacked Japanese legation Korea two killed three wounded palace threatened have advised admiral send vessel protect treaty interests suggest President to order."[2] The telegram reached the secretary of state's office on the following day. Frelinghuysen immediately arranged for the despatch of a gunboat to Korea; he telegraphed Young on the following day, August 2, notifying the minister of his action: "Admiral instructed to send vessel and communicate with you."[3] Some seventeen days of communication and preparation were necessary; but the unhesitating actions of Frelinghuysen and Young resulted in the arrival of the USS *Monocacy* in Chemulpo on August 19. Young instructed Commander Cotton, the commanding officer of the *Monocacy*, in very clear terms; the commander would, upon arriving, see first the commanding officer of the Japanese expeditionary force and tell him that the purpose of his mission was to offer his "friendly office"; he would also see the Korean authorities and give them "moral support." The minister did not neglect to remind Cotton that preserving "a strict neutrality" was his duty.[4]

The voyage of the *Monocacy* was very successful, not because Cotton had an opportunity of offering the good offices of the United States, but because all three countries involved in the crisis—Japan, China, and Korea—looked favorably on the coming of the American gunboat and thanked the American government for its support.[5] The Korean government was especially grateful for the presence of the American gunboat in Korean waters.[6] The only question to be raised is whether there was sufficient justification for the American government to send the gunboat to Korea. It is true that the presence of two armed forces in Korea—more than three thousand Chinese troops with six gunboats and a battalion of Japanese soldiers with three gunboats and three cargo ships—encouraged the impression that the war was imminent. Moreover, the maintenance of peace and prosperity in East Asia was the general policy of the United States. On the basis of these two factors, one may well argue that sufficient reasons motivated the United States to send the gunboat to Korea in the summer of 1882. But it should be pointed out that the Shufeldt treaty had not yet been ratified and that the action in question took place ten months before the official opening of diplomatic relations between the two nations. In his explanation to Minister John A. Bingham of the intent behind the sending of the *Monocacy* to Korea, Secretary of State Frelinghuysen disclosed that the purpose was to protect "American interests should any be found there in jeopardy or the person of any citizen of the U.S. who may have been there and in danger."[7] There were no American citizens in Korea at this point, nor was there any American interest in the country except one expected in the future. Hence, if protection of American interests and citizens was the purpose, the secretary missed the point. Fortunately, this innocent act of good will occurred without hurting any nation involved, and it helped protect future American interests in Korea by showing good will to the Koreans before formal diplomatic relations began.

The three East Asian countries emerged somewhat unevenly from the 1882 incident in Seoul: while Japan and China gained, at least temporarily, Korea lost, a pattern that would occur again and again. The Japanese government, having decided on July 31 not to fight, at this point at least, ordered Hanabusa back to Korea to find a peaceful settlement. With one battalion of troops and six gunboats, he had no difficulty in exacting a 500,000 yen indemnity, stationing a legation guard of unspecified size, securing the punishment of the key figures responsible for the violence against the Japanese, and requiring that a special Korean apology mission be sent to Japan.[8]

The Chinese also responded promptly and decisively. As soon as the government learned of the Seoul incident from its representative in Tokyo, and learned that Japan intended to send an armed force, it immediately decided to despatch an armed force, a decision that was supported by two Korean officials, Kim Yun-sik and Ŏ Yun-jung, who were expressing the wish of the government in Seoul. The decision resulted in the initial despatch of a flotilla of three gunboats under Admiral T'ing, which arrived outside Chemulpo on

August 10, one day before Hanabusa, and the following despatch of some three thousand troops under General Wu, which arrived thirty miles south of Chemulpo and then came to Seoul. The pronounced object of the despatch of the sizable Chinese force was to handle the crisis in the suzerain state and to give protection to the Japanese in Korea. Wu even forcefully took away to China the Taewŏn'gun, the king's father (who had taken advantage of the crisis to make a short return to power), suspected of being a key person behind the incident.[9] Thus, the crisis in Seoul gave China an excuse to send and station a not small force as the first post–Shufeldt treaty act of a positive intervention policy in Korea.

Where Japan and China gained, Korea lost: the half million yen indemnity was heavy and, above all, the stationing of the two armies, which was forced upon the country, was certainly an evil. In the long run, however, all three East Asian countries lost in this crisis as a basis for a clash of empires was thus prepared as an aftermath of this incident.[10]

Formal diplomatic relations between the United States and Korea began in May 1883 with the arrival of the first minister, Lucius H. Foote. This was also the beginning of a two-year "honeymoon" period for the two countries. During these two years, the United States tried to establish a pattern for the relationship with Korea; Korea tried to find a trusted friend in the United States in a difficult time. Foote was a happy choice to serve in such a period, because he was the ideal person for the situation. Although his diplomatic experience was meager, he had other experiences—twenty years of public service, including four years as a judge in California—and he had, more significantly, a maturity brought by his fifty-seven years, resourcefulness, and thoughtfulness—a very important virtue in a traditional society such as Korea.[11] Foote, who arrived in Chemulpo on May 13 on the *Monocacy*—the same gunboat that had destroyed the Korean forts twelve years earlier—went through the initial steps of his function in a ceremonial fashion: he entered the capital city on the seventeenth; the exchange of the ratified treaties took place on the nineteenth, and his first audience with the king followed on the next day.[12] Of course, no inappropriate words are spoken on such an occasion, but the words the American minister and the king exchanged in Seoul on the early afternoon of one spring day of 1883 sound quite symbolic: along with other good words, Foote stated, "In this progressive age, there is a moral power more potent than standing armies, and the weakness of a nation is sometimes its strength." After wishing good health for the president and expressing his joy at the appointment of Foote to his position, the king expressed his genuine happiness: "I rejoice that the friendship of the two countries is now firmly cemented, and I am certain that the friendly relations will always continue."[13] The king, who had grown up and lived in the Confucian tradition must have rejoiced to hear these civilized words; however, it is doubtful whether Foote knew that the king's words were much more than simple ceremonial rhetoric. The American minister at least thought the Oriental monarch's presence was pleasing and his manner graceful. Thus the "peculiar nature" of the mission began.

Before leaving the United States for Korea, Foote received from Secretary Frelinghuysen two instructions spelling out his tasks in his new assignment, which were put in somewhat general terms but still sufficiently clear to guide him in carrying out his duties in Seoul. The first instruction, on March 3, indicated that the minister's job in Korea would be to "maintain and strengthen the harmony and friendly relations existing between the two countries." The second instruction, of the seventeenth of the same month, was a little more detailed: the secretary of state explained the minister's task in four categories: one, to exchange the ratification of the treaty; two, to cultivate friendly relations with the government and people of Korea; three, to report fully on relations between Korea and China and Japan; and four, to report on matters of political importance or of interest to those engaged in commerce.[14] In late December and in early January of the following year, Frelinghuysen again defined the objectives of American foreign policy in Korea. The United States did not have, the secretary said, any special objective other than "the advancement of commerce and the material and general interests of Korea" and "to meet whenever possible, the just wishes and expectations of a monarch and a people."[15] All of these words were far too general as guides for situations Foote soon encountered in the Korean position; but the vagueness was in a sense convenient, for it gave him plenty of room for interpretation and discretion.

Foote had little difficulty in carrying out the secretary's instructions. His first task in Seoul was the exchange of the ratified Shufeldt treaty. He cultivated friendly relations with the Korean government. He satisfied the Department of State with detailed reports on the political and other conditions in Korea.[16] Although it was not clearly indicated in the instructions from State, Foote knew well that the main task of any national representative was to develop and protect the economic and related interests of the government and the people he was representing, and he did well in this task. During his stay in Seoul, substantial American economic interests developed: the Americans sold to the Koreans some 4,000 stands of breachloading firearms and ammunition in 1883 and the following year; an American company obtained a charter to operate steamers along the Korean coast and on Korean rivers; another American company acquired a timber concession with an estimated value of between $300,000 and $500,000; and Thomas Edison was given the right to construct an electric and telephone facility in the palace.[17] Besides these economic interests, American missionaries' and advisors' interests were important, even though they were still small in these early years. The first American missionary did not arrive in Korea until 1884, and there was only a handful of missionaries by the end of this period; but the king had already given his permission and encouragement for the construction of mission schools and hospitals.[18] The total amount of economic and cultural interests of the United States in Korea was still small in the spring of 1885, but in this short time a sound and significant footing was established.

During this and the following subperiods, the Koreans faced the formidable task of maintaining their independence against great pressure from their neighboring empire while at the same time taking steps toward modernization. In both of these tasks they received help from the Americans. These tasks can be discussed in terms of the issues and major events of the period: gunboat diplomacy, the 1883–1884 special Korean mission to the United States, the dependency issue, and the émeute of 1884.

The unfortunate connotations of the phrase "gunboat diplomacy" give the impression that the Western powers in the nineteenth century ruthlessly used their gunboats to achieve their diplomatic objectives. It is true that the industrially advanced Western powers frequently used this particular means of diplomacy; however, it is equally true that all nations freely adopted any diplomatic means within certain legal and moral boundaries. Plainly defined, gunboat diplomacy consists of the employment of naval vessels to realize certain diplomatic objectives. American use of gunboats in Korea goes back to the mid-1860s, with the most conspicuous case being the 1871 naval expedition, and extends to the early 1900s, as will be discussed in the following chapters. The only difference between the early period—the pre-1882 years—and the later period—the post-1882 years—is that, whereas the American gunboats were used against the Koreans in the early period, they were used for them in the later period.

Because Korea is a peninsula and because the United States was separated from Korea by the Pacific Ocean, ships were the only means of contact between the two nations; gunboats consequently were used for different purposes within the boundaries of diplomacy. One of them was transportation and communication. When Foote was picked for the Seoul position, Secretary Frelinghuysen asked the navy secretary, William E. Chandler, to send a gunboat to Korea to provide transportation for the new minister; the secretary also requested permission to keep the vessel in Korean waters as a means of communication. The navy responded willingly and gave excellent cooperation on this and many other similar occasions.[19] Gunboats were also used to conduct coastal surveys.[20] The third, and by far the most important, purpose for the use of American gunboats during this period was political. The first person to suggest keeping a gunboat on the Korean coast for political purposes was Minister Bingham in Tokyo. "I beg leave to suggest that an American naval vessel should be stationed permanently," wrote Bingham to Frelinghuysen, "for the time being in an open port of Korea." He continued: "I have no doubt that the Government of Korea will gladly hail our flag and representative; but I am sure that the Government will feel greater security and be in fact abler to maintain its authority in our interests as its own by the presence in Korean waters of an American man of war."[21] The State Department readily adopted the idea, and the Navy Department's response was equally prompt; this pattern of request and response was to be repeated many times in the coming years.[22] When the émeute of 1884 broke out in Seoul, two American gunboats, one of which was the flagship for the Asiatic Squadron commanded by the admiral himself, were rushed to Chemulpo; Admiral John L. Davis even invited the king to his ship in an effort to boost his morale.[23] This is not to suggest that American gunboat diplomacy maintained the security of Korea during this period; but it is clear that the government used its gunboats and the occasional landing of the marines willingly and effectively, and it did not fail to give moral support to the Korean government and even some security at times.

The most serious problem the Koreans faced soon after the conclusion of the Shufeldt treaty was the change in Chinese policy toward the peninsula kingdom from one of passive advice to one of active intervention. In their struggle to maintain their independence against the new thrust of their aggressive neighbor, the Koreans sought both moral and other assistance from the United States. Frederick Foo Chien located the origin of the change in Chinese policy during the period of September–October 1882.[24] It must have happened somewhat earlier, at least at the time of the July meeting of the same year in Seoul. Chien interpreted the change as part of the Chinese effort to fit traditional Sino-Korean relations into the legal framework of the West, with the objective of restoring the ground lost since the conclusion of the Kanghwa Treaty of 1876 between Korea and Japan.[25] If Chien's thesis is correct, China should have accepted the legal effect of the conclusion of the Shufeldt treaty—the independence of Korea; but this China did not do. Whatever the logic behind the Chinese policy, the government of the United States had to come up with a working formula to handle the issue.

Even before revealing his views on the dependency issue to the newly appointed Minister Foote, Secretary Frelinghuysen had to respond to an inquiry from John Russell Young, the American minister in Peking, on this issue. In his August 4, 1882 instruction, the secretary stated that, in view of all circumstances, he could not but regard Korean independence as an established fact.[26] Early the following year, when he was asked by Young whether the Shufeldt treaty should be ratified by the Chinese emperor he gave a firm negative answer.[27] In the spring of 1883, Frelinghuysen's mind was clear and firm on the issue. In his March 17 instruction to Foote he stated: "As far as we are concerned Korea is an independent sovereign power, with all the attendant rights, privileges, duties, and responsibilities." He then added an important statement regarding Korean-Chinese relations, explaining that the United States had no desire to interfere with the relations between the two nations unless it was prejudicial to the treaty with the United States.[28] Frelinghuysen apparently found this convenient but somewhat evasive dual policy the most pragmatic one. While China switched its relations with Korea from the sociocultural to the political realm, it also began to act in the economic realm, concluding with the Korean government in the fall of 1882 commercial regulations that were duly signed by the representatives of the two countries. To the Westerners this was the single most annoying document signed by the Koreans for a long time after that fall.[29] In his March 17 instruction to Foote, Frelinghuysen pointed out the special privileges the Chinese merchants would enjoy that the Americans would not according to the Shufeldt treaty—trading at four points in the interior, trading in the interior under passports, taking foreign goods to the four points and buying native goods in the interior, transporting native produce from one port to another, and paying low import duties. He also showed anxiety about the possibility of the monopoly of foreign trade by the Chinese merchants and instructed the minister to report fully on the matter in Korea and wait for further instructions.[30] Instead of giving the Chinese the advantage in trade with Korea, the document prematurely alarmed the European powers before they concluded their final treaties with Korea; thus the Chinese failed to reap great benefits from the scheme because the European powers obtained through the treaties many of the benefits the Chinese had tried to monopolize.[31]

Chinese control of Korea in 1883 and the following year was more successful in other areas: Chinese troops remained in Korea; the Chinese began to train Korean soldiers under the direction of General Wu; the commissioner Chin Shu-fang, who had come first as only a commercial agent of China, later became the agent for diplomatic affairs as well; and the Chinese government appointed Paul Georg von Moellendorff, who was also in charge of the Korean customs office, as foreign policy adviser to the Korean government. Both Foote and Young reported fully to Frelinghuysen the extent of China's policy in Korea.[32] This was only the initial period of Chinese control over Korea, a control that would be further strengthened in the following years.

When the king and the people of Korea welcomed the representative of the United States in the spring of 1883, they were doing more than opening diplomatic relations; they were opening the door to another civilization. Despite a large number of serious drawbacks as a king, Kojong had many virtues, one of which—a very important one—was his genuine interest in and even zeal for modernizing his country by learning from Western culture. He and his people chose the United States as the representative of this culture, and they tried to learn from its people. The introduction of steamships, telephones and electricity, schools and hospitals, and new weapons all came through American hands; they were the agents of modernization in Korea. In addition, a model farm was established with seeds and animals brought from the United States in this early period.[33]

A matter that made the king and high officials of the Korean government very anxious for years was bringing American military and political advisers and school teachers to Korea. The coming of three military advisers and three school teachers from the United States became the cause of so much anxiety that it acquired a legendary character in the history of the modernization of Korea in the 1880s. In the fall of 1883 the king first mentioned his wish to hire American military men as instructors to train a modern Korean military unit; his request was repeated many times throughout this period and continued to the latter part of the decade.[34] In the fall of 1884, the State Department referred the Korean request to the War Department; this referral was just the beginning of a long process.[35] The request for three teachers was made in the fall of 1884 and was a much easier subject for the Americans to handle. The Koreans also desired to obtain American advisers for foreign policy and other policy areas and to obtain the advice of the American minister and others in the American legation. The king expressed his desire to hire an American adviser first on October 19, 1883, and the request was later repeated.[36] This subject later became one of the most delicate diplomatic issues. An even more delicate issue was the American minister's activity as the king's informal adviser. Foote brought this matter up soon after his arrival in Seoul on July 19, 1883, and, two months later, he received Secretary Frelinghuysen's qualified approval: the secretary approved such activity if Foote acted with discretion and treated the king's request as a "personal question."[37] Not all other secretaries held the same view, and the matter later became a difficult subject between the State Department and the legation in Seoul.

The Americans were very generous in helping the Koreans in their modernization effort, and this American generosity was best expressed in the sending of the first, special Korean mission to the United States, which took place in 1883–1884. This mission was not the first of its kind for Korea; three relatively large missions, numbering between fifty-eight and seventy-six members, had been sent to Japan in 1876, 1880, and 1881; but this was the first special mission to go to a Western nation, and its impact was long-lasting and significant. On July 5, only a month and a half after his arrival in Seoul, Foote said to the king that his government would be pleased to receive an embassy from Korea.[38] The Korean monarch acted promptly: on the following day the Council of State decided to send the mission; it left Chemulpo before the end of the month. The ten-month mission arrived in San Francisco on September 2, stayed three months in the United States, and returned to Chemulpo on May 31 of the following year by way of Europe.[39] The American government was extremely generous and thoughtful in treating the mission from the Oriental kingdom: the navy provided transportation for the mission between Chemulpo and Nagasaki when it left Korea, and the government had the USS *Trenton* bring back the chief delegate and two other members all the way via Europe to Korea; the American government made every effort to maintain the mission in a suitably dignified and comfortable fashion; it bore the total expenses of the mission while in the country. The mission had the honor of being presented twice to President Arthur and carried out a very heavy schedule of observing almost every aspect of governmental, economic, and cultural facilities of the United States.[40] The mission obtained substantial information from its observations of the governmental organizations, military installations and West

Point, educational institutions, museums, post offices, hospitals, industrial facilities, and model farms. The gain was translated on a moderate scale immediately into tangible results in the establishment of the model farm and the activities of many of the mission members in the progressive movement in Korea. The only regretful outcome was that the chief delegate, Min Yŏng-ik, a nephew of the queen and an important member of the court, returned to the conservative fold soon after his return from the United States and in his later career worked almost against the advancement of the nation. His now famous statement shows well the degree of the impact of the mission on its most conservative member: soon after his return Min said to Minister Foote, "I was born in the dark, I went out into the light, and now I have returned into the dark again. I cannot as yet see my way clearly, but I hope to soon."[41] When the mission returned to the capital on June 2, 1884, the welcoming procession swelled into a march of more than six hundred people who came out of the city to welcome the emissaries returning from the United States; judging from the degree of the enthusiasm exhibited by the people, the venture was a great success.[42]

The first two-year subperiod began with violence and turmoil; it ended with more violence and turmoil. This time the American representative in Seoul was in the midst of the crisis, and the American involvement in this crisis was naturally greater than in the earlier one.

Ever since the opening of Korea to Japan in 1876, the fast-modernizing island empire's influence had grown quickly in Korea, and as is usual under such circumstances, a number of young intellectuals who wanted to see Korea advance along the same lines had begun to work together; by the fall of 1884 there was a small, tightly knit progressive party in Korea. The progressives received both sympathy and encouragement from some Japanese leaders in both Tokyo and Seoul. By 1884 there were two factions in Seoul—the progressives, supported by the Japanese, and the conservatives, supported by the Chinese. Because both Minister Foote and George C. Foulk, the naval attaché in Seoul, sympathized with the progressives, the progressive leaders revealed to their American friends their "terrible" plan before their émeute. By the fall of 1884, progressives' future seemed to be hopeless; their efforts for fund-raising and for the training of the new armed forces failed, and when they felt the danger of extinction of the group from the pressure of the ruling conservative group and the Chinese, they decided to take over the government by force and to carry out reforms.[43] Both Foote and Foulk advised them to wait for a good opportunity, and the Americans even pleaded with

Min Yŏng-ik, the leader of the conservative group, to cooperate with the progressives.[44] When he found out that the progressives intended to carry out their plan, Foulk left Seoul for a long journey to the southern part of Korea. After days of preparation, the progressives executed their plan on December 4, using the occasion of a dinner party celebrating the opening of the post office at the house of the postmaster, Hong Yŏng-sik, one of the leaders of the progressives and the former vice-minister for the special mission to the United States. In the midst of the party, a fire started in the neighborhood, and when Min Yŏng-ik, who had gone out to investigate the fire, returned bleeding from the cuts inflicted by the progressive party's assassin, the crisis escalated. The progressives began to eliminate the key conservative leaders, murdering six of them and suggesting to the king, whom they soon moved to a small palace building for easier protection, that he call up Japanese troops for security. However, General Wu, the commander of the Chinese troops in Seoul, was invited in by the conservative Min faction, and he and his soldiers entered the palace grounds and began to exchange fire with the Japanese troops. When the Japanese minister saw that his two hundred troops were outnumbered ten to one by the Chinese, he abandoned the king and retreated to the legation. Unable to defend themselves against the mob attack, the Japanese made their way, as they had done a little more than two years before, to Chemulpo and then to Nagasaki. All the key members of the progressive party escaped the calamity by fleeing with the Japanese except Hong Yŏng-sik, who remained with the king and faced death bravely.[45] Thus, the action portion of the émeute of 1884 ended, and diplomacy began.

In the post-émeute diplomacy the Japanese played their cards well and came out as sole victors; the Chinese and the Koreans were both losers; the Americans also played well their relatively minor part in the incident. When the Japanese government received the news from Minister Shinichiro Takezoe in Nagasaki on the thirteenth of the month, almost ten days after the event, it judged that the nation was not yet ready to fight the Chinese and decided to make the best of the situation. Similarly, the Peking government, which had received through Li Hung-chang the report of the émeute on the twenty-third of the month, was unable to fight against the Japanese at this point, when the war with the French was still not concluded. The Japanese goverment despatched Foreign Minister Inouye Kaoru to Seoul with two battalions of troops and six gunboats to deal with the Koreans, and it sent Itō Hirobumi to Peking to make a settlement with the Chinese. In both capitals the key concern the Japanese delegates had was to avoid admitting the guilt of the Japanese minister in the incident and to exact the price of the loss in Seoul by turning the tables. Both Inouye and Itō did their jobs well. Inouye had relatively easy work in Seoul; the death of some forty Japanese and the destruction of the legation building, an exhibition of Japanese military force, and Inouye's imperious attitude were sufficient to make the Koreans accept the terms the Japanese presented to them. The Hansŏng (Seoul) Treaty, which stipulated a Korean payment of 130,000 yen for the loss of the legation building and for the Japanese lives lost and the punishment of those Koreans guilty of the incident, has been praised as a generous treaty. Koreans, very concerned about an outbreak of war, were happy with a peaceful settlement.[46]

The negotiations between Itō and Li did not proceed so smoothly; both sides readily agreed that the presence of the armies of the two countries in Korea was an evil and decided to withdraw them; but the negotiations almost deadlocked on the thorny issue of guilt. Li argued emphatically that Takezoe's responsibility was great; to this Itō retorted with an emphasis on the responsibility of the Chinese troops for entering the palace grounds, attacking the Japanese guards, and massacring and plundering Japanese citizens. Leaving the punishment of the guilty parties and the compensation to later settlement, the two, who had already decided not to fight, at least at this point, concluded the twelve-day negotiations on April 18, 1885. In addition to the withdrawal of both armies from Korea within two months, the two agreed to recommend to the Korean king that he train the army with the help of a third power's military instructors and to notify the other party if one decided to send troops into Korea. In anyone's eyes the first two points were sensible and wise; but the negotiations, either intentionally or by misjudgment, sowed the seeds of the war of 1894–1895 in the third point. Itō was proud of his achievements in this diplomatic duel with Li: he not only got away without admitting the guilt of the Japanese minister in the incident, he also was successful in raising the Japanese position in Korea to a level of equality with the Chinese without paying any price.[47] As much as Itō was successful, Li failed; especially since the Sino-French conflict had just ended at the time of the negotiation and the Chinese situation had greatly improved, his failure was even more serious. As for the Koreans, they were relieved to find that peace, not war, had developed, but their condition did not improve by any means through either the Hansŏng or the Tientsin settlements. What emerged in the peninsula after the émeute was the establishment of the Sino-Japanese "quasi-joint suzerainty."[48] The only gain the Koreans made out of the settlements was the ten-year peace between 1885 and 1894. We will now see how the Koreans used this valuable time, which was gained at such a high price.

In the aftermath of this incident, the Americans did their best for all parties involved, especially for the Koreans. The Korean king wanted the Americans to offer their good offices to conclude an amicable settlement of the incident with the Japanese; Foote was willing to make an offer, but the opportunity to do so never developed.[49] The Japanese decided to make a peaceful settlement. Even Mrs. Foote played her role well: when all the other foreign women left Seoul and went to Chemulpo, where the Western gunboats were anchored, she alone remained in Seoul. On December 10, when the king asked Mrs. Foote to stay in Seoul, the minister answered that they would certainly comply with the request, adding that they were "the first to come and would be the last to leave."[50] This statement is worth remembering for comparison with the American attitude toward the Koreans in another, even more serious, crisis in the fall of 1905. The American navy, too, did its part well: Admiral Davis sent the USS *Ossipee* to Chemulpo as soon as he had learned of the incident in Seoul, and then he came himself to Chemulpo on the flagship the USS *Trenton*.[51]

Foote's mission in Seoul ended soon after the émeute of 1884. With his leaving, the honeymoon period of American-Korean diplomatic relations ended. During the previous summer, Foote had been notified of a change in his rank from Envoy Extraordinary and Minister Plenipotentiary to Minister Resident and Consul General according to the July 7, 1884, Appropriation Act and had been asked to remain in Seoul with the same pay. He declined the offer because of the difficulty in explaining the change to the Koreans, and he requested that the department relieve him from duty.[52] Because of the crisis in Seoul, he was asked to stay for the time being, but when he left Chemulpo on January 19, 1885, he left Korea for good. After returning to the United States, he left public service; his wife died soon because of the strain she had experienced in Korea, according to her biographer.[53] Thus, Foote's Korean mission, which had begun with such high hopes and expectations on a spring day in 1883 in Seoul ended with his departure from Chemulpo harbor in the midst of fear and uncertainty in Korea.

To be fair to Foote, to Frelinghuysen, to the king and to the many dedicated Koreans who were involved in American-Korean relations during the first two years of formal diplomatic relations, it should be said that both sides made their best efforts to promote and maintain their mutual friendship and each remained faithful to the other. The honeymoon period was a successful one.

As the first three years of American-Korean formal diplomatic relations came to an end in the early spring of 1885, the peculiarity of the "peculiar relations" between the two nations diminished, along with the curiosity that always follows in every meeting of different cultures as well as persons, and American-Korean relations found themselves in the world of reality. Historian Tyler Dennett has called the two-and-a-half-year period following the émeute of December 1884 "the critical years" in Korean affairs so far as concerns American policy.[54] If not critical, it was at least an important period, as American policy toward Korea assumed certain shape and direction. Later observers have characterized American policy toward Korea during this period as a "retreat," "retirement," or "a gradual and indecisive withdrawal."[55] Hence, it is an important question whether there was a real policy difference between this and the preceding and also between this and the following period. The most important issue for the formulation and execution of the policy during this period was Korea-China relations. There were also a number of lesser factors, such as the personalities involved, the tradition of American policy toward the region in general as well as Korea in particular, and the always important national interests.

One of the most important characteristics of America's Korean policy during this period was its posture of passiveness: it was more likely to react passively than to take active and positive actions, and there was much to react to. The *modus vivendi* arrangement between China and Japan over the Korean issue seemed to signal a tranquil period, at least temporarily. Bingham, a long-time observer of the East Asian scene, remarked: "It would seem from the terms of this Convention that neither China nor Japan can hereafter claim any considerable authority over the frightful sovereignty of the Korean Government."[56] This time his prediction was wrong; the Koreans would not be left alone to work out their own destiny. When the China-Japan pair disappeared behind the curtain, at least for some time, other pairs advanced on the stage and acted out their parts: they were the pairs of China-Korea and England-Russia. The China-Korea relationship or the dependency issue, which now escalated from rhetoric to action, was the most important issue during this period. The crux of the issue was that, even though the Chinese gave an impression through the Tientsin settlement to Bingham and other observers that they would be content with an equal share with the Japanese and with the status quo, they became very aggressive in their Korea policy and made a determined effort to make Korea a province of China. The major obstacle to this Chinese scheme was U.S. Ensign George C. Foulk, who happened to be in Korea during this period, first as a naval attaché and then as the chargé; the Korea-China issue crystalized as the Foulk issue.

During the summer of 1885, when Chinese and Japanese troops withdrew from Korea, China immediately stepped up its political control in Korea.[57] In an effort to link the two countries more closely the Chinese built the telegraphic line between Seoul and Ŭiju on the Yalu River to connect with the Chinese communication system.[58] The biggest mistake made by the Chinese government was the sending of Yuan Shih-kai as the new Commissioner of Trade replacing von Moellendorff, who had been dismissed by Li when he tried to advance the interests of Germany and Russia in Korea against Li's will. Accompanying Yuan was the Taewon'gun, who had been taken during the military rebellion of 1882 in Seoul and detained in Tientsin until this time, and H. F. Merrill, who filled the position of head of the Korean Customs Office, an integral part of the Chinese customs system.[59] The Chinese moves to gain political control over Korea were so swift and vigorous that, by the early part of December 1885, the American representatives in Seoul and Peking felt that the Chinese were trying to create a province on the peninsula.[60]

This Chinese move for ascendancy in Korea began to affect the Americans within two weeks after the arrival of Yuan and the others, as the Chinese began to pressure the Americans to transfer the legation's business in Seoul to Peking; this pressure continued throughout the whole period.[61] In Washington, Secretary of State Thomas F. Bayard encountered a severe test for American foreign policy during this period. The secretary was unequivocal on this issue: the United States would continue to treat Korea as an independent sovereign nation and would reject China's request to transfer diplomatic transactions from Seoul to Peking. In his November 16, 1885 instruction to Charles Denby, U.S. minister to China, Bayard made a reference to his predecessor's instruction of August 4, 1882, on the dependency issue, which stated that the negotiations for the Shufeldt treaty were conducted with Korea as a sovereign power and that the country would be regarded as a sovereign nation. When the Chinese minister in Washington asked if Bayard's view was different, the secretary gave a clear, negative answer.[62] Having failed in their efforts to gain American recognition of Korean dependency through transfer of the diplomatic function of the United States in Seoul to Peking, Li and Yuan went ahead in their effort to assure Chinese de facto control of Korea in the following year, an effort that became a diplomatic duel between Foulk and Yuan.

George C. Foulk's story in Korea is an interesting but tragic one.

His association with the Koreans began in the fall of 1883, when he was appointed by President Arthur as an assistant to the 1883-1884 Min mission because of his intelligence and experience. He served the mission well and, at the end of the tour in the United States, Min Yŏng-ik expressed his wish to have the ensign's service in Korea. The American government responded kindly to this request, appointing Foulk a naval attaché; he arrived in Korea on May 31, 1884.[63] His official duty in Seoul was to make reports on naval and other matters of interest to the Navy and State departments. He had another, much more important, duty of giving advice to the Korean government, a duty understood clearly by all involved in his appointment. Secretary Frelinghuysen made a special remark on this matter in his November 12, 1883, instructions.[64]

During his three-year period as a naval attaché and chargé, Foulk rendered invaluable services to the king and the government of Korea.[65] A young man of only twenty-eight when he arrived in Korea, he charmed the Koreans with his brilliance, dedication, and idealism.[66] He became the most trusted adviser and hence the most influential American in Korea, not only for his time but for the whole period of the first thirty years of diplomatic relations between the two countries.[67] Mainly because of his advisory activities for the king and the Korean government, he soon became the major obstacle to the Chinese plan for Korea and thus their target of attack. Unfortunately, his candid observations of the Korean government and the royal family were published in the *Foreign Relations of the United States*; the reprinting of this article in the English newspaper in China gave a good excuse to Li, Yuan, and the Korean Foreign Office, which was under the complete domination of Yuan at the time, to seek Foulk's removal.[68] Foulk himself, chargé William W. Rockhill, and Minister Hugh A. Dinsmore—the American representatives in Seoul—all presented a spirited defense of Foulk to the Korean government, but, responding to the direct pressure of the Chinese government through its representative in Washington and the Korean Foreign Office, Bayard finally recalled him from Korea.[69] In addition to his difficulties with the Chinese and the Korean Foreign Office, Foulk suffered from lack of financial support, from overwork, and from, above all, neglect by the Department of State during his year and a half in Korea.[70]

Both contemporary and later observers have been almost uniformly critical about the way Bayard handled the Foulk case, and one gets an impression that the secretary failed in this test dealing with the Chinese and their meddling in Korean affairs. There is less agreement about the reasons for Bayard's failure, but they can conveniently be divided into personal and official reasons. Even though the two are related, for analytical purposes it is useful to separate them. Clear evidence exists that Bayard fully appreciated Foulk's capabilities and, above all, his dedicated service.[71] If this was the case, Bayard should have given him a promotion, assigning him a position in Washington; the Chinese would not have taken such a move as an offense because their main objective was simply removing Foulk from his influential position in Korea. If it was not advisable to move Foulk to Washington, Bayard could have, and should have, allowed his appointment as the naval attaché in Tokyo.[72] If neither action was possible, Bayard should at least have given Foulk a year of leave with pay, a leave he much needed and one the Navy Department granted him later. It is difficult to defend Bayard from the condemnation of his critics that he discarded Foulk like an old shoe after Foulk's dedicated service in an impossible situation.

On the official or policy level, however, Bayard's action can be understood. His choice was between helping a small nation in which the United States had hardly any material interests and the Chinese Empire, in which the United States had much to lose or gain. Moreover, the presidential election was coming up, and there was a need to please the Chinese government because of the United States government's dealing with Chinese immigrants in California. Additionally, the British were behind the Chinese in Far Eastern affairs in the 1880s, and there was every reason to please them. Bayard was cautious in the extreme when he suggested that the Navy Department not give Foulk the naval attaché's position in Tokyo so as not to irritate the Chinese. He was probably a little too shy in dealing with the Chinese in general, but he was certainly realistic in dealing with the Chinese in this case.[73]

Foulk was a good adviser to the king and a good friend to the people, and the Koreans lost much when he left the country. Soon after his departure from Korea, Foulk married a Japanese girl and, after a year of badly needed rest in Japan, he worked for a couple of years for an American company in Yokohama. Then, he taught mathematics for three years at Doshisha University in Kyoto. He died at thirty-six; some have attributed his early death to the strains he suffered in Korea.[74]

American interests in Korea during this period remained small, although in a few areas some progress was made. By 1887 missionary work had firmly taken root, and some twenty workers from the United States were active in medical and educational works.[75] Another notable accomplishment during this period was the arrival of three schoolteachers. After three years of waiting, they finally arrived in Korea in the summer of 1886, and their arrival was significant for the advancement of Korean education. One of them was Homer B. Hulbert, who played a very important role in the political as well as in the cultural arena.[76] In other areas there was almost no progress. The area that made both the Koreans and the Americans who were involved anxious was the matter of military instructors. The king checked with Foulk almost daily on the subject, but the American military instructors never came during this period.[77] The situation of the foreign policy adviser was similar: the king awaited anxiously the adviser's coming from the United States; in this case, however, an appointment was made, and Owen N. Denny was sent to Korea.[78] Nor did trade see much progress during this period: Foulk estimated in the spring of 1885 the total American trade with Korea, both direct and indirect through Japan, to be $175,000. The major advancements in trade and concessions were the timber and fishing concessions and the sale of two steamboats and a water mill.[79] Because of Foulk's service to the king, the Americans could have had more concessions if they had tried to get them from the Koreans, but they did not. Bayard even discouraged Foulk from helping American citizens obtain new business contracts.[80] Altogether, the advance of American interests in Korea during this three-year period was not impressive.

Aside from sustaining the position of Korea as an independent, sovereign state, the American government in Washington maintained during this period a passive posture. Moreover, the secretary of state repeatedly warned his representatives in Korea to maintain absolute neutrality and not to take sides with any power in "the center of intrigues."[81] This passive posture[82] seems to have come, at least partly, from the outlook of the policy makers in Washington, the negligible amount of American material interests in Korea, and the difficult conditions in Korea. President Cleveland and Secretary Bayard were cautious in dealing with those East Asian countries where the United States had only a small interest, and American interests in Korea were small. Moreover, Chinese ascendancy and the involvement of England and Russia in the Port Hamilton affairs, which lasted for about two years from the spring of 1885 and in which Foulk was active in advising the Koreans, created a very difficult environment for American diplomacy in the area, which Bayard called "the center of intrigues."[83] For the Koreans, this was another difficult period; somewhat discouraged by the Foulk case, they began to turn to Russia as a counterforce against Chinese ascendancy, a move that caused much difficulty in 1885 and the following year in the de Speyer affair and in the Korean-Russian secret agreement of 1886. In a sense, the two-and-a-half-year period between 1885 and 1887 was a transitional one to be followed by a period of a more distinctive character.

The recent special studies focusing on a major event and a key personality in an era are very helpful for a better understanding of at least the first half of the period, from 1887 to 1890.[84] However, there is still much danger of not understanding this seven-year period in proper historical perspective because of the lack of a comprehensive study of a longer period. Even though 1887 has been treated as a dividing point (some have even treated it as a turning point), it is questionable if such a periodization is accurate. Certainly there was no policy change for the Americans at this point; moreover, the situation in Korea remained about the same in the post-1885 period. The only discernible changes were in the style of diplomacy and in the execution of policy in Seoul. To quote Robert E. Reordan, who understood well Foulk's role in Korea:

Although American friendship had in practice offered little more than good will and assured sympathy, even such immaterial support from a major power was important to a feeble state struggling for existence. The significance of the withdrawal of Foulk was not that American aid was to be henceforth withheld, for none had ever been provided, but that American faith and interest in Korea had faded and she was henceforth to be left in the world alone.[85]

We shall see if the "American faith and interest" in Korea completely faded and what policy the United States carried out in Korea during this period.

The continuing, major issue of diplomacy during this seven-year period was how to act toward China. Both Minister Hugh A. Dinsmore and Augustine Heard, who occupied the Seoul post during most of the period, had to struggle with the China issue. Only a few days after his arrival, Dinsmore, in his report to the secretary of state, made the following interesting observation: "In conclusion I venture to remark that in my opinion from all that I have seen and heard in the short time I have been in this capital but for Chinese interference all would go smoothly and well here, and the country would advance rapidly in prosperity and enterprise. But every step forward is opposed by the Chinese Minister." Then he made a very significant statement regarding American policy in Korea: "I shall not in anywhere attempt to interfere with matters arising between China or any other power with Korea when we are not directly concerned." He added: "But the effect upon these people of such presumption as we constantly witness on the part of the Chinese representative, is deplorable, and naturally and I would think unavoidably humiliating to any sovereign power in treaty relations with this unfortunate country."[86] Nonintervention in Korea, along with absolute neutrality in dealing with other powers in Korea, had been policy there from the very beginning of diplomatic relations between the two countries, but a clear expression of it had never before been made, certainly not by Foote, Foulk, or Frelinghuysen— not even by Bayard. About three weeks later, Dinsmore described the Korean situation in the following revealing words: "To my mind it appears that Korean political affairs are gradually approaching a crisis. China is slowly but surely tightening her grip upon this Government and its King. The spirit of resistance seems almost to have died out of the Koreans and there is an apparent acquiescence on the part of foreign representatives." Almost definitely, he was excluding himself from those foreign representatives. His keen observation ends with a gloomy statement: "All in all, at this time the prospect for Korean independence is gloomy."[87] Dinsmore's perceptive observation depicts well the Korean situation about the time of Foulk's departure and before the minor crisis that came up toward the end of the year.

Mainly because of Yuan's unusual tenacity and nefariousness, the sending of the first permanent Korean representative to the United States was blown up to the size of a crisis in the winter of 1887 and 1888, and American policy underwent a severe test. With the objective of reciprocating the American representation in Seoul, which had been there for a little more than four years by the summer of 1887, and, mainly, with the purpose of strengthening the independence of the nation against the intensifying Chinese effort for control of Korea, King Kojong decided in the summer of 1887 to establish permanent envoys in the capital of the United States and the capitals of Japan and the major European countries.[88] The king appointed Pak Chŏng-yang, the vice-minister of the interior, as Envoy Extraordinary and Minister Plenipotentiary to the United States on August 18 of that year, assigning him a secretary and other capable staff members.[89] Dinsmore was one of those who had suggested sending missions to the capitals of the Western powers in the spring and early summer of the year, and he soon learned the decision had been made, even though the official notification did not come until September 16.[90] Yuan, too, soon learned of the appointments and began to act to block the despatch of this mission; his actions resulted in the September 23 telegram from Li in which the viceroy stated that he had heard that the Korean government was sending ministers to other countries without first consulting him. Then, he presented his view: since Korea did not have any trade with foreign countries, there was no reason for it to send representatives to them and if it did so, it would overburden its treasury with debt. Li instructed Yuan to communicate his view to the Korean government and wanted to know the result.[91] Thus, the struggle for the Koreans to send its permanent mission to the United States began in the early fall of 1887.

The diplomatic battle between the Chinese and Korean governments began on September 23, the day on which Yuan received the telegram from Li. The Korean king, notorious for his weakness and indecision, acted quickly this time by ordering Pak to leave the capital immediately and be on his way to the United States. As soon as the mission stepped outside the South Gate, however, it was stopped by Yuan's troops, and a two-month detention began.[92] During the two-month period, very active communication took place between the Korean and Chinese governments and between the American and Chinese governments. When the king saw the failure of his effort to solve the problem by taking quick action and forcing the Chinese to accept the fait accompli, he retreated to a strategy of appeasement, which, like all other similar strategies, entailed much humiliation. He sent two missions—Yun Kyu-sŏp and Owen N. Denny, his foreign policy adviser—to China, one to beg and the other to reason with the Chinese.[93]

The other part of the struggle—between the Americans and the Chinese—was much more noble and straightforward, but not easy by any means. On October 27, four days after Yuan's physical detention of the mission, Dinsmore began his verbal battle with Yuan, which took place in four exchanges of notes. In his September 27 note, the first of the series, Dinsmore bluntly asked Yuan whether it was true that the Chinese representative had prevented the sending of the Minister to the United States.[94] Yuan's answer was evasive, but he pointed out to Dinsmore that the United States had acknowledged the dependency of Korea in the 1882 treaty and that Korea could carry out its duty as a vassal state without any outside interference. In his second letter to Yuan, Dinsmore quietly pointed out that Yuan had not answered the question but simply made a reference to the treaty and that the treaty did not contain a statement such as the Chinese minister pointed out.[95] Yuan's answer came two days later; in it he pointed out that a letter appended to the treaty clearly indicated the dependent relationship of Korea to China and expressed his surprise at Dinsmore's refusal to acknowledge it.[96] Four days later Dinsmore wrote his third letter to Yuan, in which he candidly but tactlessly stated that he had never heard of the letter.[97] Yuan was undoubtedly happy to see Dinsmore's admission of his ignorance of such an important matter, and his October 10 response frankly showed his surprise and quietly pointed out again that the United States should not interfere in a matter that concerned his country and Korea.[98] Tacitly admitting defeat, Dinsmore came out defensively in his next and last letter to Yuan; he regretted that his position on the issue should be regarded by Yuan as in conflict with the "rightful interest" of the Chinese government in Korea.[99] In his last note, Yuan sounded triumphant.[100]

Fortunately, however, the battle between Dinsmore and Yuan in Seoul did not have much impact upon the one between Washington and Peking/Tientsin; and, moreover, the battle on this level was simple and effective. Greatly irritated and disturbed by Yuan's first answer, Dinsmore telegraphed Bayard on October 5 that the Korean mission had been stopped by the Chinese outside the capital and that he had not yet received an answer from Yuan to his (second) letter, which cited the terms of the treaty.[101] In Washington, Bayard acted promptly and decisively: he telegraphed Denby in Peking, "You will express surprise and regret Chinese obstruction to Korea sending Minister here according to treaty."[102]

It is difficult to determine accurately what and how much impact Bayard's communication had upon the Chinese change of policy. The Chinese only cited the Korean request for the presentation of a memorial about the sending of the mission, not the American "protest," as the reason for the change.[103] Denby, however, thought the Chinese change of mind resulted from Bayard's action.[104] The Chinese probably decided to concede because of the American reaction, but used the king's request as a face-saving device. Once they, especially Yuan, had decided physically to detain the Korean mission, they could not have easily yielded to Korean words. Whatever their real motive, the Chinese government communicated on October 21 its concession to the Korean government.[105] The Korean mission, which had been held waiting outside the capital for more than two months since its appointment in mid-August, left Chemulpo on November 16 on the USS *Omaha*.[106] Thus the Koreans and Americans won the first battle. The war, however, was not over; it continued in the three capitals.

When the Chinese permitted the departure of the Korean mission to the United States in late 1887, it was only a small concession, not the abandonment of the intervention policy itself. They took the position that Pak's title should be changed from that of Envoy Extraordinary and Minister Plenipotentiary (EEME) to that of a third-rank minister, so that it would be differentiated from the rank of the Chinese representative in Washington.[107] The Korean government took up this issue with Yuan and Li and persuaded them that since the minister was already despatched with the rank of EEME, it would be impossible to change it without the loss of American confidence in the Korean government, and that it would be better for it to replace him later with a chargé.[108] Then, however, the Chinese government came up with three regulations, communicating them to the Korean government on November 8, eight days before the departure of the mission.[109] The three regulations the Chinese established as a tool of intervention and control of the mission were (1) the Korean representative abroad must first present themselves to the Chinese ministers and be introduced by them to the offices of the countries of appointment; (2) the Korean ministers would always yield precedence to the Chinese ministers; and (3) the Korean ministers would consult first "secretly" with the Chinese ministers on important matters of business in foreign capitals.[110] Because the Chinese ministers already had seniority in Washington and other capitals, the second regulation would not cause any problem, but the two other regulations would. The Korean government tried to convince the Chinese government to withdraw the first regulation, for it would stir up again the dependency issue. Because the Chinese government would not yield on this item, the Korean government decided on a strategy of evasion, and the American government gave full cooperation to this strategy.

After a journey of nearly two months, the Korean mission arrived in Washington on January 9 of the following year. On the next day, the Korean minister immediately communicated with the secretary of state, informing him of his arrival and expressing his wish that a date be set for his presentation to the president. Bayard arranged first to meet the minister and then made an appointment to present him to the president on the seventeenth. Bayard took these steps despite the fact that the Chinese minister in Washington, Chang Yin-huan, saw him first and then sent a note on the ninth, the very day of the arrival of the Korean minister, explaining the nature of the first regulation, which he had received from Li on November 11 of the previous year.[111] By the time Pak had communicated his arrival to Bayard, the secretary had decided to treat the Korean minister as he would any other representative on the basis that Korea was a sovereign, independent nation.[112] Thus the Chinese suffered another setback and the Korean government scored another victory.

After his arrival in Washington, Pak was pressured by the Chinese minister to submit to the first regulation; he responded that he had not received any clear telegraphic instructions from his government and showed a firm attitude in resisting the pressure.[113] Yuan in Seoul, however, was very persistent; he bombarded the Korean Foreign Office with notes, demanding Pak's compliance with the first regulation; as many as five notes were despatched in the three days between January 13 and 15.[114] The Korean Foreign Office finally gave in and sent a telegraphic instruction to Pak on the seventeenth, but it was, probably purposely, sent too late to change the schedule in Washington.[115] On the seventeenth Secretary Bayard presented the first Korean minister to the president; on the following day, Pak notified Bayard of the establishment of the legation in the capital.[116]

Thus, the crisis that some thought comparable in importance only to the Shufeldt treaty negotiations of 1881–1882, ended in early 1888 with a victory for both the Korean and the American governments. The success owed much to the courage and resourcefulness of the king and Pak and even more to the determination and good will of Bayard, Dinsmore, and other Americans involved in the event. Compared with what happened to the mission that had headed toward the European capitals, which the Chinese detained in Shanghai, the mission to the United States was a success. However, Pak himself had to endure much pain and humiliation in the following years: he had to leave the Washington position before the end of the year, using illness as a pretext, because of the Chinese government's continuing pressure; following his return to Seoul, he had to subject himself to unduly severe punishment, almost persecution, because of Yuan's persistency.[117]

It seems that the sending of the Korean mission to the United States in the winter of 1887–1888 was one of those cases in diplomacy in which the will and action of the parties involved in the event turned out to be the right mixture, and the process reached a successful conclusion. Korea, which initiated the action and which played a major role in the incident, mixed just enough courage with timidity, perseverence with submission, wisdom with cleverness; China, whose action in Seoul was vigorous but whose policy in Peking was somewhat wavering, did enough to publicize its position over Korea but would not push to the point of antagonizing both the Korean and American governments; the United States, which happened to be on the spot not by choice but by circumstances, showed enough firmness as well as caution to help the Koreans succeed, but just barely.[118] Yuan Shih-kai was a difficult man for anyone to battle with, and Dinsmore did well in waging his four-round verbal battles with him between September 27 and October 14 of 1887. Although Dinsmore definitely could not match Yuan in forcefulness, at least a part of the reason for his loss in the affair was his unpreparedness: that he was not fully informed about all the details of the 1882 treaty was really the fault of the Department of State. On October 25 he requested from the department a copy of the treaty, but this was too late.[119] In sending his telegram on October 6 to Denby to express his surprise and disappointment regarding Chinese interference in the matter, Bayard was both quick and decisive, but he was not sure where the responsibility for the execution of the treaty lay—with the Korean or the Chinese government—because it seemed to him that the power that had the authority to approve a diplomatic action also had the authority not to approve it and the responsibility came with the authority; hence, he asked Denby on November 4, 1887, to find out China's real position.[120]

The diplomatic defeat of 1887–1888, which was not a major loss in the Chinese view, did not even slow down the Chinese effort to strengthen its control of the Korean kingdom, and by early 1890 a widespread impression existed that Chinese influence in the Korean peninsula was "paramount."[121] This state continued throughout the early years of the 1890s; even the Japanese government had to go through the Chinese government to accomplish a matter of substance. The paramountcy took various forms in its expression, and the United States, as well as other powers that wanted to deal with Korea, sometimes had to respond in terms of policy and diplomacy.

On the policy level, the most significant matter during this post-1887 period was a clarification, or a restatement, of the American policy regarding Korean-Chinese relations. The instructions from the Department of State under James G. Blaine clearly stated the American policy line on the issue: in his April 25, 1890 instruction, William F. Wharton, the acting secretary of state, said that, for the execution of the treaty of 1882, Korea would be held responsible as a sovereign state but, with regard to the relations between Korea and China, the United States would not "interfere to raise any question"; Wharton had stated the same principle in his June 27, 1890 instruction to Denby.[122] This dual policy was, of course, not new; it had been the main American posture toward Korean-Chinese relations in Korea since 1882. Along with the dual policy, Blaine also restated clearly another important policy of the United States in dealing with the powers in Korea: the "impartiality" or neutrality policy.[123]

On the diplomatic level, several minor—some even ridiculous—matters came up in Seoul, some of which caused American responses and the rest of which were simply ignored. Since 1882, the Chinese government had tried to control the Korean Customs

Office, and in the winter of 1889 Denby raised a question whether the *likin*, the Chinese internal tariff, would be applied also in Korea. Blaine's view, expressed in the following summer, was to simply disregard it because it would not affect U.S.-Korea relations.[124] In the summer of 1890, Yuan intervened with regard to the employment of military instructors and foreign policy advisers by asking the Korean government to dismiss its American military advisers and hire certain persons to replace them.[125] When the queen dowager's funeral called for the landing of an American marine guard for ceremonial purposes in the fall of 1890, Yuan insisted that the Korean government should have obtained prior approval from the Chinese government for this action.[126] From the day of his arrival in Korea, first as a commercial agent and then as a commercial and diplomatic representative, Yuan perplexed the American representatives, as well as other representatives in Seoul, with his title and behavior. Yuan tried to impress upon the foreign representatives in Seoul that he, the representative of a suzerain power in the capital of a vassal state, was not one of them but was above them, much like the British commissioner in Egypt. He would not attend the foreign representatives meeting—although he sometimes sent his secretary; he would ride alone in a sedan chair through the main gate to the audience hall like a head of state.[127] Other representatives, including those from the United States, sought the same privileges but had to be content with a compromise. (Secretaries James G. Blaine and Walter Q. Gresham reproached the ministers in Seoul for their action in concert with the other representatives on this matter.)[128]

It is fair to say that the American legation was blessed with good ministers and also with better material support during the seven years after the spring of 1887. Both Hugh A. Dinsmore and Augustine Heard, who occupied the post for most of the period, were good choices. Dinsmore had an understanding of the king and the people of Korea. Cautiously, so as not to hurt his official position, he did the favor of advising the king and was actually offered the advisory job, although because of the disapproval of the State Department he was unable to take this position with its annual salary of $12,000. His service can be favorably compared with that of Foote, the first minister in Seoul.[129] Heard, an 1853 graduate of Yale University and armed with knowledge of and experience in China, was the right person, in a sense, to serve in the Seoul position when the Chinese influence was a problem in Korea. He got along well with Yuan and thought he was a good man.[130] There is no way to know how Washington took his insightful statement, which came from a real understanding of the situation in Korea; on October 21, 1890, five months after his arrival in his Seoul post, he asked, referring to the Chinese influence in Korea: "Is it not time that this should be stopped? and for the treaty powers to take counsel together and warn the Imperial Government that it goes too far?" He continued, "As a friend of China, and I am a friend of China by long intercourse and association, I would urge her in her own interests not to check Korea in her aspiration towards development and reform."[131]

After a long period of negligence, the department finally paid some attention to the logistics of maintaining the legation in Seoul; the building was purchased, a small amount was allowed for annual repair costs, and the minister was allowed a secretary beginning in 1887.[132] Gunboat diplomacy continued, and the American ministers in Seoul enjoyed the protection of the American navy. With a short period of exception during 1893, the navy gave full cooperation to the American diplomats in Seoul, especially during the period of minor crisis in 1888, when rumors were bruited that the American missionaries were eating Korean babies, and on the occasion of the funeral of the queen dowager in 1890, when a fifty-man marine guard was brought to Seoul.[133] Despite unease about the dualism on the policy level, American diplomacy in Seoul was relatively stable during this period.

Economic and other tangible interests of the United States in Korea during the seven-year period to 1894 were still in the same state as that of the previous period: small but promising. There were seventy-six Americans in Korea at the end of 1892, a much smaller number than the Japanese and the Chinese, but still the largest among the Westerners.[134] American trade interests in Korea were small, with only one firm, Morse Townsend and Company, in Chemulpo; the electric plant that had been owned by an American firm was sold to the Koreans in 1892.[135] The concession area was much more promising: American companies were exploring with the Korean government the possibility of building a railroad between Seoul and Chemulpo and of opening gold mines, and the king made a proposal to another American company to work on the gold mines.[136] The cultural activities of the various missionary groups grew continuously throughout this period; the American representatives made a serious effort to restrain their zeal for evangelical work to avoid complications with the Korean government.[137] Americans assisted in the modernization of Korea by providing technical assistance and expertise. The Americans responded generously to Korean requests for their various needs, providing a description of torpedoes for the establishment of a torpedo service in Korea, sending two mining engineers, testing Korean coal in American ships, and providing assistance for Korea's joining the Universal Postal Convention.[138] In addition to Judge Owen N. Denny, who ably served the Korean government until the spring of 1891, Charles W. Le Gendre and Clarence G. Greathouse held influential advisory postions in the Korean government during this period.[139]

The most disappointing case of American assistance was that of the three military instructors. After four long years of delay and writing, they finally arrived in Korea in the spring of 1888. But General William M. Dye and his two assistants—Colonel Elmond H. Cummins and Major John J. Lee—proved poor choices, and the "heterogeneous collection" was a great disappointment to the Koreans from the beginning; even before the end of the two-year term, the government fired the two assistants, and after much communication between the American legation and the Korean Foreign Office, the case was finally settled with full payment of the two-year salary and the return travel expenses for the two. General Dye continued his service until the mid-1890s, but the Korean government's expectation of building a modern army with the help of American military instructors was never fulfilled.[140] As a remedy to the failure, the Korean government asked the American government to educate young Koreans at American military academies; the American government responded gracefully to this request and agreed to receive one each at the military and naval academies.[141] The three schoolteachers brought from the United States rendered better service than the three military instructors: they were much more capable and decent human beings; two of them, however, Daniel A. Bunker and George A. Gilmore, left Korea before the end of the period, leaving only Homer B. Hulbert to complete his distinguished service in Korea.[142]

American business interests in Korea during the seven-year period did not amount to much. Trade, still indirect and all coming through Japan, was only three percent of Korea's total foreign trade. Americans obtained no new concession during this period; if anything can be counted in this category, it was only a hope for the future. The export of American technology to Korea was substantial and important in the long run, but it was not conspicuous. Viewed against this background of limited American interests in Korea, it should be said that the American policy toward Korea was fair. Bayard, who has been considered as one of the most inactive secretaries of state, sustained the policy of providing assistance to the Koreans as they tried to keep their independence and sovereignty by receiving the first permanent Korean mission in Washington; Blaine, who was very active elsewhere, quietly maintained the dual and neutrality policies toward Korea. Together, they maintained passively but well the traditional American policy toward Korea from the time of Frelinghuysen. During this period, no more than this policy was needed.

For the Koreans, the years preceding the Sino-Japanese War were years of calm. There were some minor incidents, but no major crisis of any kind, foreign or domestic, occurred during this period. The major fact of life during this period was Chinese dominance, against which the king wished to find a counterforce. Japan showed no interest in those years in spending its energy in a political struggle with China, preferring to quietly strengthen its economic position on the peninsula and wait for a future opportunity. Turning to Russia, which had been tried in the past and would be tried again in coming years, was too risky for Korea. England, which took a very large share of Korean foreign trade and whose main political interest in Korea was to check the Russian advance, made common cause with China. The United States was thus the power the Koreans wished to serve as the counterweight to Chinese pressure. However, the most this "disinterested power," in the king's own words, would do for the Koreans was to sustain the position of continued recognition of independence and sovereignty of the kingdom through verbal battles.

In 1891 the king toyed with the idea of the neutralization of his country with an international guarantee, somewhat similar to the situation of Switzerland.[143] Japan, Russia, and possibly even England and the United States were interested in the scheme, but China, which would lose most through such an arrangement, would pay no attention to it in this period, and nothing came out of the king's effort. An important point to be made here is that whether an institutional mechanism for neutralization existed or not, the imbalance in power and interest that existed in Korea in this tranquil period between China and Japan and between England and Russia was not conducive to its realization. To be sure, there was the Chinese paramountcy in this period; at the same time the Japanese were very quietly increasing their economic and their real power.

Another point to be made is that in this rare tranquil period, the Koreans should have made a heroic effort to strengthen themselves; unfortunately, they did not. They certainly made some effort: communication was improved through the establishment of a telegraphic line between Seoul and Pusan, the postal service was reestablished in 1893, and the torpedo service and the navy department were organized.[144] These technical advancements were certainly helpful for Korea's self-strengthening and modernization effort, but they were not enough for the needs Korea had in this period. What Korea needed in the latter part of the 1880s and the early part of the 1890s was an overall, great step forward—a great reform movement, close to a revolution—and the Koreans failed to meet this need.

There is no question that the first twelve years of official diplomatic relations were very important for American-Korean relations. The main policy line of the United States toward Korea was firmly established and executed during this period; Korea also experienced the extent of the role that the United States would play in its independence and development. The United States policy toward Korea during this period was twofold: the republic would help the Korean kingdom survive and develop as a strong, independent sovereign nation; at the same time, in dealing with the other powers involved on the peninsula, it would act with absolute impartiality and neutrality. This twofold policy was clearly established at the outset by Frelinghuysen,[145] and it was maintained by Bayard and Blaine.[146] There was a difference in intensity of activity and interests: Frelinghuysen was more active and interested in Korea than Blaine and Bayard. But there was only one policy line; and even Bayard, who gave an impression of extreme conservatism and passivity, stood firm in resisting Li Hung-chang's pressure to transfer the business of the American legation in Seoul to China.[147] It should also be noted that during the Bayard period the word "intervention" became an important part of the vocabulary of American-Korean relations.[148] The single most important issue for American-Korean relations during the period was China, and the American government had to decide on its posture on this issue. There was no question that China had a very forceful policy in Korea, whether it was a continuation of an old policy or an entirely new one. Concerned about the advance of Japan and the danger posed by Russia, China wanted to enhance its security by obtaining a tight control over Korea. Its problem was too much success; in the subtle balance of power in the East Asian subsystem of international relations, there was a delicate point of equilibrium, and China's mistake was going beyond this point, a move that Japan could not tolerate, as will be shown by the events of 1894–1895 in Korea. In dealing with this important China issue, the United States had a definite policy line: the dual policy of maintaining the position that Korea was an independent, sovereign state as far as the treaty powers were concerned, but that it had, at the same time, a special relationship with China.[149] But this dual policy was a temporary measure of convenience, and it was inevitable that the two parts of the policy would conflict.

As to the Korean alternatives, the small, helpless kingdom relied as much as possible on the United States in its heroic effort to maintain its independence against the aggressive hands of the Chinese; but, despite some wishful thinking, the Koreans must have realized the limit of what their "disinterested" friend could do for them and they tried to counter power with power by approaching Russia during this period; at the same time, they tried to strengthen themselves by training a new army with American military instructors and by importing modern technology from the United States and elsewhere. But, regretfully, their effort was too small, and they ended up wasting the invaluable twelve years when the peninsula was relatively quiet. Thus, by the time the 1894–1895 Sino-Japanese War came, American-Korean relations had been established on a firm basis and had been tested by twelve years of experience.

4

THE SINO-JAPANESE WAR
AND AMERICAN DIPLOMACY

The second twelve years of American-Korean relations, from 1894 to 1905, were the most crucial years not only for Korea in the modern era, but probably also for the American-Korean relations. During this period, a systemic transformation took place in the East Asian subsystem of the world international society; and when a one-power domination replaced the earlier balance-of-power system in the region, the independence of Korea, which had been sustained largely by the power equilibrium among the major powers in the area, was first jeopardized and then almost lost by the end of the period. When the Japanese, who had achieved brilliant success in their drive to modernize through a courageous process of Westernization during the previous twenty-five years, were ready to test their newly acquired military power, first against the Chinese and then against the Russians in an effort to eliminate the competitors and to establish their domination over the whole region, the United States and other Western powers faced a serious challenge. Because of the relatively small degree of interest the Western powers had in Korea, there was no way they could individually play a significant role in the two crises.[1] The real question was what role the Western powers—five, the United States, Russia, England, France, and Germany for the Sino-Japanese War and four, the United States, England, France, and Germany for the Russo-Japanese War—would play jointly as a balancer.[2]

Of the two crises, the Sino-Japanese War was the more significant, for both Korea and East Asia. Even though, because of unexpected events in Korea in the fall of 1895 and the spring of the following year, Japan had to wait ten years to complete its domination of the region and Korea had a sixteen-year grace period, Japanese hegemony in the region was virtually assured by this war through the elimination from the Korean political scene of China, one of the two major contenders in the region, and the fate of Korea was sealed. Faced with the real danger of the closing of the Korean door, which had been opened only a little more than a decade earlier through its own efforts, the United States faced the question of what to do to prevent the closing of the door by preventing the coming of war. The following pages will be devoted to a study of American policy and diplomacy as the United States dealt with this question.

The Sino-Japanese War of 1894–1895 surprised no one. The confrontations between the two powers in Seoul in 1882 and 1884 were in a sense rehearsals for this war; Japan was not quite ready in the early or middle 1880s to settle the Korean issue on the battlefield; instead it spent a decade building additional military power to defeat China. In addition to the military readiness of Japan by 1894, there was also an internal political reason for the war; the Japanese government, which found the opposition in the Diet against the oligarchs who carried out the Meiji Restoration too obstructive, sought a way to unify the nation through an external conflict.[3] The third factor contributing to the war was Japan's desire for territorial expansion. For nearly two decades, Japanese leaders had found that expansion toward Formosa and Korea was a handy outlet for excessive energy and dissatisfaction at home; in a sense, this emulation of Western imperialism was one important way for the Japanese to demonstrate their capacity to learn from an advanced culture. The war between China and Japan in 1894 and 1895, as many American newspapers and magazines articulated it at the time, was a war between two cultures.[4] Another very important factor was that, mainly because of its geopolitical importance, Korea would not be allowed to fall under the control of any one power for too long—China, Japan, or anyone else.

In addition to these underlying causes, there was a direct cause—the Tonghak Rebellion of 1894. The Tonghak (literally, "Eastern Learning," against the "Western Learning," which signified Christianity), was a political, social, and religious movement that emerged in 1892 and rapidly spread in the southern provinces of the Korean peninsula, mainly because of its appeal among the oppressed.[5] In the spring of 1894, the movement was transformed into a rebellion as a response to excessive corruption and oppression in Cholla Province. When government forces failed to suppress the rebels, the Korean government, despite the objection of most of the king's advisers, asked Li Hung-chang to send troops to Korea.[6] This was the greatest mistake the Korean government had made in its external affairs since the opening of the nation to the Western world. The sad result for Korea was that the king and his advisers either did not see clearly the obvious consequences of the move or were not decisive enough to block Min Yŏng-jun's scheme to bring in the Chinese troops. After some hesitation, Li decided to send a force of 1,500 soon to be augmented to more than 2,000—an equally important step toward the crisis.[7]

On June 6, the day on which the Chinese troops landed at Asan, south of Seoul, the Chinese government duly notified the Japanese government according to the agreement of 1885 between the two governments that Chinese troops were being sent to Korea in response to a request from the Korean government to suppress the rebels and assured the Japanese government that the troops would be withdrawn immediately after completion of the mission.[8] The Japanese government immediately seized the opportunity and sent its armed forces to Korea; within ten days, by June 15, there were at least 4,500 Japanese troops in Korea including infantry, cavalry, and artillery, obviously too large in anyone's eyes for protection of their legation, consul general's office, and citizens; even Edwin Dun, the American minister in Tokyo, who was usually optimistic with regard to the Japanese, was suspicious about the motivations behind the sending of this large number of troops ready for a military action.[9] Both the Korean and the Chinese governments explained to the Japanese government that there was no reason for it to send such a large force to Korea and requested its immediate withdrawal. The Japanese government, however, did not heed the requests.[10] By June 20 the situation in Korea was ominous; two armies were poised in the short distance between Seoul, where a large portion of the Japanese troops were situated, and Asan, where the Chinese forces were. The *North China Daily News* observed correctly that the Japanese government had committed too large an army in Korea and that it would be impossible for Japan to withdraw the troops without any "material compensation" from China.[11] Two days later, the Japanese foreign minister, Mutsu Munemitsu, told Otori Keisuke in Seoul that war was inevitable.[12] Sensing the inescapable consequences of the war between the two contending powers for his small kingdom and after repeated direct appeals to the Japanese government, the Korean king turned to the United States for help.

On June 21 Minister Yi Sŏng-su in Washington delivered to the American government the king's message asking the United States "to take steps to avert war in Korea."[13] Secretary of State Walter Q. Gresham acted promptly. On the following day he telegraphed John M. B. Sill, the American minister in Seoul: "In view of the friendly interest of the United States in the welfare of Korea and the people, you are, by direction of the President, instructed to use every possible effort for the preservation of peaceful conditions."[14] Meanwhile, the Korean government made similar appeals to the representatives of the other Western powers in Seoul.[15] The Gresham instruction and the Korean appeals in Seoul to the Western representatives resulted in the joint note of the four representatives (from the

United States, England, Russia, and France) of June 25, in which the four pointed out that they had received requests from the Korean government to offer their "friendly offices" for the simultaneous withdrawal of the Chinese and Japanese troops from Korean soil and that they were asking for a favorable consideration of the proposal by the representatives of the two nations.[16] Otori and Yuan each acknowledged receipt of the note and added that each would refer it to his home government.[17] The note, the only joint offer of good offices in the crisis and in that sense a remarkable document, failed to produce a satisfactory response from the two governments. Of course; the target of the message was the Japanese leaders in Tokyo, but apparently deciding to disregard the diplomatic gesture in Seoul, the Japanese government did not even give an official reply. When Sill pushed Otori for a reply two weeks later, the Japanese minister gave him a discourteous note indicating that the representatives in Seoul would be able to "acquaint" themselves better through their representatives in Tokyo.[18] Within the ten days following the presentation of the joint note, the Japanese government advanced two new ideas—concerning reform measures in Korea and the dependency issue between Korea and China—which were used later by the Japanese as an excuse for occupying the palace in Seoul. Otori first brought up the Japanese desire for carrying out certain reforms in Korea during his audience with the king on July 26; two days later, he began to scrutinize the dependency issue, and he persistently pursued these two issues.[19] Pressed by Otori's demand for a radical reform, the king turned again to the United States for aid. In Washington, Yi presented the second appeal of the king on June 28 for a "powerful conference to adjust the difficulty and avert a conflict."[20] The next day, Gresham telegraphed Minister Dun in Tokyo: "The United States cherish the most friendly sentiments toward Japan and Korea and in view of the helplessness of the latter, you will ascertain and report Japan's reason for sending military force to Korea and demands Japan has made upon Korea with reasons therefore. Gresham."[21] It is clear that Gresham desired more information directly from the Japanese government regarding the Korean crisis, but there is also a definite tone of accusation in the inquiry. The Japanese foreign minister's answer to the query was that larger force was despatched to prevent the recurrence of what had happened in the 1882 and 1884 crises and that the radical administrative reform was asked of the Korean government "to guarantee peace in future."[22] This formal and perfunctory reason was far from the real reason for Japan's sending a large number of troops and forcing the reforms upon the Koreans, and it is doubtful if this answer helped to reduce the secretary's suspicion and perturbation. Two days before the arrival of Dun's telegram, the Department of State had received a third appeal from the Korean minister in Washington. This time the Koreans asked the American government to instruct its representatives in Tokyo, Peking, and Seoul to make efforts to avert conflict and to seek withdrawal of the troops of the two countries.[23] On July 5 Yi delivered another telegram from the king, the fourth and last during this crisis. It read in part: "The Japanese Minister declined to withdraw Japanese troops. Please ask the government of the United States to adjust the difficulties."[24]

Prodded by these pleas from the Korean king and annoyed by the elusive Japanese responses, Gresham sent to Dun on July 7 a truly remarkable telegram, probably one of the most remarkable documents in American-Korean relations:

> The government of the United States has heard with sincere regret that, although the insurrection has been suppressed and peace prevails in Korea, Japan refuses to withdraw her troops and demands that radical change be made in the domestic administration of Korea. This demand is more remarkable in view of the fact that China favors the simultaneous withdrawal of both the Japanese and the Chinese troops. Cherishing sincere friendship for both Japan and Korea, the United States indulges the hope that Korea's independence and sovereignty will be respected. You are instructed to say to the government at Tokyo that the President will be painfully disappointed should Japan visit upon her feeble and defenseless neighbor the horror of an unjust war.[25]

Dun immediately delivered the message to the Japanese government and received a reply two days later. The reply was characteristic: the object of Japan in Korea, the Japanese government said, was "not to make war but essentially to insure peace, order, good government and independent sovereignty of Korea."[26] In a formal sense the Japanese were not telling a lie; they were not waging war against the Koreans, but against the Chinese; furthermore, they were proclaiming a high ideal—if their proposal would be carried out it would not only bring "peace, order, and good government" to Korea but assure its independence. But to everyone who knew what Japan's real objectives in Korea were, this was a remarkably deceptive and evasive response.

American actions—or, more accurately, avoidance of actions— were conspicuous and are important for understanding the fundamental nature of American-Korean relations; they therefore deserve a careful analysis. In view of the long-maintained American policy in Korea—absolute nonintervention and strict neutrality—the American diplomatic activity of June 22–25 (the joint offer of the good offices), was an aberration. In the past, the United States had been willing to offer its good offices, and an actual offer had been made more than once in the 1880s and early 1890s, but a joint offer had never been made. The American action in Seoul in late June was definitely a deviation from the nation's traditional policy in the region, and after the June 25 offer, it was carefully avoided during the crisis. The July 7–8 action of the United States in Washington and Tokyo, which definitely went beyond an offer of simple good offices but was not quite an act of intervention, may be defined as a "protest" and should also be labeled an aberration. An important question arises: Why did the American policy makers in Washington deviate even temporarily from their traditional policy with regard to Korea in late June and early July of 1894?

The main reason for the actions Cleveland and Gresham took on behalf of Korea in early summer of 1894 seems to lie in their personal outlook and style of diplomacy. President Cleveland, who was responsible for the general line of foreign policy during his administration,[27] was a conservative who adhered strictly to the traditional policy of isolation. In his first inaugural address he declared that his foreign policy would be the policies of independence, peace, neutrality, and the policy of Monroe and Washington and Jefferson.[28] Morality, honor, and justice were all important underlying principles in Cleveland's handling of international relations. A moralistic tone is very clear in these words of the president: "The United States, in aiming to maintain itself as one of the most enlightened nations, would do its citizens a gross injustice if it applied to its international relations any other than a high standard of honor and morality."[29] In his annual message delivered at the end of 1894, Cleveland explained to the Congress the efforts he had made for the Koreans the previous summer:

> Acting under a stipulation in our treaty with Korea (the first concluded with a Western power), I felt constrained at the beginning of the controversy to tender our good offices to induce an amicable arrangement of the initial difficulty growing out of the Japanese demands for administrative reforms in Korea, but the unhappy precipitation of actual hostilities defeated this kindly purpose.[30]

His kind disposition toward the Koreans is evident in these words.

Gresham's personal outlook was similar to Cleveland's. With his lawyer's background and humane attitude, he displayed a strong sense of justice, one that had been abundantly revealed in his Hawaiian policy of nonannexation. Writing in early 1894, he said, "I am not at all disturbed about the Hawaiian question. My action has been with sole regard to justice and our national honor."[31] Gresham thought that to endorse "a selfish and dishonorable scheme" of American adventurism in Hawaii would lower the standards of the country and that it would be better for the national honor if the president "condemned the wrong and expressed a desire to see it rightened."[32] Gresham, too, thought morality to be an important factor in international relations. In connection with the Hawaiian question, he said that he thought there was such a thing as "international morality."[33] It is not difficult to imagine that, because of his strongly anti-imperialistic feelings and his inclination to side with the underdog, he had much sympathy with the Koreans.

Why did the American offer of its good offices and its protest fail in 1894? Three major reasons lay behind the failure. The Japanese, first of all, had sent a large force to Korea with a definite purpose to accomplish; moreover, by late June, the Japanese plan had advanced so far that they could not withdraw their troops without seeing an action. The second important factor was the Japanese image of the American threat. It is true, as will be shown later in this chapter, that the Japanese feared the possibility of the Western powers' intervention in the crisis; but the powers they most feared were England and Russia, not the United States. Actually, the United States was the most reliable power for the Japanese during the war. In addition to these reasons, there was an incident that must have had a bearing upon the Japanese actions. On July 7, the very day on which Secretary Gresham sent his remarkable instruction to Dun, he held a conversation with the Japanese minister. After reviewing the situation in Korea, the secretary said to Tateno: "You understand, Mr. Minister, that the United States is equally friendly toward both Japan and Korea. We claim no right to intervene in controversies between the two countries otherwise than by our good offices, in the hope of preserving peace. . . ."

The secretary then informed the Japanese minister of his conversation with the minister from Korea: "I told the Minister frankly that the government was equally friendly to Korea and Japan; that it could not and would not intervene in behalf of Korea otherwise than with its good offices; that, under no circumstances, would it go to the extent of a forcible intervention."[34] The conversation could not fail to have had an impact upon the Japanese policy makers in Tokyo. Although Gresham's statement was undoubtedly an honest description of the American policy, it was hardly a tactful one.

In retrospect, it may be said that there were only two actions with which the United States could have had an impact upon Japanese responses and hence have prevented the war: a one-power forceful intervention or a joint intervention backed by armed force. The United States would not undertake either of them. Tyler Dennett, a leading authority on American–East Asian relations, argued that the United States did not intervene because an intervention would necessarily have had to be a forceful one and, further, because such an act would have helped the European powers' ambition to weaken Asia, which was contrary to traditional American policy in the Far East.[35] The argument, although supported by an array of evidence, is not completely satisfactory. In view of the conservative policy makers in Washington, the even more conservative American public, the negligible amount of American interest in Korea, and, most important, the level of American military forces available for such an action, a forceful American intervention in Korea was not even conceivable at this time.

The American press had a definite opinion on the question of the offer of the good offices by the American government in the Far Eastern crisis. When newspaper editors learned about the American offer of the good offices, they turned furiously on Secretary Gresham. "It was hardly credible that Mr. Gresham should have used the words," a *New York Herald* editorial said, "attributed to him in relation to the interference of Japan in Korea."[36] Another New York paper lamented the secretary's action: "Neither the Farewell Address nor the old-time tradition of the State Department have deterred him from intervening most offensively and injudiciously in Korean affairs."[37] Three days later the *New York Herald* expressed the mood of the American people in even clearer terms: "It has been reported that Mr. Gresham has promised the good offices of the United States in mediating between China and Japan. But we do not need to act the part of mediator. That is none of our business."[38] Cleveland is known not to have had great respect for public opinion,[39] but he could not go far against this strong reaction of the American public, even if he had wished to take a stronger action against the Japanese.

American action to prevent the coming war reached its peak in the protest of July 7–9. It was to be three weeks before the outbreak of hostilities; meanwhile, the American government was asked to intervene in the Korean crisis; the request came from two directions —England and China—and it was for a joint intervention. On June 8, a day after Gresham's instruction to Dun for a protest, the British minister in Washington delivered the British invitation for a "joint protest" in Tokyo against the commencement of hostilities by

Japan. The American reply was firmly negative: Secretary Gresham said that the United States had already offered its good offices and would not participate in a joint intervention with any power.[40] Three times in July—on July 8, 12, and 15—the Chinese asked the American government to take the initiative for a joint action to preserve peace in Asia.[41] The American posture remained firmly against any joint action. Thus, by the middle of July, the danger of a joint, forceful intervention by the Western powers had gone, and Japan took by force the palace in Seoul and initiated military action, which began on July 25.[42] When the Japanese troops forced their way into the palace and occupied the palace grounds, the Koreans appealed again to the United States and the other Western powers, but it was too late for anyone to do anything to prevent war at this point.[43]

As soon as the fighting broke out, diplomacy took a back seat, and the American government maintained without much disturbance its traditional nonintervention and neutrality policy in Korea. Sill wrote to Gresham: "It is likely, however, that in view of the apparent sympathy of England with China, [the Russian] government may be particularly favorable to Japan. I imagine that I must remain quite neutral."[44] On the eve of the outbreak of the war, Gresham wrote to Dun: "It is hardly necessary to remind you of the absolute neutrality of your government in the present unhappy contest."[45] In late November, Gresham proudly stated that diplomatic history showed no departure from "a wise policy of avoiding foreign alliances and embarrassing participation in guaranteeing the independence of distant states."[46]

American neutrality toward the two belligerent powers, however, was a pro-Japanese neutrality. Minister Kurino Shinichiro in Washington, a close friend of Gresham, learned from the secretary the attitude and policies of the European powers toward Japan. The secretary informed the Japanese minister that his government had twice rejected the British overtures for a joint intervention.[47] Gresham also informed Kurino of the substance of the two conversations between himself and the French minister concerning a joint intervention proposed by the Western powers.[48]

The failure of the United States and the European powers to prevent war in East Asia in 1894 did not keep them from making efforts to stop the war in its early stage. Since it was certain that the time and manner of ending the war would have a great impact upon Korea, as well as on the two belligerent powers, American involvement in the movement to bring an earlier peace was important for the future of Korea and also the future of American-Korean relations. When the small but efficient Japanese army and navy won smashing victories against the larger but much less efficient Chinese armed forces—especially after the important battles at P'yŏngyang and near the mouth of the Yalu River on September 16 and 17— against the expectations of the Western powers, including the American diplomats in the Far East, the British diplomats, who still stood by China, began to take steps to end the war at an early stage with a minimum sacrifice by China. On October 6, three weeks after the P'yŏngyang battle, the British government, through its representative in Washington, asked the American government if the latter would be willing to join four European powers—England, Russia, France, and Germany—in intervening between China and Japan on the basis that the independence of Korea would be guaranteed by the powers and China would pay an indemnity for the expenses of the war.[49] Six days later Gresham replied by saying that although the president desired a peace honorable to both belligerents and not humiliating to Korea, the United States would not be able to participate in an intervention in concert with the European powers.[50] Two days later the British government sent another note explaining that the intervention they had proposed would be limited to "diplomatic action."[51] Apparently, even the British would not support China as far as a military intervention.

Nevertheless, the Japanese worried about the danger of the Western powers' intervention. On August 20 Japanese Foreign Minister Mutsu Munemitsu despatched a special mission to Seoul to find out, through the representatives of the Western powers in the Korean capital, the inclinations of their home governments regarding intervention.[52] On October 8, while the British were probing the possibility of a joint intervention by the powers, Mutsu sketched to Itō Hirobumi, the prime minister, three alternatives: (1) compel China to recognize the independence of Korea, to promise not to interfere any more with the internal affairs of the kingdom, and to cede Port Arthur and Dairen to Japan; (2) get the Western powers jointly to guarantee the independence of Korea, and compel China to cede Formosa to Japan; and (3) find out the Chinese peace terms. Mutsu added that he preferred the first alternative and added his wish for a delay of ten days to respond to the British overture.[53] A few days after this communication, the British government abandoned the idea of a joint intervention because of the difficulty of moving other powers, especially the United States and Germany. By October 17, the Japanese government had decided not to worry any more about the Western powers; on that date Mutsu confidently suggested to Itō that he disregard the Western powers and proceed in carrying out the war plan.[54] Within ten days of this communication, the Japanese carried the fighting into Manchuria.

It was clear that the United States would not join the European powers in an intervention or even in an "intercession" against Japan to restore an early peace in East Asia; this did not mean that it would not offer its good offices for the prompt ending of the hostilities. The Chinese appeal to the American government for an offer of good offices for a peace initiative reached Washington on November 5, exactly a month after the British overture. This was a request for neither a joint nor a forceful intervention but simply for the one-power good offices. The American government responded promptly; Gresham telegraphed the next day to Dun, and the Japanese answer came ten days later.[55] The Japanese candidly told the Americans that, because the Japanese army so far had enjoyed "universal success" in the war, the government did not need the cooperation of friendly powers for peace. Then the Japanese added that if the Chinese wished peace they should directly contact the Japanese authorities through the American legation in Peking, thus opening a door for a direct communication for peace.[56]

Without doubt, preventing war or stopping it early was the most serious task in the crisis. But in addition to these major foreign policy issues, there were some minor although not negligible issues in this war-time diplomacy. One was the sending of American naval vessels to Korean waters; another concerned the reform measures the Japanese presented to the Korean government; the third involved the American public image of Korea.

In early May, Minister Sill had asked Admiral J. S. Skerett to send a naval vessel to Chemulpo.[57] In response to this request, Admiral Skerett hurried to Chemulpo on the flagship USS *Baltimore*, and at least one vessel remained in Chemulpo throughout the crisis.[58] Retaining the American naval vessels in the Korean port during the crisis served two major purposes: the protection of the American citizens and their properties in Korea and the protection of the political interests of the United States in the country—issues that were interrelated and not new during this period. Once described by Sill as little more than "preventive medicine," the American naval vessel in Chemulpo met real needs by giving a sense of security to some eighty Americans and to various other tangible and intangible interests in Korea.[59] Sill kept a legation guard of up to 50 men, with a possibility of increasing it to 120, detached from the vessels in Chemulpo during the war period, and it did not leave the legation until July 19, 1895, more than three months after the end of the war.[60] The other, political, objective was not insignificant. The "suggestion" that brought the first American naval vessel to the Korean port during the crisis originated with the Korean monarch;[61] on June 25, 1894, Sill connected his decision to give asylum to the Korean king and his family with keeping a naval vessel in Chemulpo;[62] both Admiral Skerett and Admiral C. C. Carpenter, the commanders of the Asiatic Squadron, were treated "very graciously" by the king.[63] Even though Admiral Skerett tried to correct the king's erroneous impression that the American naval vessels were in Chemulpo to protect him and his family, it is doubtful whether the helpless monarch ever changed his view.[64] It may be argued, of course, that almost every act of a foreign government in Korea, especially keeping a naval vessel in Chemulpo, had a political implication in time of crisis. This State-Navy cooperation in the field was not without some minor difficulties coming from differences of opinions and even some distrust; but, in general, Sill and the naval commanders cooperated well throughout the war.[65]

The reform measures the Japanese tried to carry out in Korea in 1894 and 1895, which are interesting and important in their own right, had a significant bearing upon American-Korean relations. Starting on June 26, 1894—twenty days after the landing of the first group of Japanese troops in Korea—the Japanese made a drastic effort to transform completely the Korean administrative and social systems. Day after day the reform decrees fell "like hailstones" over the Koreans' heads.[66] There is no question that Korea needed large-scale reforms and that the reform measures the Japanese tried to carry out had much validity. Because of the corruption within and oppression by the government, Korea often attracted outside interference. Until the health of the nation could be restored through radical reforms, Korean independence could not be expected; and not until Korean independence could be realized would Japan feel secure. If the reform had been fully carried out in the mid-1890s, Korea would have greatly benefited; its modernization probably would have gained a half century. But the program had grave defects: first, it was forced from outside, and the speed was too great. The Japanese tried to accomplish in Korea in only a few years what had taken twenty-five in their own country. Furthermore, they mixed clever realism with idealism: they used the reform as a pretext for the forceful occupation of the Korean palace and for initiating the war.

The Americans were involved in the movement at two levels: the minister in Seoul and public opinion at home. When Minister Otori asked the Korean government to establish a council to consider his reform proposal, the king turned to Sill for advice. Sill advised the king that he should grant the council the sole power to listen to and report upon the Japanese demands. Following Sill's suggestion, the Korean government told the Japanese that although many of the Japanese proposals were similar to the policy that it had been trying to pursue for the past decade, such proposals could not be accepted in the face of the military occupation of their country.[67] The American public was enthusiastic about the Japanese reform program in Korea, hailing it as a great missionary effort of the Japanese for civilization. The *New York Daily Tribune* praised the Japanese: "[The reform program] glorifies her pride to occupy a position of a social and political pioneer in the Far East and to be recognized as indicating the advanced principles to which she committed herself twenty-five years ago."[68]

As has already been indicated in connection with the intervention issue, the American public's image of Korea played an important role for the first time since the bilateral relationship began. Both magazines and newspapers in the United States published a large number of articles during the war; the number of magazine articles, to which the more elitist or "attentive public" had easy access, was usually more stable. Nevertheless, *Poole's Index* and *Readers' Guide* list a large number of articles for the war period—34 articles in 1894 and 9 in the following year—for an annual average of 22. These indexes list, for the preceding twelve years from 1882 to 1893, an annual average of 4.2 articles and, for the following eight years from 1896 to 1903, an annual average of 7. The increase in the exposure of Korea and the war in the mass media was much more dramatic in the United States: the *New York Times Index* lists 235 articles for 1894 and 195 for the following year (an annual average of 215), which was a truly large number when compared with the annual average of 6 for the preceding 10-year period from 1884 to 1893 and 8.6 for the following 10-year period from 1896 to 1905.[69]

The American public was in general very pro-Japanese throughout the war, even though some apprehension began to be expressed toward the end of the war about the possibility of the Japanese making excessive demands of the vanquished power. Two closely related themes dominated both newspaper and magazine articles on the war and Korea: the Japanese were representing the West in a form of cultural warfare against the Eastern culture, and a Japanese victory would be good for Korean independence and welfare. The *New York Times* articulated Americans' wonder and surprise about the accomplishments of the Japanese: "The progress that Japan had shown for the past quarter of a century has extended the wonder of all, but few were prepared for the exhibition that has been made during the past year of her ability to take first rank among the powers of the world."[70] The same paper summarized succinctly the feeling of the American public on the cultural issue when it editorially stated, "The war is often called a conflict between Eastern and Western civilization. It would be more accurate to call it a conflict between civilization and barbarism,"[71] The *New York Daily Tribune* was equally loud on the other theme—that Japan was fighting for Korean independence and welfare. In the fall of 1894 the paper declared, "And, indeed, she has entered upon this war very largely for the purpose of establishing Korea's independence, and of maintaining it against China's claim of suzerainty."[72] The same paper also said soon after the war broke out in Korea: "The present war may decide many things, including whether or not Korea is henceforth to exist as an independent nation. But one of its most important results will be to decide this question, which was its own cause, whether Korea is to march forward or to be carried forward with Japan on the high road of civilization or whether she is to remain with China in the stagnant slough of semi-barbarism."[73] The American image of Korea and the war created by these newspapers and magazine articles must have influenced the policy makers in Washington as they formulated and executed policy in the crisis.

American representatives in Peking and Tokyo helped end the Sino-Japanese War by becoming a communication channel according to the wish of the governments of the two belligerent powers. On November 22, the day after the fall of Port Arthur, the Chinese government, through Minister Denby, made a direct overture to the Japanese government for peace on the basis of the recognition of the independence of Korea and the payment of a reasonable war indemnity.[74] This was the beginning, and after five exchanges of communications in forty days, a peace conference was finally agreed upon on the last day of the year; the first meeting was held on February 1 of the following year.[75] At times, the American ministers in Peking and Tokyo showed frustration about the attitude of the victorious power, but they patiently carried out their role.[76]

The peace treaty, which was signed on April 17, 1895 by Itō and Li, the most important politicians of Japan and China, at Shimonoseki, ended the war and one epoch of Far Eastern history. In the first article China recognized the independence of Korea, a simple but deceptive statement. Japan extorted from China 300 million taels along with Taiwan and the Liaotung peninsula.[77] The Japanese acquisition of land and money was certainly significant for future international relations in the region, but the most important outcome of the war and peace was the new Chinese position in Korea. The treaty marked the end of China as a power factor on the Korean peninsula, and Japan was given a free hand in Korea as far as China was concerned. Because of the unexpected events of the fall of 1895 and the spring of the following year (see the following chapter), the completion of Japanese control of Korea was delayed, but the outcome of the war was decisive for the future of the kingdom.

The American public's pro-Japanese sentiments extended to the peace treaty: on April 11, still a few days away from the announcement of the terms of the treaty, the *New York Times* said that it would be the duty of the Japanese negotiators to use their advantage to obtain what would be most useful to the interests of their country.[78] When the terms of the treaty were announced, the *Times* editorialized: "The amount of the money indemnity, as reported, is surprisingly small," adding that the territorial cessions seemed to have been "very judiciously exacted."[79]

American diplomacy during the Sino-Japanese War is both interesting and significant for understanding the fundamental characteristics of American-Korean relations; it shows well how far the nation would go to help Korea, a nation in which the United States did not have much interest but in which it had an emotional involvement as the nation that opened the door to the United States and other Western powers. As the British acting consul, Christian C. Gardner, aptly remarked, the United States acted during the crisis as a "godfather" in dealing with the Korean problems.[80] More than once in the past the United States had acted in the same manner for Korea, especially during the crises of 1882 and 1884, but it had never shown as much eagerness as this time; nor in the future would it act as it did during this crisis. In late June and early July of 1894, the United States went as far as it could to help its "godchild": it made an offer of joint good offices and it lodged a one-power "protest," both of which were rare incidents for the United States in dealing with any nation. But, unfortunately, it was not quite enough to move the Japanese to react as the United States wished. As was pointed out in the preceding pages, Japan's plans were set, and Japan was not in a position to alter its course of action unless faced with either an armed intervention by a power or a joint intervention of the powers with definite willingness to use force. And because the United States would not go so far as to take either of these courses at this time, the failure of its diplomacy was inevitable. In the sense that the American actions in June and July of 1894 were beyond the usual line of its diplomacy, American policy was defined as an "aberration" in this study. With the exception of this brief period, however, the United States successfully maintained its policy of nonintervention and neutrality. This success seems to have come from the weight of tradition—the tradition of strict neutrality and a policy of absolute nonintervention in the region—and the conservative and isolationist impulses of both Cleveland and Gresham.

As for Korea, it is doubtful if the Korean leaders were happy with what the United States did for their country in the crisis. Korea was an unhappy nation at this time, primarily through its own fault but partly because of the circumstances, and nothing short of an extreme act close to a miracle could change its situation. The Koreans tried to rely on the United States not just as a "godfather" but as an "elder brother nation," who solves all of his young brother nation's problems. Therefore, it is doubtful if they realized that the United States went to the limit in trying to help them in the crisis. The only "elder brother" upon whom Korea could truly rely was its own strength. If the nation could not change overnight because of the centuries-old burden of tradition, what Korea needed was a dozen, if not a hundred, heroes like Kim Ok-kyun—who was sacrificed before the crisis and became one of the causes of it—who would turn the country around with their wisdom, dedication, and courage. The Koreans paid a heavy price in 1894 and 1895 for the time idled away during the previous decade.

In the spring of 1895, the future of Korea and of American-Korean relations was uncertain. No one knew what the Japanese would make out of the new situation. Korean independence from China did not mean independence for Korea, but dependence on Japan; under normal circumstances, the establishment of a Japanese protectorate in Korea was a sure course, soon to be followed by annexation. But history is full of abnormalities, and unusual events soon began to occur that influenced the course of history in the coming decade.

5

THE INTERWAR
YEARS

The years of the interwar period, between the spring of 1895 and the winter of 1903, was another period of testing for American-Korean relations. There were changes in the major actors: China, which had been the major power in the previous decade, was replaced by Russia, which was being pushed to the front of the stage by the need to oppose the major protagonist, Japan; and England, which stood behind China, changed sides and became an ally of Japan before the period ended. Mainly because of a series of unexpected incidents that had come about soon after the end of the war with China—the three-power intervention of the spring of 1895, the murder of the Korean queen in the fall of the same year, and King Kojong's escape to the Russian legation in the following spring—Russia emerged as a formidable challenger. However, Russia's seizure of Port Arthur in the spring of 1898 changed somewhat the Russian position on the Korean peninsula; and when Russia was unwilling to give up peacefully what Japan wanted in Korea and Manchuria, Japan decided to take the issue to the battlefield in the winter of 1903–1904. The question confronting the Americans, both in Washington and Seoul, was how to maintain their traditional policy toward the peninsula kingdom and at the same time protect their national interests in these years, so filled with changes in the power configuration. The turn of the century was, further, a time of significant change for American policy as a whole toward East Asia: the occupation of the Philippines, the emergence of America as a full-fledged Asiatic power in 1898, and the declaration of the open door policy in 1899 and 1900 changed the American position. A question to be raised is whether these changes had any impact at all upon its policy toward Korea. Another point of concern in this chapter is the impact of personnel changes upon the conduct of policy and diplomacy: William McKinley replaced Grover Cleveland in 1897; he in turn was replaced in the White House by Theodore Roosevelt in the fall of 1901; a change of hands took place also in the Department of State and in the Seoul legation: Richard Olney, John Sherman, William R. Day, and John Hay succeeded Gresham in turn, and Horace Allen took over the minister's position in Seoul in 1897.

For the Koreans, this also was an important period, in a sense the most important period in the late nineteenth century. The Russo-Japanese pair was definitely much more dangerous for Korea than China and Japan had been; nevertheless, the nature of the power equilibrium created by the Russo-Japanese rivalry gave the Koreans another valuable opportunity for self-strengthening—the most important opportunity because of the timely emergence of national consciousness. Another point that deserves attention is the process and outcome of the Koreans' effort to achieve neutrality, even though it had little chance of success.

The first three years of the interwar period, between the spring of 1895 and the early spring of 1898, which began with the three-power intervention and ended with the peaking of the Russian ascendancy, was turbulent and filled with a number of extraordinary events. The first and most significant event in terms of its later impact was the three-power intervention. Earlier, the European powers had failed both in preventing the outbreak of the war and in stopping the war in its early stages; but they succeeded, at the end of the war, in preventing Japan from taking too much from China, denying her the acquisition of a foothold in continental Asia. The major force behind this move was Russia. As soon as the Japanese peace terms were known, the Russians were compelled to act, and they decided through a series of cabinet meetings between April 6 and 15, 1895, to prevent the Japanese from becoming too strong by acquiring the southern tip of Manchuria including Port Arthur and, then, to cooperate with the Japanese for their own benefit in Korea and Manchuria.[1] When the Russians approached the three European powers about participating in this venture against the Japanese, the British decided that their interests in the Far East were only commercial and declined to be involved in an apparent political act; the Germans, fearing a Russian-French-British combination, showed no hesitation in joining the Russians; and the French had no choice but to go along with their ally.[2] The Russians did not even bother to contact the Americans about the joint intervention, for they had been standing aloof from the beginning of the conflict. Because of the relationship between the two powers and because of the general policy line of the United States, the Japanese tried to rely on the Americans in dealing with the intervention. On March 19, the Japanese foreign minister, who had learned of China's plea to the powers to intervene on behalf of China, instructed Minister Kurino in Washington to ask Secretary of State Gresham to ascertain for the Japanese government, through the American representatives in the European capitals, the intentions of the powers with regard to the proposed intervention.[3] Gresham replied that the U.S. government would not be able to comply with the request, because such an action "would excite suspicion" among the powers and might cause embarrassment to the government.[4] A few days later, however, the secretary showed the Japanese minister a despatch from the American minister in St. Petersburg, which revealed Russian ambitions in China.[5]

On April 23 the representatives of the three powers in Tokyo presented identical notes to the Japanese government claiming that "the possession of the peninsula of Liaotung claimed by Japan, would be . . . a perpetual obstacle to the permanent peace of the Far East" and advising Japan to renounce its demand.[6] Three days after receiving these notes, Minister Kurino asked Secretary Gresham to mediate between Japan and the three powers and to advise China to ratify immediately the Treaty of Shimonoseki.[7] Gresham carried out the second part of the Japanese request, but because he died soon after the communication, no action was taken in favor of mediation. It is doubtful if he would have favored mediation had he lived longer. The Japanese government, realizing that the identical notes from the three powers were much more than "friendly advice," accepted the inevitable on May 5, four days after ratification of the treaty.[8] Thus, American involvement in the three-power intervention was minor, but the event itself had many repercussions. The Japanese were naturally bitter about the outcome,[9] and since the following three major events in the two-year period—the assassination of the queen, the king's flight to the Russian legation, and Russia's taking over of Liaotung peninsula—were causally connected, it should be said that the event itself was significant for international relations, and hence also for American-Korean relations, in Korea in the following years.

The five-month period after the conclusion of the peace treaty and the three-power intervention was quiet in Korea. But beneath this surface tranquility preparations were being made that would result in another five months of extreme violence and change. As soon as the news of the intervention reached the peninsula, its impact upon the power configuration in the kingdom was inevitable: Japanese influence declined, and the influence of the Western powers, especially that of Russia, rose. The party who gained the most from these circumstances was the Korean queen, who had been retired from her position of power when the series of Japanese reform measures were introduced. Since her violent death in early October turned the already lively Korean stage even more so in the following years and since her removal from the scene also had a great impact upon Korea for at least a decade and a half, it is desirable to understand what she was. From various sources we can construct a reasonably clear picture of Queen Min—a lady of middle age, shrewd, tactful, strong-minded, and capable. She was also selfish, often cruel, and single-mindedly dedicated to the prosperity of her family and the Min clan. From 1876, when her husband Kojong took over the governing authority from his father, the Taewŏn'gun, she, "the only man in the Korean court," was a powerful force behind the throne. She took full advantage of the outcome of the three-power intervention, and before long, she succeeded in forcing the Japanese minister, Inouye, to retreat to a conciliatory policy. Probably there were enough reasons for the Japanese government to replace Inouye, but it made a serious mistake in sending Miura Goro, a soldier-diplomat, to replace Inouye in the fall of the year. Before forty days had elapsed, he shocked the world with an unusual act by a diplomat. On the early morning of October 8 the Korean queen was hunted down by a group of armed intruders and was mercilessly murdered in one of the inner palace buildings. Her body, soaked with kerosene, was burned in a palace park. It was alleged—with good cause—that the Japanese minister had conceived the idea and made and executed the plan,[10] but the following spring a Japanese criminal court in Hiroshima acquitted Miura and his associates on the basis of insufficient evidence.[11]

After the October incident, a new government was organized in Seoul under the auspices of the Japanese minister, and the king became a virtual prisoner in his palace; the very security of his person was in danger. Along with other Westerners, the Americans in Seoul—both diplomats and others—were heavily involved in the developments of the ensuing months. American and other Western diplomats visited the king every day to assure him of their sympathy and to indicate to the Japanese their concern about his safety; American missionaries and their wives even brought food to the king to forestall the possibility of poisoning.[12] The American legation also admitted Korean political refugees, refusing to give them up to the Korean government.[13]

American and Western representatives in Seoul went much beyond this, however. They requested the Japanese minister to investigate the incident carefully and to punish the criminals; they refused to recognize either the decrees issued by the new Japanese-controlled Korean government or even the government itself; and they requested that Komura Jutaro, who had come to Seoul as the investigator of the incident and who remained as the minister, use Japanese troops to oust the new government and to restore the safety of the king.[14] What was rather unusual was that American and other diplomats in Seoul took all of these actions without instructions from their home governments.

The Japanese government gauged the significance of the acts of the Western diplomats in Seoul and tried—successfully—to limit their activities by exerting pressures upon their home governments.[15] When Secretary of State Olney learned what Sill and his secretary Allen had been doing in Seoul, partly through the Japanese minister in Washington and partly from the American representatives themselves in Seoul and Tokyo, his reaction was prompt and decisive.[16] In his instruction of November 20, 1895, he exploded: "Confine yourself strictly protection of Americans citizens and interest. You have no concern internal affairs. Your actions to be taken independently of other representatives unless otherwise instructed."[17] The instructions of the following day had a definite tone of accusation: "It is in nowise his [the American minister's] function, unless acting under instructions from this department, to take action with the representatives of other treaty powers in calling the government to account, or in any way mixing with the internal affairs of the country." After stating that the minister should not shelter Korean refugees, the instruction continued: "The department sees with disfavor disposition to forget that you are not to interfere with local concerns and politics of Korea, but are to limit yourself strictly to the care of American interest."[18]

Thus a temporary gap appeared between the line of policy in Washington and the spirit of diplomacy in Seoul, this despite the fact that the representatives in Seoul knew full well that the American policy of neutrality and nonintervention had been firmly established by this time in Washington and equally well that their function was to carry out the policy made in Washington, not to make it. This temporary breakdown in the normal foreign policy-making and execution apparatus happened because of the breakdown (both literal and figurative) of normal channels of communication, because of the urgency for some kind of action demanded by the grave situation, and because of differences in the emotional make-up of the persons involved. When the crisis came to Seoul, Minister Sill was vacationing in Japan, planning to return to his post two weeks later. Allen, the secretary, now in charge of the legation, sent despatches almost daily to Washington through Dun in Tokyo because of the breakdown of the telegraphic line between Korea and Japan.[19] Dun necessarily played an important role as a channel of communication. But his job did not stop with that role; he probably, as part of his duty, also checked with the ranking officials of the Japanese government about developments in Korea and communicated his own views as well as this information to Washington.[20] Consequently, Washington was troubled because it had at times two sets of information and views on the same subjects.[21] Allen was so upset by this incident that his emotional state influenced his words as well as his actions. In his October 10 telegram to Olney, Allen said, "I am forced to believe that the queen was murdered by these Japanese ruffians and that her body was burned by prearranged plan to conceal the crime"; four days later, he telegraphed again to Olney, describing conditions in highly emotionally charged words: "The condition of His Majesty is pitiful; Queen murdered; murderers in full power; his own life in imminent peril, compelled to act abhorently."[22] Allen was also obsessed by the sense of being important in the crisis. "I am just now occupying," he wrote to his sister, "a more important position than I ever expected to fill. I say the peace of Asia probably of Europe in a great measure depends upon me."[23] When Sill returned to his post in late October, he approved, using strong words, what Allen had done and pursued a similar line of diplomacy himself.[24]

The Japanese government, troubled by its envoy's blunder, sent Komura, one of its ablest diplomats at this time, to Seoul to succeed Miura, who left the country in late October to go to Hiroshima, where he was immediately arrested and tried.[25] Being an ambitious diplomat, Komura would not undo what his predecessor had done, even though he saw clearly the wrong the Japanese minister had done. Japanese policy makers in Tokyo also held the same posture; surprised by the unusual news from Seoul, they first insisted that the Japanese government did not have anything to do with the atrocity in Seoul, which they claimed was done by the Taewŏn'gun and an unemployed Japanese samurai; however, by October 17, in an effort to retain the advantage that had been obtained at such a high cost, they had switched their strategy and begun to claim that the new Korean government, which had been organized by and was controlled by the Japanese minister, was "completely autonomous and independent."[26] Meantime, the king remained a prisoner of the puppet government, and there did not seem to be any possibility of change or improvement in Seoul. A group of Koreans soon hatched a plot to free the king from his hopeless position. According to a report of Komura to his home government, eight hundred former palace guards, forty assassins, a number of Korean refugees in foreign legations, and five Americans—General Dye (a military adviser to the Korean army) and four missionaries—attempted to break into the palace to rescue the king.[27] The attempt failed because of poor coordination and the betrayal of the leaders by certain of the guards.[28]

American involvement in this venture was extensive. Both Sill and Allen admitted that American missionaries had participated in the plot. It is difficult to determine how deeply the two American diplomats themselves were involved, since there is considerable disagreement between their reports and those of the Japanese diplomats. Sill claimed that when he first learned of the plot on the afternoon of the previous day he tried to contact the Japanese minister. That night, when awakened by a legation guard who had heard noise coming from the direction of the palace, Sill had gone to the palace with the Russian and British ministers and the legation secretaries to appraise the situation. He also claimed that he had sent a note to the attacking party suggesting that they disperse.[29] Allen said that he had had nothing to do with "the revolution."[30] However, the Japanese minister, Komura, stated in his report that a Japanese legation secretary had seen Allen returning from the direction of the palace with an officer and ten marine guards.[31] In the following spring, Komura proposed to his government that an attempt be made to have Sill and Allen recalled by their government for their alleged involvement in the November countercoup.[32] It is difficult to believe all of what the Japanese secretary claimed, but it is also true that a number of Korean refugees who stayed in the American legation were involved in the incident and that, at least because of this, Sill and Allen must have known what was taking place on that evening, even if they were not directly involved in any part of the plot.[33]

Far from helping the dreadful situation, the unsuccessful countercoup of late November made it even worse. In the following two months, the American policy and diplomacy apparatus was under much stress, and Olney and Sill exchanged many harsh words. Secretary of State Olney in his instruction of December 31 announced that the legitimate place for policy making in American diplomacy was within the Department of State.[34] Early in the following month, Olney became furious about Sill's activities in Seoul. After referring to the minister's despatches regarding his expression of satisfaction to the king on having confirmed the revocation of the decree regarding the late queen and the trouble of American missionaries because of their expression of anti-Japanese feelings, Olney said: "Your course in continued intermingling with Korean political affairs in violation of repeated instructions noted with astonishment and emphatic disapproval. Cable briefly explanation you have to make, also answer whether you intend to comply with instructions given."[35] Sill frankly admitted his mistakes and expressed his intention of obeying the orders of the Department. He answered, "I did err unintentionally in certain points recited in my 175 and 176." Then he continued, "No harm resulted Korea. There will not be henceforth any cause for criticism. I will act according to instructions scrupulously."[36] In his despatch soon after, Sill explained:

> Positively the circumstances by which I am surrounded have influenced me unconsciously for I live in an atmosphere of continual and often arbitrary and violent interference in Korean affairs. Sometimes this interference is directly antagonistic to American interest. Sometimes, in my judgment, it endangers the peace and order of Korea and by consequence, the safety of American life and property. In other cases there is some temptation to interference with counter-interference.[37]

He added that he would make no further mistake in the same direction.[38]

One of the basic factors for an abnormal operation of the decision-making process is here succinctly indicated. It should be added that the American diplomats were not the only foreign representatives in Seoul who were acting on their own without instructions from their home governments; other Western diplomats did exactly the same, indicating that there was a systemic, not just a personal or operational, factor behind this abnormality.[39] By his forceful actions, however, Olney pushed the operation back to a normal channel of functioning.

Even though the failure of the November 27 attempt was a setback for the anti-Japanese and hence the pro-king factions and the pro-Korean groups, they would not abandon the idea of rescuing the king from the hands of the Japanese and their helpers. Although the next scheme was not quite honorable, it was planned well and, most important, it worked. In the early hours of a February day, the Korean monarch slipped out of his palace in an unceremonious way in a carriage used to carry the court ladies and went to the Russian legation. This ignoble and furtive act, which removed the king from Japanese hands and put him into Russian, had great repercussions for Korean affairs, more than the dramatic event of the preceding fall.

Yi Hi (Kojong), the twenty-eighth monarch of the Yi dynasty, was forty-four years old in 1896, of medium height and pleasant appearance. Well-educated in the traditional Oriental educational system, he was a hard-working and intelligent man. He was an ideal country gentleman, perfectly at home in a study far away from the capital. Despite his many fine qualities as a man, he had some serious deficiencies as a ruler, especially during an era of continuing crises: not only was he weak, he also lacked a vision for the future of the nation. A weak, clever, and often cruel ruler, the king had committed numerous dishonorable acts in his life, but none equaled the disgrace of his act of February 11, 1896.

American involvement in the king's flight was minor. On February 10, the day before the flight took place, the king asked Allen whether he should take refuge in the Russian legation. Allen, hesitating to take the responsibility for advising the king either way, arranged for the royal emissary to confer with the Russian minister. Yi Pŏm-chin and others who had a connection with the Russian legation made careful preparations. Lady Ŏm, a court attendant, played an important role in the preparation and the execution of the flight. On February 10 the Russians brought 15 officers and 107 men, armed and supplied, from Chemulpo to Seoul.[40] The American guard, which had been in Seoul since the October incident, was ordered to leave the capital four days before the Russian guards were brought in—evidence that the Americans did not know what was to occur within a few days.[41]

Throughout the months of crisis, American diplomats were fortunate to enjoy excellent cooperation from the American navy. When the October 8 violence broke out in Seoul, the USS *Yorktown* was in Chemulpo, and fifteen marines were sent immediately to Seoul, where they stayed until early February of the following year.[42] With only a few days' rest, the guard returned to Seoul because of the February 11 incident; a guard of eleven bluejackets and ten marines was despatched from USS *Machias*.[43] This twenty-one-man party did not leave its position until early July of the year, when tranquility was restored to the city and the security of the legation was assured.[44] A naval vessel stayed on after the withdrawal of the guard, and its change to the status of an occasional absence did not come until the early spring of 1897, when "absolute assurance of future tranquility" was seen by the commanding admiral of the Asiatic Squadron.[45] Besides the excellent service provided by the physical presence of military force in the center of the fierce power play, officials of the Department of State as well as those of the Navy Department often benefited from the valuable information and keen observations provided by the naval officers who visited Seoul.[46]

With the sovereign now in the Russian legation, the Japanese lost the control they had gained at the high cost of Miura's crime; the Russians, on the other hand, enjoyed their period of ascendancy during the ensuing two-year period until the spring of 1898. The desire of the two rival powers on the peninsula to avoid a collision and to adjust the losses and gains accumulated through the transfer of the royal person resulted in the Waeber-Komura and Lobanov-Yamagata agreements, signed in the spring of 1896 in Seoul and St. Petersburg, respectively.[47] Views as to the success and failure of the two parties in the agreements vary, but essentially what the two powers achieved on paper was the establishment of a two-power condominium over Korea.[48] Russia, however, soon began to seek monopolistic control of two important aspects of Korean life—the army and finance—jeopardizing the arrangements made in the two agreements.

The Americans in Korea enjoyed this period of Russian ascendancy between the spring of 1896 and the spring of 1898. The continued friendly relationship between the Russian minister, Waeber, and the Americans in Seoul was a great help to American diplomacy. Waeber's relatively mild imperial diplomacy in Korea left enough room for American action in the nation. Actually, there was more cooperation between the representatives of the two countries than the Department of State wanted.[49] Trade between the United States and Korea, which was carried out indirectly through merchants in Japan, was still small, almost negligible; however, in the post–Sino-Japanese War years, two major concessions were obtained by the Americans in Korea, a significant move from the Korean viewpoint. The concession of the Unsan gold mine, which proved to be not only the best gold mine in Korea but also the most profitable one in all of Asia, was given to James R. Morse in August 1895, before the Russian ascendancy began but while the Japanese influence in the peninsula was waning.[50] Also granted to Morse was the concession of the Seoul-Inchon railway, the first and most important railway concession in Korea, which was given in the spring of 1896, when the period of Russian ascendancy had already begun.[51]

The United States successfully maintained its traditional policy of neutrality and nonintervention in Korea during the three years immediately following the Sino-Japanese War. Mainly because of circumstances in Korea, the foreign policy-making system experienced a temporary period of abnormal operations in the fall and winter of 1895, but the Department of State managed well in general to keep its representatives in the regular track of the policy-making process. A number of factors made this possible: the weight of the policy line (which was firmly established by this time), the relatively small amount of American interest in the peninsula, the degree and nature of American public opinion on Korea, and the personality factor. A few additional comments are necessary with regard to the last two items: after the explosion of information on Korea and the war in the United States in 1894 and the following year, the American news media practically deserted the kingdom (the *New York Times* printed twenty-one articles in 1896 and five in the next year, and *Poole's Index* lists only two articles for the first postwar year and six for the following year),[52] and if a small number of Americans had an image of Korea, it must have been a poor one.[53] Secretary of State Richard Olney, who handled the policy side of the Korean problem was quite different from his predecessor Gresham; he was realistic and efficient to the extent of being crude at times. On the Korean side, many, especially the king, clung as much as they could to Sill and Allen and other Western diplomats in the difficult months of the fall and the winter of 1895; to be sure, the helpless king must have wished that he had chosen the American legation after slipping out of his own palace where he had been a prisoner, for the Russian legation was not much better than the Japanese legation. Humiliation and risk were the price the Koreans were now paying for their weakness.

The four-year middle section of this period, which roughly coincided with the McKinley administration in the United States, was in a sense a transitional period for American-Korean relations, not so much because of any change in the line of the policies, which remained the same, but because of the change of the mode of diplomacy or the execution of the policy. One of the two key factors in this change was personality; the other was a change of conditions. William McKinley, the new president, brought a host of new personalities into American-Korean relations: John Sherman, William R. Day, and John Hay into the Department of State and Allen into the American legation in Seoul. For the direction and general line of the foreign policy of the McKinley administration, the president himself was most important.[54] McKinley made but few statements indicating the general principles of his foreign policy; his overall conservative orientation, however, can be discerned from some of his public remarks. In his first inaugural address, he declared:

We have the policy of non-interference with the affairs of foreign governments wisely inaugurated by Washington keeping ourselves free from entanglement; either as alliance or foes, content to leave undisturbed with them the settlement of their own domestic concerns. It will be our own aim to pursue a firm and dignified foreign policy, which shall be just, impartial, ever watchful of the lawful rights of American citizens everywhere.[55]

In the spring of 1900, speaking to a small group of people in New York, he said, "We are neither in alliance nor antagonism nor entanglement with any foreigner [applause]."[56]

None of the three men—Sherman, Day, and Hay—who headed the Department of State expressed any particular interest in Korea. Sherman, who occupied the secretarial position from March 1897 to April 1898 and who was probably appointed as a result of a political deal, was "senile" and a weak secretary of state.[57] Sherman was concerned about the involvement of American missionaries in Korean politics, but the degree of his involvement in the process of policy making with regard to Korea is questionable. Whatever attitude he had, it could not have had much impact upon the policy-making process. While Sherman was secretary of state, the burdens of the department were actually carried on by Day, a close friend of the president. Day was assistant secretary from May 1897 to April 1898, and then secretary to September of the year.[58] Although lacking any experience in foreign affairs, Day was an able man, and he carried out his duties well. His view of Korea cannot be found; concerned with the important Cuban problem, he probably could not pay special attention to this small Oriental nation. John Hay, one of the abler secretaries of state, headed the department for the last three years of the McKinley administration beginning in September of 1898. Although there is not much evidence regarding his views on Korea, he had responsibility for Far Eastern policy and must have played an important role in formulating policy concerning Korea.[59]

The person who was most involved and probably also most important in American-Korean relations during the period was Horace N. Allen. He replaced Sill as the minister in the early summer of 1897 and stayed in that position for almost eight years, until the spring of 1905. When he took over the post, he had lived for fourteen years in Korea and had been the legation secretary for seven years. One of the foremost Western experts on Korean affairs, he was certainly well qualified for the position. Although the *New York Times* reported that his appointment was made because of his knowledge of Oriental affairs, much political support was involved in it; for the long-coveted position, Allen had the support of such prominent men as John Sherman, Joseph B. Foraker, George K. Nash, and William W. Rockhill.[60] The tall, thin, bald-headed Allen was a native of Ohio. After his education at Ohio Wesleyan College

and Miami Medical School, he went to China as a medical missionary in 1883 and then to Korea in the following year. Although Allen
was intelligent and capable, his short temper, his "lack of Christian
charity," and his narrow-mindedness did not aid him as a diplomat.
He could avoid difficulties with both the Koreans and foreigners,
but not with Sill and the American missionaries in Korea.[61]

Allen was frankly pragmatic in carrying out his diplomatic duties
in Seoul, probably much more so than anyone in the State Department. His view of international law reveals much about his character; Allen said, "International law, like treaties and conventions,
you know, are to be violated at will by the stronger party. If each
party is of equal strength, the stipulations and provisions will be
carefully lived up to."[62] Neither McKinley nor any of his aides in the
State Department could make such a Machiavellian statement.
Some of Allen's diplomatic techniques were extremely realistic.
"Meantime the troubled waters," Allen said in the latter part of his
diplomatic career in Seoul, "afford the fine fishing and a 'show-
down' will show that some large fishes have been captured."[63] He
even used his attendance at the emperor's New Year's audience as a
diplomatic tool.[64] Possessing a low opinion of the Korean ruling
class, he thought little of either the ruler or the government. He
thought highly, however, of the common people in Korea—"docile,
good-natured, a patient and hard working race."[65] From this mixture
of ideas—a bad ruling class and a good common people—Allen
emerged with a view that the Korean populace would be better off
under foreign domination.[66] A brief examination of the personal
outlook and the attitudes toward the Koreans of those who were
involved in the policy-making process and the execution of policy
indicates that the Koreans did not have a friend either in Washington or in the American legation in Seoul during this period.

Allen had the advantage of receiving in late November 1897, soon
after he took over the duties of the chief delegate's position in Seoul,
a clear instruction as to the policy line he was supposed to follow.
Secretary of State Sherman's instruction ran:

> You are appointed to this interesting mission at a time when there is rea-
> son to believe that rival purpose and interests in the East may find in
> Korea a convenient ground of contention, and it behooves the United
> States and their representatives, as absolutely neutral parties, to say, or
> do nothing that can in any way be constructed as taking sides with or
> against any of the interested powers.[67]

Then, after stating the undesirability of partiality, the instruction
continued: "This government is in no sense the Counselor of Korea

as to its internal destinies, neither is it bound to Korea by a protective alliance." Further, Sherman expressed the hope that not only would the legation stay aloof from Korean affairs, but also that all American subjects in Korea would maintain an attitude of "absolute neutrality."[68] The McKinley administration never deviated from this line of policy toward Korea. Allen, grateful for the position he had long desired, made a firm determination to execute loyally the instructions from Washington. In his first despatch, he said: "I am deeply grateful to the President for the high honor he has conferred upon me, and I shall do all in my power to carefully carry out the spirit of the instructions I have been favored with."[69] He tried to hold to this spirit, although, as we will see, it was not always easy.

The winter of 1897–1898 was an important period for international relations in Korea. Russian domination reached its peak in late 1897 under the vigorous minister Alexis de Speyer. In the fall of the year, Allen wrote: "The Russians are taking a very decided stand and I fancy the next four years will not be as quiet as some years I have seen here."[70] The Russian grip in Korea, however, did not last long. When Russia decided to lease from China Port Arthur, the very port the three-power intervention had forced Japan to return to China two years before, it was willing to make a concession to Japan in Korea.[71] In the spring of 1898, Russia withdrew its military and financial advisers from Korea, and the Rosen-Nishi agreement of April 25 was signed.[72] Allen thought that this settlement established a "joint control of Korea."[73] Russia seemed to be leaving Korea, but in the light of later developments, it is clear that the departure, based on convenience, was only temporary. In the early summer of 1898, Allen shrewdly observed: "She will probably come back when the time comes for her inevitable conflict with Japan."[74] It is more appropriate to say that because of geopolitical reasons, Russian interest in the Korean peninsula was to be permanent.

The rise and fall of Russian influence in Korea provided a test for American diplomacy in the country. In early October 1897 Allen optimistically thought that the Russians would not object to American interests on the peninsula.[75] But the Russian minister de Speyer turned out to be hostile to the Americans, and Allen was naturally very much concerned. In early October he reported to Sherman: "It has been reported to me several times that Mr. de Speyer had spoken in a very heated manner against American missionaries, Americans in general and the American publications in Korea, saying he would drive them out of Korea." "Later it was told me," continued his report, "by Korean friends of mine he had assured them that no Korean with sentiments friendly to Americans would be allowed to remain in office."[76]

A subtle sense of the power balance seems to have been the reason behind the Russo-American hostility in Korea during this period. Whenever the Russians seized excessive power in Korea, the Americans and the other Westerners rose to counter them. In 1897, for example, the Russian minister complained that, when Russia wanted to bring in more military advisers (sixteen of them), the Americans raised an objection; Allen also tried, at about the same time, to prevent the Russians from getting a coaling station at Pusan.[77] De Speyer once succinctly explained the cause of Russian distrust of the Americans. In the middle of October 1897, in one of his conversations with Allen, he responded to Allen's remark that the Russians received more sympathy from the Americans than the Russian minister was aware of: "O Yes, when the Japanese controlled everything they were very willing to come to us to get their friends out of trouble, but lately, No."[78] This is a very revealing statement, and the principle it implied was later borne out by the turn in American-Russian relations on the peninsula. In the early part of 1898, as Russian influence declined, Russian feelings toward the Americans improved: on January 10 of the year, Allen said that he was on good terms with the Russians.[79]

In dealing with the Koreans, Allen strictly observed the policy that he had pledged to follow. One of the privileges many American ministers in Seoul enjoyed was their role as advisers to the king and the government, a privilege that their superiors in Washington had long tolerated. During the McKinley era, however, the rule was changed, and Allen was clearly instructed to give no advice to the Koreans.[80] Allen strictly carried out the instruction, and when the Koreans were hard pressed by the Russians in the fall of 1897 and turned to Allen for advice, the American minister carefully refrained from counseling them. In mid-November he reported his utmost caution to Sherman: "I wish to say emphatically that, in view of the Russian complications, I have been particularly careful to keep away from all the Koreans directly concerned with the difficult question."[81] Allen refused to counsel the Koreans regarding the Japanese request for the Seoul-Pusan railway concession.[82] And he denied asylum to Koreans during this period, a courtesy that the American representatives had always been willing to accord to Korean dignitaries.[83]

As the relative power positions of the major powers in Korea changed, a new factor entered Korean politics: nationalism. Independent for more than two thousand years, Korea only became a nation in the modern sense in the 1890s, with the year 1898 being the crucial date. Allen showed a great interest in this movement in

Korea without deviating from the policy line of the United States. The Korean nationalist movement of 1898 centered on the Independence Club, a politico-cultural organization organized in the spring of 1896 under the leadership of Dr. Sŏ Chae-p'il (Philip Jaison), a Korean-American who had participated in the 1885 coup.[84] The history of the movement in 1898 was that of the club itself. Allen diligently reported its progress to Washington. In late 1897 Allen described the nature and composition of the organization: "The club is composed of the best elements among the Korean officials and will undoubtedly continue to do a great deal for the country if unmolested. The members seem all to have taken America as their model."[85] The club fought to reform the administration with publications, lectures, memorials, mass meetings, and demonstrations. Allen was especially impressed by the demonstrations organized by the club. "It was such a demonstration," Allen reported to Washington in the fall of the year, "as Korea has never known before, all was done quietly and in an orderly manner, but a demonstration was shown that would brook no interference."[86] He praised the *Independent*, the bilingual newspaper, as "one of the greatest instruments of enlightenment and progress."[87] And Allen watched with astonished eyes the awakening of Korean women from their seclusion through the club's activities.[88]

Without a doubt, the movement was significant, and there was a reason for Allen's excitement. The club had some successes: it forced the government to drop six corrupt cabinet members, and it pushed for the organization of the Privy Council, a semirepresentative organization.[89] However, there were more ideals and hopes than achievements, and its successes should not be exaggerated. After its peak in October, the club declined quickly, and before the end of the year, its active but short life ended.[90] Some years later Allen looked back at the failure of the movement: "This attempt at self-government has shown that the Koreans are very far from ready for it as yet."[91] Certainly, Korea's unreadiness for a democratic system was one of the basic causes of the failure. But there were other reasons: the members of the club were inexperienced and the monarch was jealous.

Although active in informing the department, Allen was cautious, and he successfully avoided being involved directly in the movement. When the emperor (the king had promoted himself)[92] asked the American minister's opinion about a struggle between the club and a group of armed peddlers—armed by the emperor himself —Allen declined to give advice.[93] A few days earlier the foreign representatives had learned about the Korean government's use of force to disperse mass meetings sponsored by the club. Allen, the dean of the diplomatic corps in Seoul, acted as their representative in expressing to the Korean government their desire to see no more bloodshed. However, he refused to join the other Western representatives when the British representative suggested a joint move to "protest" the use of force.[94] Allen held firm to a policy of independence.

The year 1898 was important in Korea also for a change in the international power configuration; as Russian influence declined, Japanese influence increased. Allen gingerly watched the change. In the spring of 1898, Allen said, "At present Japan is moving quietly in Korea";[95] a year and a half later he found the Japanese had become aggressive and their treatment of the Koreans was "most cruel and unwise."[96] Allen astutely discerned another current of the Japanese movement—colonization—a quiet but steady policy and one that was much more formidable in the long run. In March 1901 he wrote that the Japanese were intending to settle 100,000 colonists and "quietly absorb the country."[97] Allen's view was confirmed by the testimony of a responsible Japanese government official: the Japanese Foreign minister confidently declared in the middle of 1900, "There is every indication that we can make whatever agreements we like with Korea at present."[98]

As Japan became stronger in Korea, an important question for the Americans was how this Japanese ascendancy would affect their business interests, which were growing at this time. Allen was optimistic. In early 1899 he wrote to his friend James R. Morse, "When Japan shall have quietly succeeded in allaying the political disorder as she is bound to do, there will be opportunities for development, and the very preponderance of Japanese influence will assist in throwing things our way."[99] A year and a half later he expressed the same view to Hay: a Japanese peace in Korea would bring an order that would be conducive to business conditions in the country. But this was only one side of the picture. The other side was that Japanese political domination would be used to drive the Americans out of economic competition. This side of the picture became clearer before long. In late 1899 Allen deplored the Japanese attitude toward American business: "The Japanese have begun to regard Americans, and American business in Korea, with much dislike."[100] He repeatedly lamented the hostile Japanese attitude and the actions taken against American businessmen.[101] Under these circumstances, the pragmatic Allen tried a logical tactic—he simply tried not to antagonize the Japanese. In the summer of 1900 he told Hay that he regretted that the Americans should seem to be antagonistic to Japan; he himself was trying to promote friendly feelings between the two countries.[102] It seems that Allen had considerable success with his approach; by late 1900 the Russians were complaining that the two countries were cooperating well in Korea.[103]

The years 1899 and 1900 were very important for American policy in the Far East, for in these years the open-door policy was declared. When the idea arose in connection with China, Korea was also interested. In the spring of 1899 the Korean emperor read in a newspaper report that American minister Edwin H. Conger in Peking had announced that the United States would "maintain the integrity of China." He immediately asked Allen to obtain the same promise for Korea. Allen expressed his doubts about the report, but promised the emperor that he would talk to the president on the subject when he had occasion to do so. Allen recalled his interview with President McKinley and Secretary Hay on the subject in a later despatch to Hay: "It was for this reason that I went to Lake Champlain, where I had the honor of mentioning the matter to President McKinley and yourself. You assured me promptly that there was nothing in the report and the President heard me patiently and told me to make a negative reply in suitable form.[104] The Korean monarch had apparently been misinformed, for no such declaration was made by the United States in the spring of 1899. Later, when the policy was declared, the American government stated that it was only for China; that Korea was not included.

Before the end of the McKinley era, American policy met one more challenge in Korea, though not a formidable one. It was the neutrality question. Because of Korea's geographical position and the nature of power distribution in Northeast Asia, neutralization had been an ever-recurring issue since the opening of the country to the Western world in the 1880s. History has repeatedly demonstrated what the neutrality of a weak nation amounted to when backed only by international agreements and moral sanctions. However, unable to find a better means of protection, the Koreans wished to see their country neutralized like Switzerland or Belgium. They made a serious effort in this direction in the fall and winter of 1900. In September of the year, the Korean minister Cho Pyŏng-sik approached the Japanese government with the suggestion, but the Japanese did not take it seriously.[105] Then the Russians came in; and in the early part of the following year, their government, through its representatives in Tokyo, made a proposal to the Japanese for the neutralization of Korea.[106] After some delay the Japanese replied, advising the Russians to postpone the question.[107] The issue then temporarily disappeared from the surface of international society in East Asia.

The United States was involved in the issue of Korean neutralization in Seoul and Tokyo. In October 1900 the Korean minister Cho in Tokyo asked the American minister Alfred E. Buck to "urge" his government to "take initiative" to get the cooperation of the powers for the neutralization of Korea. Buck suggested to Cho that the proper channel of communication would be the Korean minister in Washington.[108] The Korean court incorrectly believed for some time that Buck had told Cho that he would see the president about an American proposal concerning the question to the powers.[109] Allen was against the neutralization of Korea because he believed that it would be harmful to American interests in that country. Minister Cho sent a report to his government that Japan would propose neutralization of Korea if the Korean government would increase the army to 50,000 men. When the emperor received this report, he asked for Allen's opinion. The American minister told the emperor that he did not see how Korea would be able to double the taxes, which were already too heavy for the people, to pay for the larger army.[110] "Such an international guarantee as could protect the Koreans from all outside interference and allow them to 'stew in their own juice' has long been a cherished object of the present ruler," Allen said on the issue in early October 1900, when he heard the rumor that Black would talk to the president about the problem.[111] At the end of the month, he expressed his view in even clearer terms: "It would be a very bad thing for Korea, and for our own interest here, since the Koreans are sufficiently difficult now to get along with, while with such international agreement they would undoubtedly be much more difficult to handle."[112]

The subject of Korea's neutralization was a strange one. Certainly the Koreans had wished for its realization since the early 1880s. Japan and Russia, the powers most interested in Korea, wanted it at one time or another, but not at the same time. When one of the contending powers proposed this scheme, the real motivation was either to halt the rising ascendancy of the other power or to stop its own decline by freezing the status quo. Japan was serious about the neutralization of Korea in the spring of 1895 when Russia seemed to be taking away all the fruits of its efforts through the joint intervention of the powers;[113] Russia, on the other hand, made such a proposal when it seemed that it would not be able to regain the power it had been losing since 1898. Since both powers refused to write off their political ambitions in the peninsula, and since it was very difficult to catch a moment of balance of influence, the powers would not seriously consider neutralization until it was too late. This was the very reason for the failure of the effort in the winter of 1900; Japan would not give up the position it had gained since the spring of 1898.[114]

During the McKinley era, American economic interests in Korea showed a small but steady increase; some of the increases were significant. Trade doubled, though it remained moderate; the Unsan gold mine concession was extended for thirty years; and concessions for the Seoul electric plant, electric railway, the Seoul waterworks were all obtained in this period.[115] Allen as usual was helpful to the American businessmen,[116] especially in the sale of Morse's Seoul-Chemulpo railway to the Japanese, an act that made the Koreans very unhappy.[117]

As missionary work increased—the number of converts almost quadrupled in this period—Allen's duties also increased. Allen's major concern with the missionaries was always to restrain them from becoming involved in domestic politics.[118] A circular especially aimed at the missionaries and circulated at the very beginning of the McKinley administration read in part: "They should strictly refrain from any expression of opinion or from giving advice concerning the internal management of the country, or from any intermeddling in its political question."[119]

The McKinley era was a transitional period, between the old and new, between the traditional and the modern, in the history of American foreign policy. However, changes in the national policy orientation little affected American policy toward Korea. From the outset, the McKinley administration's Korean policy was clear and firm: neutrality, nonintervention, noninvolvement, and independence. The major difference between this and the preceding period was that the policy was more strictly carried out and that diplomacy between the United States and Korea became much cruder. To be sure, the growth of both economic and cultural interests during this period was substantial, but both were still very small; by the end of the period, direct annual trade amounted to a little more than $200,000, and not more than 30,000 converts had been made. Another aspect important in the change in diplomatic style was the personal factor: the McKinley-Sherman-Day-Hay-Allen team was different from the teams of the previous periods—it was much more realistic. One might assume that, since the United States opened the door of Korea to the Western world, its open-door policy, which was declared during this period, would have included Korea. Unfortunately, Korean trade did not promise much. Nor did Korea seem to be on the verge of disintegration at this point (probably it did not matter anyway). Moreover, Korea did not have Alfred E. Hippisley and William W. Rockhill as advocates. For the Koreans, the four-and-a-half-year period that began in 1897, when Russia was retreating and Japan was still not strong, was a golden opportunity. Unfortunately, however, Kojong's lack of vision undermined the Independence Club, the sole nationalist movement in the nation. The Koreans turned again to the Americans, hoping that this time they would aid in the neutralization of the peninsula kingdom; but McKinley was too far away emotionally for them to reach, and Allen, not only realistic but also very selfish, was almost too cynical on the issue. For all of these reasons, the period was a transitional one, and a new era was at the door, with a far more unpleasant mood and events for American-Korean relations.

When Theodore Roosevelt became president, following McKinley's assassination in September 1901, a new era of American foreign policy opened. That this change would have an impact upon American-Korean relations was inevitable, even though its full impact did not come until the Russo-Japanese War and the postwar period. The main line of American policy toward Korea underwent no modifications or deviations during the two-year period between the fall of 1901 and the winter of 1903. Even the personnel in the Department of State remained the same; Hay, a good friend of the new president, remained head of the department until his death in the summer of 1905. Had there been no war in 1904–1905 and had conditions not changed during the war and the postwar years, the degeneration of American-Korean relations during the Roosevelt years would probably have not gone beyond the level of indifference.

Korea was calm during the two-year prewar period—the calm before a storm. Korea was also despairing, more despairing every year; it was at the lowest ebb of the five hundred–year history of the Yi dynasty.[120] Centralization, ineffectiveness, corruption, and oppression were bleeding the country. The government exacted impossibly high taxes from the people and spent the money lavishly. The court often hired highly paid dancing girls; it spent as much as $5,000 for the entertainment of one visiting foreign admiral; and it planned to spend $3,000,000 to celebrate the fortieth anniversary of the emperor's accession, a sum that included the purchase of 350 horses from the United States for a parade.[121] Allen remarked late in 1902, "There seem to be millions for celebration and other things that please the vanity of the ruler, but not one cent for supporting proper enterprises or for paying off obligations."[122]

These two years in Korea were also marked by the steady progress of Japanese colonization and by the strengthening of Japan's already dominant position. "The Japanese scheme is to build railways and colonies along the line, much as Russia is doing in Manchuria. They have colonies in most of the large cities in the interior," Allen wrote late in 1902.[123] In the summer of 1902, a Japanese adviser came to Korea to work in three departments: agriculture, commerce, and public works.[124] As the Japanese grip became firmer, the Koreans sought friendship with the Russians, but the latter never regained enough power in Korea to match that of the Japanese.[125] Toward the two antagonists Allen acted tactfully, trying not to antagonize the Japanese and to maintain the good relations with the Russians.[126]

Although England and the United States became friendly after 1898, in Korea they oscillated between cordiality and antagonism. At the beginning of the Roosevelt era, the relationship was cordial; then it turned antagonistic. Roosevelt's presidency ended with a period of cooperation.

The first important diplomatic event in Korea during the Roosevelt period was the Anglo-Japanese alliance of early 1902. The motivation behind the treaty is debatable, but it is clear that the treaty had great consequences for international relations in the Far East, especially in Korea. It became one of the cornerstones of Japanese diplomacy in the Far East until the Washington conference of 1921–1922, and it was at least one of the important factors leading to the fall of Korea three years later.[127] The text of the treaty reveals that it was a defensive rather than an offensive alliance and that it was made to preserve the independence of China and Korea and to protect the open-door policy in both nations. These were negative and minor aspects of the treaty, if any degree of sincerity was in it. The agreement also had a positive and more important side. The treaty aimed at isolating Russia from its ally France in case of a future war. Moreover, England frankly acknowledged, in the first article, Japan's "peculiar degree" of not only commercial and industrial but also of political interest in Korea and recognized the necessity of its taking proper measures in the event of an invasion or internal disturbances in the country.[128] The record of negotiation shows that, as far as Japan was concerned, the real motivation was to clear the way for domination of Korea.[129] The isolation of Russia was only a means to this end.

The American government did not know anything about the negotiation of the treaty until the Japanese government notified it, through the Japanese minister in Washington, on the morning of the publication of the treaty.[130] Neither the American government nor the American public paid much attention to the treaty at this time, although their concern increased later. Hay's reaction was expressed to the Japanese minister when the latter first gave him the information about the treaty: Hay thought the objective of the treaty was consonant with the Far Eastern policy of the United States—maintenance of the status quo and equal commercial opportunities.[131] A *New York Times* editorial said: "It seems odd that it should be left for us to learn by way of St. Petersburg the very interesting and important news of the Anglo-Japanese agreement, which also virtually includes the United States."[132] Whether this was an opinion widely held by the American public is not known. At least some Americans held this idea and welcomed the alliance. Those Koreans who correctly read the future implications of the treaty must have been greatly disturbed; but, oddly enough, the Korean minister in London conveyed the reaction of his government in Seoul, which regarded it with "much satisfaction."[133] Whatever the reactions of the people in the United States and Korea, the treaty—in view of its future role—was the most significant diplomatic act to occur during the two-year period.

During this period Russia tried once again for understandable reasons to arrest Japanese ascendancy by proposing the neutralization of Korea. While Japan was busy planning the alliance with England, the Russians approached the Japanese with the idea of neutralization. The Japanese, as they had done a year before, refused to take it seriously.[134] The idea was very attractive to the Russians and they tried again in the following year; this time they expanded the idea to include not only Russia and Japan but also the United States as the guarantor of the neutrality of Korea. Naturally, the United States was involved, and much more than before because of the nature of the proposal. In the middle of August 1902, the Russian minister in Tokyo, Alexander P. Isvolsky, explained to Minister Buck the necessity for the neutralization of Korea under a three-power guarantee and the desirability of an American initiation of the proposal. Buck did not encourage the Russian minister, and the case was shifted to Washington.[135] When the Japanese learned that Minister Pavlov, the Russian representative in Seoul, who was visiting the United States, might bring the neutrality issue to the American government, they became anxious and took preventive action through Minister Takahira Kogoro in Washington. The Japanese minister asked Hay whether Pavlov had raised the issue with him.[136] Pavlov had never presented the issue to the American government. As Hay surmised, the Russians may have dropped the idea, anticipating how the Americans would have received it.[137] Hay soothed the anxious Japanese minister; in mid-October he told Takahira that, in his opinion, his country would not abandon its traditional policy by involving itself in the neutralization of Korea, although the decision would be made after a discussion with the president if the Russians made such a proposal.[138] When the Japanese minister touched upon the issue again a month later, the secretary assured him that even if the Russians raised the question, the American government would not take it seriously; then he added that the Russians had not brought up the question at all.[139] Allen, who was not directly involved in the neutralization issue this time, expressed his view: "It would also be a mistake for us to play into the Russian hands in this matter and annoy the Japanese by so doing." His reasoning was the same as before: if the Koreans achieved political security, they would be too difficult to deal with in business transactions.[140] He was short-sighted in thinking that the Japanese or Russians in control of Korea would be easier to deal with than the independent Koreans. In any case, the American policy of nonintervention was again maintained in Korea without much difficulty.

A small incident in the fall of 1903, a minor confrontation between the president and a minister holding a position not important in anybody's eyes, revealed the nature of American policy toward the northeastern corner of Asia. In the summer and fall of 1903, Allen made a long trip to the United States through Siberia and Europe. He thought he had something important to tell the president, and, while in the United States, he had a dramatic interview with him toward the end of September. Even though he had a missionary background, he had not come with a missionary spirit to "save Korea."[141] Later, Allen said: "I had not talked with him about Korea, where I have all along held that Japan should have the paramount influence"; the conversation, instead, centered on Manchuria. While traveling through Manchuria, Allen was much impressed by the volume of American exports to the area, seventy-five percent of the total Manchurian imports, and he told the president that his pro-Japanese policy would not only encourage Japanese bellicosity but also endanger the American trade interest in Manchuria, thus antagonizing the Russians, who had helped develop this area of foreign trade.[142] Roosevelt did not disagree with Allen on the nature of the American interest in Manchuria—trade; even so, his policy was the opposite of Allen's. Flanked by Rockhill, an East Asian expert, Roosevelt asserted that the Japanese could not rely on America to back them up in a reckless policy, and the American government had an assurance from the Russians that they would not deny the open-door policy in Manchuria. When asked who would win in the event of war between the two powers, Allen answered that on the basis of his observation in Siberia Japan would. Why then, Roosevelt demanded, should the United States side with a losing power?[143] Roosevelt's thinking seemed to go against his principle of a balance of power; but perhaps he simply doubted Allen's judgment. At any rate, it was a "stormy evening" for Allen.

During the interwar decade the American government maintained successfully, as it had in the preceding decade, the established policy toward Korea: neutrality and nonintervention. There was no deviation from this policy throughout the whole period; any variations occurred in the execution of policy or in diplomacy. The style and spirit of diplomacy, however, was quite different during this period from both the preceding and the following periods; it can be characterized as strictness of neutrality and absoluteness of nonintervention. The words "strict neutrality" and "absolute neutrality" had been heard also in the previous decade, but from the time of Arthur-Frelinghuysen-Foote through the time of Cleveland-Gresham-Sill, there was a great deal of understanding and sympathy in the execution of the policy, and the good offices of the United States could be readily offered. Furthermore, the American representatives' informal advisory role was usually allowed, if not encouraged. During the first six and a half years of this period, under Cleveland-Olney and McKinley-Sherman-Day-Hay, the policy was carried out literally, "strictly," and "absolutely," and its observation was asked even of individual American citizens. In the last two years of the period, between 1901 and 1903, under the Roosevelt administration, the style and spirit of diplomacy saw a further change—to indifference. This was only a prelude to another turn that would come in the following period and was discernible even in those relatively quiet years.

This change of style and spirit from understanding and sympathy to strictness and absoluteness and then to inattention and indifference must have had reasons; these seem to have included the size of American interests in Korea, the general spirit and tone of the age, the outlook of the persons involved, and conditions in Korea. Although American interests during this period were growing fast—especially in the concession area and in missionary work—they still were small and negligible from the American viewpoint; the soft, idealistic, traditional diplomacy was replaced by the hard, realistic, modern diplomacy during this period; the teams of Cleveland-Olney-Sill, McKinley-Sherman-Day-Hay-Allen, and Roosevelt-Hay-Allen were quite different from those of Cleveland-Gresham-Sill and other previous teams; and the rough conditions in Korea at this time, with the fierce rivalry between Russia and Japan—all were key factors.

For the Koreans the most conspicuous and deplorable fact about the period was their loss of a ten-year grace period for self-strengthening. For most of the period, a state of power equilibrium was maintained in the kingdom between the two contending powers, and the Koreans had a rare opportunity for their development. Emperor Kojong himself was most responsible for the waste of this opportunity; his lack of vision for the future of Korea and lack of courage in both the internal and external affairs of the nation were very costly to the country. The latter part of the nineteenth century was a time when revolutionary changes were taking place everywhere in the world, and Korea was the very spot where the diplomacy of imperialism was played out in its crudest form. Of course, the Koreans had 1898—the year of reforms; however, because of the seriousness of conditions, Korea needed not just one Sŏ Chae-p'il, who returned from the United States to serve the country for $40,000 a year, but at least half dozen men like Kim Ok-kyun, the most brilliant reformer of the time in Korea. Under the given circumstances, perhaps it could not have been otherwise; but it is regrettable that the American government did not pay attention to the Koreans' pleas for the inclusion of the nation in the open-door policy and that it denied them a helping hand in achieving the neutralization of the country.

After all, the two nations were still able to indulge themselves in the luxury of indifference and in wasting time during this period mainly because of the still existing power balance on the peninsula; when Russia left the stage and the balance-of-power system was destroyed, the two nations were to face a much more severe test.

6

THE RUSSO-JAPANESE WAR, THEODORE ROOSEVELT, AND KOREA

The two years of 1904 and 1905 were very significant for American-Korean relations, as significant as the two years of 1881 and 1882. The two nations had begun formal diplomatic relations in the early 1880s; two decades later, they faced a critical point, and relations between them practically ended. The ending of the diplomatic relationship was a logical consequence of the end of the very independence of Korea, which, in turn, was an outcome of the war between Japan and Russia. The most important change that took place as a result of the Russo-Japanese War of 1904–1905 occurred in the East Asian international system. The previous war in the area, the Sino-Japanese War of 1894–1895, which ended the rivalry between the two major powers in the region and eliminated one of the three powers trying to dominate the peninsula, fortunately did not end the balance of power; the East Asian international system was sustained for another decade because of continued Russian participation. When this war ended with the Russian defeat in the early fall of 1905 and Russia ceased to be an important factor on the Korean peninsula, the balance-of-power system in the area ended and a new system, one of one-power domination, began. Korean independence also disappeared. Thus, significantly, at the end of the two-year period, the balance-of-power system, the independence of Korea, and American-Korean diplomatic relations all ended at the same time.

The outbreak of war between Japan and Russia presented the American government with another—and the last—test of its policy toward Korea. During this period the Roosevelt administration was forced to take up the general policy of dealing with the war; the nation's policy toward Korea, as well as toward the other powers involved in the conflict; the maintenance of the open-door policy in the region; and a concern for the restoration of a regional balance-of-power system in the postwar period. Before an investigation of these issues can be undertaken, an examination of the foreign policy-making system in Washington needs to be made.

During the Roosevelt administration the president himself was the most important force in the making of foreign policy. And since

Theodore Roosevelt was, to a large extent, a man of principle, his conceptual framework was an important element in his views about foreign policy. There were a number of important conceptual components in Roosevelt's philosophy of international relations; one of them was the concept of power. Roosevelt was one of the few American statesmen before the 1940s who understood clearly the place and role of power in international relations. "The main point," he wrote in the fall of 1904, ". . . is that in international affairs, as things are in this very human world, each nation, while striving to act fairly by other nations, must rely for its safety upon its own foresight and industrial efficiency and fighting edge."[1] The following spring he said: "[The German emperor] respects us because he thinks that for a sufficient object and on our own terms we would fight and that we have a pretty good navy with which to fight." Then he continued, "I shall hope that on these terms I can keep the respect not merely of Berlin, but St. Petersburg and Tokio both."[2] Roosevelt saw clearly that power, especially military power, counted most in international politics.

The concept of the balance of power, one of the many possible forms of power configuration, was an important principle in Roosevelt's foreign policy, especially in his Far Eastern policy. At the turn of the century, one of the main concerns of the United States in Asia was Russia's thrust into the Far East, and when the Russo-Japanese War broke out, Roosevelt thought the Japanese were playing the American game, and he rejoiced in the Japanese victory.[3] As the war progressed, however, he began to worry about the possibility of Russia's elimination as an East Asian power. He also worried about the possibility of an alliance between the two belligerents.[4] Roosevelt's concern about the balance of power in the Far East was best expressed in a statement he made in the summer of 1905: "It is best that she [Russia] should be left face to face with Japan so that each may have a moderative action on the other."[5]

If McKinley was a transitional figure, so was Roosevelt; and if McKinley was a transitional figure by circumstance, Roosevelt was so by temperament and principle. Like other transitional figures, Roosevelt was a mixture of a realist and an idealist, even though the characteristics of the new age were more dominant in him than were these of the old. While putting a great emphasis upon power, especially the balance of power, Roosevelt retained a great respect for morality in international relations, an important tenet of his idealism. He could not discuss foreign policy without using such terms as righteousness, justice, and peace; and it was much more than just idle rhetoric. In his annual message of 1906 he declared: "It is a mistake, and it betrays a spirit of foolish cynicism, to maintain that all international governmental action is, and must be, based upon mere selfishness, and that to advance ethical reasons for such action is always a sign of hypocrisy." "This is no more necessarily true," he continued, "of the action of government than of the action of individuals."[6] He held on to this view throughout his years in the White House. In his last annual message he said that the foreign policy of the United States was based on the theory that right must be done between nations as between individuals.[7] Thus Roosevelt was subscribing to one of the most important elements of idealism—the extension of morality from the individual to the international level.

Like other transitional personalities, Roosevelt had the problem of possessing two ideals—new and old—that struggled for supremacy in his mind.[8] A man more of the new age than of the old, Roosevelt was attracted more by the new than the old, but in most cases a compromise was worked out. An illustration of this can be found in his concept of peace. Peace was one of his key ideals throughout the whole period of his presidency. But peace in his mind was of a special kind. He declared in late 1905, "We wish peace, but we wish the peace of justice, the peace of righteousness," adding, "We wish it because we think it is right and not because we are afraid."[9] He spoke of peace in the vocabulary of a warrior; it was a fighting word.

Another of Roosevelt's concepts that had a great impact on his making of foreign policy was his idea of race. Racist ideas were quite common to the people of his time, and the fact that Roosevelt had a theory of race is not peculiar. But what was peculiar were the characteristics of this racism. Unlike other racists, he disregarded color of skin or kind of language as determinants of race, equating, instead, race with nation. "I am not much affected by the statement," he said in 1904, "that the Japanese are of an utterly different race from ourselves and that the Russians are of the same race."[10] He indignantly declared in the same year: "What a nonsense it is to speak of the Chinese and Japanese as of the same race!"[11] In general his concept of race did not have anything to do with the physical makeup of the people of a nation; what counted most was the character and achievement of the country. According to this criterion, he could rank different nations from the most superior to the most inferior. Not surprisingly, the position the Koreans had in this racial scale was important for his policy toward that country. He could not separate Korea from the Far East, and he had to weigh the maintenance of Korean independence against the preservation of the balance of power in the Far East. Saving Korea from a predatory power could be a noble act, but his moral consideration was subordinated to a more important principle in his concept of international relations, that of the balance of power. Moreover, since the Koreans had shown no evidence of courage to Roosevelt, it is not hard to imagine the place occupied by the "Korean race" in his racial hierarchy.

Emotional elements usually play an important role in the process of foreign policy making, and this was especially so in the case of Roosevelt. He had, in addition to a strong ego, very strong likes and dislikes. One important factor in his Korean policy was that he greatly liked the Japanese; he liked a number of Japanese characteristics, especially their fighting spirit. Roosevelt's admiration of the "Japanese race" was several years old by 1904. His attitude toward the Japanese had shifted from unfavorable to favorable during the Boxer Rebellion, when he was impressed by the conduct of the Japanese soldiers in China, and he held this impression up to the outbreak of the Russo-Japanese War.[12] Then, when he observed victory after victory by the Japanese in the Russo-Japanese War, he was not only thrilled, but also convinced that the Japanese were wonderful people.[13] Even toward the end of the Portsmouth peace conference, when American feeling turned away from the Japanese, he did not lose his admiration for the Japanese. He wrote the peace commissioners that he was far more pro-Japanese than ever.[14]

Two persons in particular intensified Roosevelt's pro-Japanese feeling; one was the well-known pro-Japanese, anti-Russian journalist, George Kennan, and the other was a Japanese friend, Baron Kaneko Kentaro. Roosevelt had enjoyed a long friendship with Kennan and was much influenced by his views and attitudes toward the Japanese. "I cannot write you in full," wrote Roosevelt in the early part of 1905, "but I am sure you understand how I look forward to seeing you and to talking over with you not merely what you have seen, but the conclusions which you have reached as to the war and as to what is to come after the war."[15] Baron Kaneko, a graduate of Harvard Law School, was sent by the Japanese government to Washington to cultivate a friendship with Roosevelt and to exploit his association with him. Kaneko approached Roosevelt as a fellow alumnus and stood informally between the two governments throughout most of the period of the war and the ensuing peace conference. Roosevelt not only transacted official business with Kaneko, but also learned more of the virtues of the Japanese people through him.[16]

Roosevelt's admiration for the Japanese, however, became mingled with fear and suspicion as Japan grew more successful in the war. We can find evidence of a slight dislike for the people. "Yet

Japan is an Oriental nation and the individual standard for trustfulness in Japan is low," he wrote toward the end of 1905.[17] Within two months after the outbreak of the war he feared that "if the Japanese win out, not only the Slavs but all of us will have to reckon with a great new force in Eastern Asia."[18] In the following spring he said: "I will like the Japanese but of course I hold myself in readiness to see them puffed up with pride if they are victorious, and turn against us, or Germans, or any one else."[19]

Toward the Russians Roosevelt felt simple distrust. His criticisms were aimed not at the people but at the upper classes and at the political and social system of the nation. "No human being, yellow or white," Roosevelt said in the summer of 1905, "could be quite as untruthful, as insincere, as arrogant—in short as untrustworthy in every way—as the Russians under their present system."[20]

The implications of Roosevelt's feeling toward the Japanese and the Russians for American-Korean relations are clear: his pro-Japanese feeling became an important factor in his pro-Japanese policy and one that worked against the Koreans; his anti-Russian sentiments strengthened his pro-Japanese attitude.

Finally, of most importance for our analysis was Roosevelt's attitude toward the Koreans. We have little direct evidence about his attitude; he paid little attention to them. How much he knew about Korea and Koreans is hard to judge. It is clear, however, that he read at least what George Kennan and Arthur J. Brown wrote.[21] Judging from the degree of his confidence in Kennan, it cannot be doubted that he was influenced by Kennan's unfavorable descriptions of Korea. Late in January 1905 he wrote an often quoted statement in a letter to Hay: "We cannot possibly interfere for the Koreans against Japan. They could not strike one blow in their own defence."[22] About a week later he wrote a few more words regarding Korea; in his letter to George V. Meyer he added parenthetically: "Of course, the military situation may alter; but if peace should come now, Japan ought to have a protectorate over Korea, which has shown its utter inability to stand by itself."[23]

It is well known that Roosevelt acted as his own secretary of state, relying for advice on his friends, including those who were representing the major European powers in Washington and other capitals.[24] Despite Dennett's claim that Hay was solely responsible for the nation's Far Eastern policy,[25] it seems that Roosevelt was more responsible for its Korean policy. Moreover, Hay's role in policy making ended by the middle of March 1905 because of his illness.[26] Hay undoubtedly played an advisory role in Roosevelt's foreign policy: Roosevelt said in a letter written during Hay's last illness that he used to stop by Hay's house every Sunday and talk with the secretary, when he "often decided important questions of public policy."[27] Whatever influence Hay had in the formulation of Korean policy could not have been pro-Korean; Hay also was interested in Kennan's articles, and it cannot be doubted that he was influenced by Kennan's anti-Korean writings. In November 1904 Hay remarked cynically, "I cannot imagine why Korea keeps a Legation here."[28]

Elihu Root succeeded Hay as secretary of state, taking over the office in late July 1905. By this time Korean policy had been decided, and there was little room for innovation even if he had wished to make changes. Able, cautious, and realistic, Root played a restraining role in Roosevelt's policy making.[29] Judging from a statement he made many years after his service, we can safely surmise that his view of Korea and Koreans were very similar to those of Roosevelt and Hay: the Koreans were incapable of governing themselves and would be better under the domination of the progressive Japanese.[30]

Next to Roosevelt himself, the person who played the most important role in making Korean policy was William W. Rockhill. One of Roosevelt's old friends, he acted as a trusted adviser to the president throughout the 1904–5 period.[31] It is evident that Roosevelt turned to him for expert knowledge of Korea.[32] Rockhill, who had first-hand knowledge of Korea, knew more about the country than anyone in the foreign policy-making circles in Washington at this time; he, too, thought that Korea was helpless and that the people would be better off under Japanese domination.[33] Rockhill, like Roosevelt, Hay, and Root, was influenced by Kennan's writings on Korea.[34]

The Russo-Japanese War was one of the most important wars in modern East Asian history. For both Korea and Japan the war was a turning point: Korea lost its independence for the first time in its long history, and Japan emerged as a formidable imperial power, a big step toward further developments in the 1930s and 1940s. Like other historical events, the war gave a sense of inevitableness to the people of the time. In late 1901 Allen already foresaw that the war was coming and wrote to Hay: "In view of importance of Korea as a prospective field for future military operations, I think it would be well to have a Military Attache accredited to this Legation."[35] Widespread opinion agreed that the key issue in the coming crisis would concern Korea, and as early as the middle of 1903, the *New York Times* informed the American public that the two powers who were searching for a way to resolve their differences had deadlocked on Korea.[36] However, exactly what role Korea played in the outbreak of the Russo-Japanese War is an important question still worth raising. It is true that the Korean issue was so important to the Japanese that, even before beginning the final negotiations with the Russians, they had determined not to compromise. John L. White was correct in observing that the roots of the problem lay in the fact that neither side could allow either Korea or Manchuria to fall into the hands of the other. Both Korea and Manchuria were important factors in the Far Eastern crisis in 1904 and 1905. The Manchurian issue, however, was much more important than the Korean. The Russians were slow in compromising and clumsy in handling the negotiations with the Japanese, but they recognized from the beginning the special interests of Japan in Korea, including the islanders' right to advise the Koreans in military affairs, and they eventually gave to the Japanese all the latter wanted in Korea except one point—they denied the Japanese the right to use Korean territory for strategic purposes.[37] In other words, the Japanese domination of Korea was assured without firing a shot. The real stumbling block in the negotiations was Manchuria; the Japanese would not stop with the acquisition of Korea, arguing that certain Russian assurances were needed for the security of Korea.[38] Further, an even more important factor in the conflict was the "national aspiration" of the Japanese. Japanese public opinion was so much in favor of war by the end of 1903 that it was practically impossible for the Japanese government to retreat from war. Early in February of 1904 the inevitable took place, and the nineteen-month war began.

The major policy of the United States in the war was to maintain its traditional policy of neutrality. As soon as the war broke out, the American government declared neutrality and maintained it throughout the crisis.[39] President Roosevelt was definite about this policy: "I am entirely sincere in my purpose to keep the government neutral in the war."[40] Secretary Hay was also clear in his instruction to Allen: "Presumed you will do all possible for the protection of American interests consistent with absolute neutrality and respecting rights of the belligerents in theatre of actual war."[41]

The American attitude regarding the neutrality of China and Korea is rather revealing. Soon after the outbreak of the war, even before the news of China's declaration of its neutrality reached Washington, the American government sent notes to the belligerent powers and to China in which it expressed its desire that the neutrality and administrative integrity of China should be respected.[42] Roosevelt and Hay were very anxious that China remain neutral; and although the belligerent powers received the American notes with conditions and the Russians later defied them completely, the two American statesmen were well satisfied with the results and thought that the note-writing had been successful.[43]

Anxious to avoid the certain injury that would come through war, Korea declared its neutrality to Japan three weeks before the outbreak of the war and notified the other powers as well.[44] When the Korean minister in Washington delivered the declaration to the American government, the latter simply acknowledged it.[45] When a rumor was heard about American support of Korean neutrality, Hay wrote Allen: "Respecting your apprehension as to the rumor that this government had approved Korea's declaration of neutrality, I have to inform you that the declaration, which was comm**u**nciated to the Department on January 22 by the Korean Minister, was merely acknowledged, with the remark that due note had been taken for the declaration."[46] American policy regarding Korean neutrality was clear: no support, just simple recognition.

Unlike the Sino-Japanese War of 1894–1895, the main battleground of this war was Manchuria, not Korea; within three months, by the end of April, the fighting crossed the Yalu River to the north. But the crushing impact of the war on Korea soon became evident. After the first round of Japanese victories at the beginning of the war, the Korean government began to disappear; Japan took various measures to ensure control of the country.[47] First, the Korean army disappeared: the 3,000-man "partially armed" defense force was turned, after very little resistence, into the Japanese army's transportation corps. Policing, transportation, communication, finance —one by one, all these functions came under Japanese control, and Seoul soon became a Japanese city.[48] An American author proposed in the spring of 1904 that the name of the country be changed from "the land of morning calm" to the "land of cold gray dawn of the morning."[49]

The stormy year and a half of the war was a quiet time for Allen in Seoul, a queer kind of quietness at the center of the storm. He carefully watched the progress of the war and reported it to Washington. He knew full well the impact the Japanese victory would have on American interests in Korea, and he made every possible effort not to antagonize the Japanese.[50] Optimistic about his relations with them, he wrote early in March 1904: "I am working along with great harmony with the Japanese."[51]

Desperate, the Koreans turned for aid to the American minister, but he successfully carried out the policy of neutrality and noninvolvement in Korea during the war period.[52] The Korean emperor asked Allen for asylum in times of crisis, but the American minister firmly denied it to him.[53] When the palace building in which the emperor was living burned down and he moved into his library, which was surrounded by American properties, Allen reduced the size of the legation guard and assured the Japanese minister that he would not take advantage of the situation.[54] He even went so far as to suggest that the emperor seek the protection of the Japanese commander in Seoul.[55]

As the war progressed, the Japanese consolidated their control over Korea. In 1904, in an early stage of the war, the Japanese obtained two protocols from the Koreans as a step toward their complete control of the peninsula. Two weeks after the outbreak of the war, the Japanese, through an agreement with the Koreans, laid the legal basis for the actions they had already taken, the use of the territory of Korea, a neutral country.[56] Six months later, in August, they obtained another agreement, this time to control Korean external affairs and finance through advisers.[57] Replying to Allen's inquiry as to whether he should telegraph the text of the February agreement, Hay instructed: "Not necessary to cable text of the Japanese-Korean agreement. You will observe absolute neutrality."[58] The Department of State did not receive the text of the agreement from the Japanese minister in Washington until August 26,[59] and it is clear that the American government was extremely cautious in handling Korean affairs. When the Japanese minister notified Hay of the conclusion of the agreement, Hay replied with a short note of acknowledgment, observing the objectives and effects of the treaty given by the Japanese.[60] Thus, whatever the real reaction of the American government was, its outward expression was reserved.

Allen was articulate as ever in responding to the conclusion of the Korean-Japanese agreements. Two days before the signing of the first protocol, Allen informed Hay that the emperor had intimated to him the Japanese intention to conclude the agreements and had expressed a great concern for American assistance.[61] Allen said in his telegram of February 24 to the department, "Last night articles of agreement were signed establishing the Japanese protectorate of Korea. It is very strong."[62] But when talking to the Japanese, he was more faltering; he told the Japanese minister in Seoul that the powers, especially the United States, considered the protocol unexpectedly mild and that the Japanese would gain more sympathy in the future.[63] The American government printed Allen's despatches with the protocols in the *Foreign Relations* of the year under the caption "Protectorate over Korea by Japan."[64] Although not plentiful, the evidence clearly indicates the attitude of the American government toward the consolidation of Japanese control over Korea—acquiescence to an established reality.

Against the expectations of most, the underdog Japanese demonstrated well the effectiveness of their armed forces against one of the great powers of the Western world, and after three brilliantly executed battles in the spring of 1905—the fall of Port Arthur in January, the victory at Mukden in March, and the destruction of the Russian fleet in the Tsushima battle in late May—they were ready for peace and made the first move for a peace conference on the last day of May, a process that ended with the signing of the treaty three months later at Portsmouth. Even though Korea was not the main cause of the war, it remained the main fruit of the war for the Japanese, and they showed great effectiveness in their diplomacy in the summer of 1905 as they made sure of their acquisition of the Korean peninsula; within thirty-nine days they successfully obtained the assurances of the three Western powers in three diplomatic moves— the Taft-Katsura Memorandum of July 29, the second Anglo-Japanese treaty of August 12, and the Portsmouth Peace Treaty of September 5.

Of the three successes of Japanese diplomacy in the summer of 1905, the Taft-Katsura Memorandum comes first, both in terms of chronology and importance for this study. Because of its uncertain nature and importance, the subject has long been controversial among historians. Many authors, notably Tyler Dennett, A. Whitney Griswold, and Howard K. Beale, have considered the memorandum as a "secret pact" and hence an international agreement.[65] Raymond A. Esthus viewed it not as an international agreement but as a simple "exchange of views."[66] It seems that, since neither side had any intention of creating a legally binding agreement, it is not possible to consider the memorandum an international agreement.[67] But although clarifying the legal status of the document is not meaningless, an even more meaningful exercise is to determine its historical significance.

The memorandum is the official record of a conversation between two men, William H. Taft, the secretary of war of the United States, who was on his way to the Philippines, and Katsura Taro, the prime minister of Japan, in Tokyo on the morning of July 27, 1905. Taft first observed that Japan's only interest in the Philippine Islands would be to have the islands governed by a strong and friendly nation like the United States; Katsura confirmed Taft's view, denying that his country had aggressive intentions toward the islands. Katsura even proposed making an Anglo-American-Japanese "good understanding or an alliance in practice" for the preservation of peace in Asia; and Taft, although declining an alliance as impractical because of the American tradition of making no alliances with any country, assured Katsura that, without any agreement, Japan could rely on the "appropriate action of the government of the United States [regardless of] whatever situation[s] arise" in the Far East. Finally Katsura, turning to the Korean question, expressed Japan's feeling "constrained to take some definite step" to prevent Korea from falling back into its former condition; Taft admitted the "justness" of the count's observation and added that Japanese suzerainty over Korea was "the logical result" of the Russo-Japanese War.[68] Two days later Taft received and then passed on to the Japanese prime minister a telegram from the president: "I confirm every word you have said."[69] The memorandum remained a secret in the United States for almost twenty years, until Dennett found it among Roosevelt's letters. Both sides understood full well what the conversation on the two subjects—Korea and the Philippines—meant: the Taft-Katsura Memorandum amounted, to them at least, to an understanding, more than a mere exchange of views.[70]

The historical significance of the Taft-Katsura Memorandum can be understood best in terms of the relationship between this and two other diplomatic acts, the second Anglo-Japanese alliance and the Portsmouth Peace Treaty. A single document, Roosevelt's letter of November 1, 1905, to his friend, clearly indicates the relationship; it reads in part: "By my direction, Taft reiterated this [the President approved the second Anglo-Japanese treaty before the ratification] in a talk with the Japanese Prime Minister, Katsura; saying specially that we entirely approved of the Japanese position about Korea as set forth in the Anglo-Japanese treaty and as acknowledged in the treaty of Portsmouth."[71] Roosevelt was clearly aware that the Taft-Katsura conversation sanctioned what England and Russia would do in their forthcoming treaties with Japan. In the summer of 1905, Japan received green lights from three stations—Russia, England, and the United States—to proceed to settle its "Korean question," and the station that sent the first signal was the United States.

The second Anglo-Japanese treaty, which was signed on August 12, 1905, is significant not only because it shows what Roosevelt was approving through Taft, but also because the American government and public displayed a decisive reaction to it. In the third article of the treaty, England recognized the rights of Japan "to take such measures of guidance, control, and protection in Korea as she may deem proper and necessary" for her "paramount political, military, and economic interests" in the country.[72] This was the green light for the creation of a Japanese protectorship over Korea from the British station.[73]

In contrast to the first treaty, the two governments kept Roosevelt informed about the negotiations, even though they withheld the news of the conclusion of the negotiations until the time of the publication of the treaty late in September.[74] Then both Roosevelt and Root hailed the treaty as a great stride toward peace in the Far East and the world. Roosevelt later recalled what he had told the treaty powers: "I entirely approved of the treaty, was glad that it had been negotiated and believed that it was advantageous to the peace of Asia, and therefore, to the peace of the world."[75] Root also thought the treaty would be good for the peace of the world.[76] American newspapers showed a reaction similar to that of the government. While recognizing that the treaty "bristled with threats of war," the *Washington Times* welcomed it as a large step toward world peace.[77] A *New York Times* editorial appearing on the day following the publication of the treaty argued: "We say at once that the treaty serves our purpose well enough. It contains the customary guarantee of the 'open door' in Korea and China." Then it added: "It remains for Japan to tell us just what the 'open door' means."[78] The paper was very critical, however, about the way in which the treaty making was handled by the British and the Japanese. It criticized the British for negotiating a treaty with a belligerent power while peace negotiations were underway and for leaking the news of the negotiations to the public as a "breach of international good manners."[79] The *Boston Evening Transcript* clearly recognized the impact of the treaty upon Korea and hoped the lot of the Koreans would not be too harsh.[80] Apparently the Americans did not see in the new treaty any threat to their traditional policy in the Far East.

Owing to Roosevelt's efforts, the Portsmouth peace conference finally began on August 9, and the treaty was signed a month later, on September 5, after much difficult discussion about two thorny issues—territorial cessions and an indemnity.[81] Korea was naturally the most important item for the Japanese, and it occupied first place in each of the three most important categories of the Japanese peace terms. Russia readily recognized Japanese possession of "preponderant political, military and economic interests" in Korea and, after ironing out some controversial aspects of the issue of recognizing Korean sovereignty in the treaty and two other relatively minor issues that Sergei Iulievich Witte had raised, agreed in the treaty not to interfere with the Japanese "measure of guidance, protection and control" of Korea.[82] Roosevelt took very seriously his role as a peacemaker, undertaking an intervention—a correct legal term— through Baron Komura Jutaro and Ambassador George Meyer when the two powers deadlocked on the two difficult issues of territorial cessions and the indemnity. The two major reasons for the successful conclusion of the peace negotiations at Portsmouth in the summer of 1905 were Japan's desperate condition and Witte's courageous stand to make peace despite great reluctance on the part of the authorities in St. Petersburg. Roosevelt's last-minute contribution was also significant in preventing the negotiations from foundering. Thus, by early September 1905, Japan was given the last of the three green lights for its subjugation of Korea. Because Roosevelt had decided a long time earlier that Japan should have Korea, the fate of the peninsula empire was not even a concern of his at the conference. Maintaining the balance of power, not the wishes of either Japan or Russia, was the key concern of his Far Eastern policy, and again, he acquiesced in the reality of the power configuration in the peninsula.

If the spring of 1883 was the most pleasant season for American-Korean relations, with the arrival of the first American minister in Seoul and the exchange of the ratification of the first treaty between the two nations, the fall of 1905 was the most unpleasant one for the two-nation relationship, with the departure of the American minister from the Korean capital and with the unsuccessful and unhappy Korean missions of appeal to the American capital. Under the circumstances and given the conditions and people involved in the developments in Seoul and Washington, what took place between the two countries in this season probably could not have been otherwise. By the early part of the season the active portion of the play ended with the conclusion of the war between Japan and Russia, and the last act, at least for this stage, was over; whatever was left was largely ceremonial.

After the exit of Russian influence, Japan remained the sole force on the Korean stage, and the only question left was the speed with which the island empire exercised its control over Korea. It did not take more than two months for the Japanese to exact the treaty of protectorship from Korea; the signing of the treaty was successfully forced upon the Koreans on the night of November 17 and the early morning of the following day in Seoul. The first article of the treaty reads: "The government of Japan, through the Department of Foreign Affairs at Tokyo, will hereafter have control and direction of the external relations and affairs at Korea, and diplomatic and consular representatives of Japan will have the charge of the subjects and interests of Korea in foreign countries." Thus the foreign affairs of Korea, which had been controlled in fact by Japan since August of the previous year, came officially under the jurisdiction of the Japanese government. The third article of the protectorate document stipulated the establishment of a resident general in Seoul, with residents in provinces primarily to handle the external affairs of Korea.[83] Ten days later, the American government closed its legation in Seoul, terminating diplomatic relations with Korea that had lasted a little more than two decades from the spring of 1883. From these two basic facts, all the problems of the postwar bilateral relations emerged.

The withdrawal of the American legation in Seoul was preceded by a change of ministers in the Korean capital; Edwin V. Morgan replaced Allen in June 1905. Many factors were thought to have contributed to Allen's recall. Allen himself thought that the main reasons behind his replacement were his unworkable personal relationship with Roosevelt after the stormy interview of September 1903 and his close relationship with the Koreans.[84] He also thought Roosevelt removed him to create a position for Morgan, a friend of the president and his daughter Alice.[85] None of these seemed to have been the real reason for the change; it was probably simply one of the many changes in diplomatic posts undertaken by the Roosevelt administration at this time; Allen had already been in his ministerial position in Seoul for seven and a half years.[86] It should be added that Morgan had some experience in Korea as a legation secretary and was a good choice.[87]

When the American government closed the legation in Seoul, the action aroused indignant feeling on the part of many Americans and Europeans, as well as Koreans. Some thought that an agreement between the United States and Japan had been made behind the scenes.[88] The most severe criticism came from two Americans who were present in Korea at that time, Willard Straight, the vice-consul and secretary to the American legation, and Homer B. Hulbert, an American educator. Straight wrote: "[The Koreans] all realized that the legation would go, I think, and that their country was turned over, but it came as a cruel blow that the United States should have been the first to take such a step."[89] Hulbert was also bitter about the American move: "When the pinch came we were the first to desert her, and that in the most contemptuous way, without saying good bye."[90] Former minister Allen resented the nasty action, saying: "[The Koreans] have trusted us so much, and have had so many fine promises from Washington, even as late as in Mr. Hay's time, that it would seem we might have at least given them an expression of our sympathy and waited till the funeral was over before nailing the coffin."[91]

Although critical about the early withdrawal of the legation, Allen had said as early as 1897 that he did not see why the United States should maintain one in a dependent country. In March 1904 he clearly saw the inevitable: "If the Japanese succeed in the present war it would seem to be better if diplomatic matters were to be discussed in Tokyo with a responsible government."[92] This was a mere expression of a feeling, and action was not taken until after the war. When, however, the feeling became a reality, many were surprised to find the United States taking the initiative. On November 8, ten days before the conclusion of the protectorate treaty, Roosevelt asked the Japanese minister in Washington whether Japan wished withdrawal of the American legation in Korea. Takahira answered by asking the president to wait until the result of the mission of Itō Hirobumi, who was in Korea for the negotiation of the treaty.[93] On November 23, six days after the conclusion of the convention, Takahira asked the American government to withdraw the legation; Root said he would take proper measures after a discussion with the president.[94] The record shows how quickly the American government acted: on the following day, it sent instructions to Morgan and Griscom, notifying them of the withdrawal of the Seoul legation and giving Griscom in Tokyo authority for relations with Korea.[95] The American government terminated its relations with Korea not only unhesitatingly, but also quite willingly. Perhaps it was a typical characteristic of Roosevelt's diplomacy.

The Japanese were very pleased, or in their own words, "profoundly satisfied." The Japanese foreign minister thanked the Americans for the "friendly disposition again shown by the United States government by favorably entertaining the desire of the imperial government and promptly taking the initiative action."[96] The *Jiji*, a Japanese newspaper, praised the action as that of a great power, greater than any power except Japan.[97] The praise sounds almost a snarling criticism.

The hasty withdrawal of the legation reflected in essence a conviction reached by the summer of 1905 by Roosevelt, Hay, and Rockhill that Japan could have, or even should have Korea. In the year of the Boxer Rebellion, a year before entering the White House, Roosevelt had said, "I should like to see Japan have Korea. She will be a check upon Russia, and she deserves it for what she had done." Continuing, he expressed his hope that China, however, would not be partitioned.[98] The historical record has nothing to show for the next five years, but in the early part of 1905 Roosevelt noted: "We cannot possibly interfere with the Koreans."[99] Once he adopted the position that the United States could not intervene to save Korea from Japan and that Japan should have the peninsula, he held it throughout the spring of 1905. On February 5 he said, "If peace should come now, Japan ought to have a protectorate over Korea";[100]

on the following day he wrote Hay in a similar vein.[101] Two and a half months later, when the Russo-Japanese peace talks dominated his mind, Roosevelt said, "I heartily agree with the Japanese terms of peace, insofar as they include Japan having the control over Korea."[102] Throughout the summer, he never deviated from the line that Japan should have Korea.[103]

Roosevelt's advisers held similar convictions. Hay wrote to Allen late in 1904, "I cannot imagine why Korea keeps a legation here. It is positively no use to them." When the Chinese minister asked Hay for the American view of "reasonable terms" of peace, Hay included the "existing relations of Japan to Korea" in his "reasonable terms." Rockhill was even more explicit. Soon after the outbreak of the war he wrote, "I cannot see any possibility of this government using its influence to bolster up the empire of Korea in its independence. I fancy that the Japanese will settle this question when the present war is finished." Then he went on, "The annexation of Korea to Japan seems to be absolutely indicated as the one great and final step westward of the extension of the Japanese empire."[104] While his prediction was wrong, he saw clearly that Korea would inevitably be annexed by Japan and that the United States could and would do nothing to prevent it.

By the fall of 1905, the Koreans had few possibilities for preserving their independence. The ideal course was to stand up and defend themselves against the military force of Japan. The emperor and two of his ministers did in fact refuse to sign the November convention against the Japanese guns. But what did the Koreans have to fight with in 1905? The 3,000-man defense force had evaporated in a day at the beginning of the war. The government was hopelessly corrupt and ineffective; trade, industry, communication, and transportation were negligible; and the education system was poor. Above all, Korea had an apathetic people and a timid ruler—such were Korea's "strengths" in the winter of 1905. The country simply lacked the strength to face the Japanese troops in Korea under General Hasegawa Yoshimitsi. It is true that later the "Righteous Army" arose all over the Korean peninsula and harassed the Japanese army for some time, but resistance by an organized force in 1905 was impossible.

Although the Koreans could not fight with any hope of success, they also could not give up their country without an effort to save it. Consequently, they chose a third alternative; as a last resort, they tried to appeal to the great powers, attempting several times to send missions to England, Russia, and France. But because of the vigilance of the Japanese government, all of these attempts failed.[105] Even if the Japanese preventive tactics had not been successful, the missions would not have brought about any results. Both England, an ally of Japan, and France, a friend of England by this time, would not do anything to hurt Japan. Germany had no such alliance and so could, theoretically, have acted against Japanese interests, but it had already pledged Japan a benevolent neutrality in the Far Eastern crisis.[106] The missions to Europe were doomed even before the attempt began. Much more important were those directed to the United States.

The bases of the Korean appeals to the United States were both legal and moral. The legal basis of the Korean claims was that the Japanese had obtained the November convention from them under duress and that, according to international law, the convention was therefore null and void. Anyone who goes through the record of the negotiation of the convention can hardly deny that the Japanese applied force during the negotiation process.[107] The Koreans thought that if Roosevelt learned the truth about the treaty negotiations, he might take a step to help them.[108] The emperor also remembered what Allen had told him—that the Americans were his friends, that they were the only people who could speak "a strong and disinterested word" for him, and that, if it became necessary for the emperor to invoke the good offices clause of the treaty of 1882, he could be sure that the request would receive the "prompt and kindly attention" of the Americans.[109] It is doubtful that the Koreans did not understand the legal meaning of the good offices concept after more than twenty years of diplomatic transactions with the Western powers, as some authors suggest.[110] An important factor behind the Korean appeal was psychological or cultural; the emperor and others in the ruling class had a vague feeling that the Americans, who were not only benevolent and unselfish but also happened to be the nation that had opened the hermit kingdom to the Western world, would have some sense of moral obligation and would come to help them in their time of need.

The Koreans made several attempts to appeal directly to President Roosevelt before November 1905. In the winter of 1904, Chase W. Needham, the president of George Washington University, who was the counselor of the Korean legation in Washington, saw Secretary Hay and conveyed a message from the emperor—which was received "very gracefully" by the secretary—asking the United States to "exercise a proper influence in the final adjustment of the Eastern affairs for the maintenance of the integrity and independence of Korea."[111] But Hay took no action for the Koreans. Sŏl Pyŏng-kiu, another emissary of the emperor, left for the United States in the early part of 1905 but soon returned.[112] The third

Korean pre-November effort was made in the summer of 1905, when it was known that the peace conference was about to convene. The emperor asked Minister Morgan whether Korea should attempt to be represented at the peace conference and, if representation was not possible, if the United States would use its good offices to obtain favorable terms for Korea. Morgan advised the emperor against the idea, and it died unborn.[113]

Four Korean missions traveled to the United States in the fall and winter of 1905. The first of them came just before the peace conference convened at Portsmouth. Syngman Rhee, later the first president of the republic founded after the end of World War II and then a young man, and Yun P'yŏng-ku, a Korean pastor in Honolulu, obtained a letter of introduction to the president from Taft, who was on his way to the Philippines and who soon would perform an interesting role in Tokyo, and proceeded to Washington.[114] Having failed to procure aid from the chargé d'affaires in Washington, who was already under the influence of the Japanese, the two men proceeded to Oyster Bay to see the president. After describing Japanese activities in Korea, the two asked the president to help the Koreans preserve their independence. Roosevelt had no problem in turning away empty-handed these practically unknown Koreans; he told them that they should present their case through proper diplomatic channels, a course of action that was not open to them.[115]

In Rhee's failure, Minister Morgan's role was important. Morgan wrote to the secretary of state on July 20: "A considerable sum of money had been obtained from the Emperor by two minor officials who desire to visit America for the avowed purpose of enlisting public sympathy in Korea's behalf." Morgan continued: "These men, however, may not be permitted to enter upon their mission." The minister gave the reason: "The powerful influence of the Japanese Minister is against them, and their undertaking is regarded, in general, as unwise, since they command confidence neither at home nor abroad."[116] The youthful Rhee did not have any chance of success.

The next mission appeared to have a slightly better chance of success. Homer B. Hulbert, who had made great contributions to Korea as a teacher, author, and editor, left Korea toward the end of October and handed the emperor's message to Secretary Root a few days after the conclusion of the November convention.[117] Root soon conveyed the letter to the president at Oyster Bay. In his reply to Root, Roosevelt showed that he had deliberated on the emperor's message. "I have carefully read through the letter of the Korean Emperor handed to you by Mr. Hulbert," the letter began. Then he reasoned that the very fact that the Korean emperor wished his letter to be kept secret made any official action on the part of the American government impossible. Moreover, Roosevelt continued, after the letter was written the Korean government had made an arrangement with the Japanese, which the emperor in the letter had said he did not desire to make. Roosevelt concluded: "All things considered I do not see that any practical action on the letter is open to us."[118] Roosevelt's reasoning was "logical and flawless," as one historian has written.[119]

Morgan in Seoul also played a part, although a minor one, in the failure of Hulbert's mission. After informing the State Department of the mission, he added his comment: "Although of good intelligence and energetic character, Mr. Hulbert's judgement is not infrequently colored by prejudice and his statements should be tested before being accepted as facts."[120]

The Japanese were well informed as usual of the progress of the mission by their representatives and by American advisers and officials.[121] When the Japanese minister brought up the subject of the Hulbert mission in a conversation with Secretary Root and asked whether the secretary had already seen the emissary, Root answered that, because of the good offices clause in the treaty of 1882, a Korean appeal could not be ignored, but that he would do his best to avoid taking action on behalf of the Koreans by resorting to formal and informal diplomatic channels.[122]

When Hulbert failed to move the American government, he turned to the legislative branch. He interested Senator John T. Morgan in the case and tried to have him introduce a resolution in the Senate to look into the actions of the administration regarding the Korean problem.[123] He also tried to appeal to the American public through newspaper articles.[124] Hulbert did not get far in this one-man campaign to save Korea, and, discouraged, he soon returned to Korea.

The third mission was somewhat similar to the first Rhee-Yun mission. Min Yŏng-ch'an, the Korean minister in Paris, crossed the Atlantic Ocean with a telegraphic message from the emperor, which asked the American president to ignore the November convention because it was obtained by the Japanese under duress. He saw Root at the Department of State on December 11, 1905, and delivered the emperor's message.[125] Eight days later Root replied to Min. The American government, he said, could not take action on the basis of the message for the emperor, which was presented through unofficial channels and was contrary to the content of an official communication from the Korean legation and the Japanese government.

Moreover, Root continued, Japan actually controlled Korea as a consequence of the two agreements made in 1904, the validity of which was never contested by Korea, and the application of the first article of the treaty of 1882 was impossible.[126] A lawyer, Root had no problem finding grounds for not being able to help the Koreans. He even could tell them that there was no such thing as duress in international law, because forcing a nation to act against its will was legally not possible. Root did not neglect to inform Takahira of what he told the Korean emissary.[127]

The fourth and last Korean effort was made at about the same time as the Hulbert and Min missions. Former American minister Allen was the main character in it, and although it died stillborn, this case clearly shows the nature of the Korean problem. The emperor provided $10,000 for Allen and two American businessmen with enterprises in Korea, Henry Collbran and Harry Bostwick, to find an able international lawyer to present the case to President Roosevelt. Allen, who did not mind doing a favor for the emperor with his own money, turned for advice to General James H. Wilson, a retired military man with business interests in the Far East. Wilson suggested Joseph Choate, former ambassador to London, as a proper advocate. Partly because of Allen's overcautiously phrased letter, with its exposure to the Department of State in mind, Choate declined to take up the case.[128] Wilson then suggested ex-Senator Anthony Higgins, who also declined the offer. After much worry, Allen finally decided to return the money to the emperor with an explanatory note.[129] The $10,000 mission failed, partly because the emperor's desire to keep the proceedings secret aroused Allen's suspicions that, if the effort failed, those who were involved would be blamed and hurt. Allen's caution also went beyond the customary. With timidity multiplied by timidity, no action could have been expected.

Before turning to an evaluation of Roosevelt's policy toward Korea, a few observations can be made regarding the communication problem involved in the four missions that were tried in the fall and winter of 1905. First, because of the Japanese control of the communication channels between Korea and the United States and between the American and Korean governments, an official channel of communication was not available to the Korean court, and this greatly hampered delivery of the emperor's message to Washington. Second, even when the American policy makers received the message, the emperor's desire to keep his appeal for American aid secret made American action difficult, if not utterly impossible. Third, communications between the American representative in Seoul and

the policy makers in Washington and between the American officials and the Japanese officials in Washington and elsewhere hindered the Korean action. Without doubt, the heart of the problem
was the purpose, intentions, and policies of the United States and
the other powers involved, but since the case could not even exist
until and unless it was properly brought to the attention of the other
treaty power, as clearly specified in the first article of the American-
Korean treaty of 1882, the communication problem was significant
for American-Korean diplomacy in the fall and winter of 1905.

Roosevelt's Korean policy has been considered controversial for
many decades, and it will probably remain so for many more
decades to come because of its importance and complexity. This
case, like many other similar cases, has both legal and political
dimensions. Root had fears about the legal basis of the case, and
Roosevelt also showed some concern about it; hence, the legal
dimension should not be altogether neglected. But in real life legal-
ity has to be interpreted in practical terms, and political dimensions
often assume more importance. Assuming there was a legal basis to
the case, an important question is what alternatives Roosevelt had.
Defending Roosevelt's policy later, Root wrote in 1930: "Many people are still angry because we did not keep Japan from taking Korea.
There was nothing we could do except fight Japan." Then he added
that Congress would not have declared war and that the people
would have turned them out if they had.[130] Roosevelt himself used
the word "interfere" regarding his Korean policy, and an effective
interference naturally had to be a forceful one. But it is hardly conceivable that the United States under Roosevelt's leadership would
have fought the Japanese to save Korea in 1905.

The real alternatives left to Roosevelt were to offer good offices
for the Koreans, to respond to the Korean appeal, or to acquiesce to
reality and help the Japanese.[131] Two leading historians who support
Roosevelt's pro-Japanese Korean policy—Tyler Dennett and Howard
K. Beale—thought that Roosevelt's decision to cooperate with the
Japanese was based on the president's view of the balance of power
in the Far East and the unworthiness of the Koreans. Critics of
Roosevelt's Korea policy, on the other hand, argue that the president
held false assumptions and had too little information to make a wise
policy. Frederick A. McKenzie thought Roosevelt adopted a policy of
noninterference to please the Japanese.[132] Philip L. Bridgham argued
that Roosevelt's assumption that the United States and Japan had
common interests in the Far East was no longer tenable, that
Roosevelt was wrong in thinking that the Koreans were timid, and
that the American representatives in Korea remained uncommuni-

cative and gave false counsel to the Koreans in suggesting that they surrender their independence.[133] Many of the points made by these critics, especially Bridgham's view that the United States and Japan no longer had common interests in the Far East, are valid; but it should be pointed out that Dennett and Beale put their fingers on important points, especially from Roosevelt's point of view, in isolating the problem of the balance of power and Roosevelt's image of Korea as significant factors for the president's Korean policy.

During the Roosevelt era, the security of the Philippine Islands became important, adding a new dimension to American interests in the Far East. The two main concerns of the Roosevelt administration in the Far East were the protection of the Philippines and the preservation of the open-door policy in China, especially in Manchuria. For these two objectives, Roosevelt played the balance-of-power game, countering the Russian threat with Japanese force. And since the author of the policy himself stated it clearly, there is no room to doubt the importance of Roosevelt's view of Korean character in the creation of his policy.[134]

There were additional important bases for Roosevelt's Korean policy. One of them, probably just below the balance-of-power factor in terms of importance, was his feeling toward the Japanese. He liked the Japanese so much that he was blind to certain matters in Japanese affairs; and even when he saw them clearly, his emotions prevented his perceptions from being translated into action. For example, had he not been so fond of the Japanese, he might have learned more about Russia and Korea and about some of the defects of the Japanese. We also now know that, if the war continued a little longer, Russia might have won it; but in 1905, when the Russians were refusing to make peace with the Japanese, Roosevelt thought they were simply stubborn and foolish. Although Dennett blames Roosevelt for not foreseeing the future shift in Japanese policy, Roosevelt did in fact see the shift coming. From the outbreak of the war, Roosevelt feared Japan. Only four months after the war began, he wrote, "The Japanese interest me and I like them. I am perfectly well aware that if they win it may possibly mean a struggle between them and us in the future."[135] In early spring of the following year, when Roosevelt's fears and uneasiness had increased, he said, "It may be that the Japanese have designs on the Philippines. I hope not; I am inclined to believe not; for I like the Japanese, and wish them well, as they have much in their character to admire."[136] What could be a better testimony of Roosevelt's mixture of suspicions about the Japanese and his emotional faith in them?

Roosevelt was as pessimistic about the Koreans and the Korean situation as he was optimistic about the Japanese. Some contemporaries thought Roosevelt did not have any knowledge about what the Japanese were doing in Korea in 1904.[137] This is not entirely true. Morgan's reports, although they were admittedly incomplete and clouded by his personal biases, were sufficient to give Roosevelt and his aides in Washington a fairly accurate picture of the situation.[138] But there was little in that picture to encourage him to support Korean independence. Already firmly in the hands of the Japanese, Korea could not be saved by any country.

It is generally known that economic concerns were not a significant factor in the making of Roosevelt's foreign policy.[139] However, it is doubtful that the comparative picture of American economic interests in the Far East escaped his attention. The difference between American trade interests in Korea and those in Japan in the mid-1900s was conspicuous. On the eve of the Russo-Japanese War, American trade with Japan was twenty times as large as the $3,500,000 value of the Korean trade.[140]

Given these four major factors—the importance of balance of power in the Far East, Roosevelt's poor image of Korea, his affectionate feeling toward the Japanese, and the great American trade interest in Japan—and other factors and conditions, Roosevelt could not possibly have acted otherwise than he did for Korea in the fall of 1905. Just how much possibility there was for him to offer American good offices for the Koreans—the other alternative—is a good question. As both a realist and an idealist, Roosevelt had an ample sense of justice, which was best expressed in his belief in the "square deal," and mobilizing some sense of justice and sympathy for the Koreans was not a total impossibility. If he had made a formal offer of good offices at a certain point in the fall of 1905, the Japanese would undoubtedly have responded with an equally formal negative answer, and nothing would have came out of the effort. At least it would have made the Koreans feel better if they had the feeling that they had done their best and that the Americans had carried out their duty. In the final analysis it may be said that, given his personal outlook, his personal philosophy, his pro-Japanese and anti-Korean sentiments, and, above all, the already hopeless conditions in Korea, President Roosevelt's Korean policy could not have been much different from what it was.

7

CLOSING THE DOOR
IN KOREA AND
THE UNITED STATES

All that happened, or was left to happen, in Korea after the fall of 1905 was in a sense anticlimactic. Although the November treaty gave the Japanese the formal authority to handle only the external affairs of Korea, no one familiar with Japanese policies in Korea thought that the island empire would stop in Korea with what it had acquired up to this time. According to Hayashi Tadasu, a prominent Japanese diplomat, Korea was one of the two major projects of Meiji Japan, along with the revision of the unequal treaties with the Western powers.[1]

The first important institutional change that took place in Korea after the fall of 1905 was the establishment of the resident general and the adjustments the powers had to make following this change. Acting in accordance with the third article of the November treaty, the Japanese government soon established the offices of the resident general in Seoul and the offices of the residents in the treaty ports; the doors of these offices were opened on February 1, 1906.[2] Even though the Foreign Minister in Tokyo handled all diplomatic matters for Korea, leaving consular business to the offices of the resident general, and even though the resident general's jurisdiction was confined to the external affairs of Korea at the beginning of the period, the resident general, partly because of the prestige and capability of Itō Hirobumi, the first resident general, but mainly because of Japanese policy, soon became the virtual ruler of Korea.[3] The consular instruction of January 30, 1906, to Gordon Paddock was very clear: "You will therefore, after February 1, address the Residency General of the Japanese Government in all cases which may arise and which therefore have been addressed to the Korean Government."[4] American consular officials would henceforth deal with the Japanese resident general, not with the Korean government, in handling problems in Korea.

Mainly because of the transitional and semi-independent status of Korea, the United States was not clear about certain aspects of institutional arrangements in Korea during the five-year period. Following the usual procedure with regard to a protected state, the American government asked the Japanese authority whether it should appoint an "Agent and Consul General."[5] Apparently fearing that there were diplomatic implications in the title of "Agent," the Japanese government objected to the use of this word and suggested the simple title of "Consul General." The Japanese government also revealed its view on the role of the resident general in communication: the main function of the office was to "handle only local affairs with the foreign countries."[6] The "local" in this case, of course, meant Korea, and the job was narrowly defined, at least in the early stage. The United States had no problem in sending an application for the exequatur for the consul general in Seoul to the Japanese government. Because some other powers raised a question about this issue, the Japanese foreign minister had Ambassador Aoki Shuzo in Washington express his own "personal view" that the American government should send the application to the Japanese, not to the Korean government.[7] However, despite Japanese efforts to eliminate any political or diplomatic implication from the consular positions in Seoul, and despite whatever the title said, American representatives in Seoul, especially Thomas Sammons, thought it was at least a "semi-diplomatic" position.[8] The Department of State also had no hesitation in reminding Sammons that the post had "a diplomatic aspect" and that it had "political importance."[9]

Some European powers caused the Japanese more concern about the institutional arrangement in Korea than did the United States during this period. Within three months after the announcement of the November 1905 treaty, the Western diplomatic representatives left Seoul one after another, turning their business over to consular officials.[10] A total of eight powers maintained their consuls general or consuls in Seoul, and none of them had any problem with their titles.[11] Russia, however, raised a serious question regarding the nationality of the authority to whom the application for the exequatur should be made. The Russians argued that the Portsmouth peace treaty did not change the sovereign status of Korea and insisted that the application should be made to the Korean, not the Japanese, government. The Russians sounded out the views of other Western powers—the United States, Great Britain, Germany, and France— but none of them wished to join the Russians in taking up the issue, and the matter ended as a protest by one nation on the issue of Korean sovereignty.[12]

There is no doubt that Itō Hirobumi was a good choice for both the Japanese and the Koreans: the Japanese government needed a person of his experience and prestige to handle the difficult task in Korea; and, under someone else, the situation could have been much worse for the Koreans.[13] The record of the Japanese work under Itō in Korea has received a mixed reception: most Japanese and many foreigners thought Itō and his fellow Japanese did excellent work for the helpless Koreans; practically all the Koreans and some foreigners, however, were sure that what the Japanese did in Korea during the short period amounted to the worst kind of imperialism, combining the ruthless exploitation of the subjugated people and land by the most greedy group of people with an extreme sense of arrogance and cruelty on the part of the victors. In truth, the record of achievement is mixed—a mixture of idealism and realism, humane service and extreme selfishness, progress and setbacks, and success and failure. The land grabbing and the overbearing behavior of some Japanese were the worst mistakes made by Japan. On the other hand, Itō also was sincere in his efforts for the improvement of the Korean people, especially the commoners. Itō's rule may be defined as a benevolent dictatorship, although one may point out that there was too little benevolence and too much dictatorship.[14]

Sammons, who occupied the Seoul position longer than any other American representative during this period and knew Itō and his rule, highly praised Itō's objectives in Korea in his comprehensive report of July 1, 1907, to the State Department. Sammons pointed out that Itō's purpose was "to improve vastly the condition of the Korean people and his policy was carried forward step by step." Even though Sammons was not sure whether the Koreans should "eventually submit freely to the Japanese control," he was largely optimistic about the Korean situation: he thought Japan's inauguration, through Itō, of a civil administration in Korea might afford "a larger measure of satisfaction of the natives."[15] In carrying out his duties in Seoul, Sammons was guided by clear and specific instructions from the Department of State: in his instruction of April 22, 1907, Huntington Wilson, the third assistant secretary of the department, told Sammons: "You will take special care to be sufficiently noncommittal and circumspect in your attitude."[16] Given the traditional American policy in Korea, his capability, experience, and sagacity, and the generally friendly attitude of the Japanese,[17] Sammons did not have any problem in effectively managing his job in Seoul.

The first year-and-a-half period to the summer of 1907, a transitional stage to a "new era," was relatively quiet in Korea—even though certain trends had already begun to emerge, such as the flocking of Japanese immigrants to the peninsula and their arrogant behavior as members of a "superior race"—and American relations with Korea, through the Japanese in Korea, were also quiet. In this quiet period, however, unusual—not because of the nature of the actions but because of the outlook of the persons involved—events occurred: Roosevelt did some service for the Koreans. Already in the fall of 1905, news about the deplorable conditions in Korea were reaching the United States through various sources, and the news could not escape Roosevelt's ears. He made an inquiry through diplomatic channels, and the Japanese government responded: after thanking Roosevelt for his friendship and kindness, Katsura assured the president that the Japanese authorities in Korea would "carefully watch over the conduct of their people" and would make an effort to prevent "injustice and ill-treatment" of the Koreans. The Japanese prime minister was also apologetic about the Japanese control of the Korean government.[18] This was the best service Roosevelt ever gave to the Koreans.

The American mass media, which had been somewhat optimistic about the changes in Korea in the fall of 1905, brought some gloomy news to the American public. The *New York Times* reported on the plight of the Korean emperor in an article entitled "Korean Ruler a Prisoner." The Japanese, reported the Seoul correspondent of the *Daily Mail*, had made the emperor of Korea a virtual prisoner in his own palace.[19] The *New York Evening Post* was loud in reporting the magnitude of the Japanese immigration to Korea: after stating that the Japanese did not enter into "a land flowing with milk and honey and waiting for occupation," the paper gave the number of Japanese immigrants since the war began—85,000 in 1904, 115,000 in 1905, and 118,000 in the following year.[20] In a somewhat cynical tone, the *New York Times* even tied Japanese immigration in Korea and Manchuria to labor troubles in California (an observation that irritated both the American and Japanese governments) by saying that one Japanese laborer in Korea or Manchuria producing foodstuffs and raw materials for the island empire would be worth much more than half a dozen "coolies" in California sending home only surplus wages.[21] The magazines, which reached a more selective audience, printed articles dealing with similar issues. The April 1906 issue of *Forum* published an article by Count Okuma Shigenobu, one of the most prominent Japanese statemen, in which the eloquent politician defended Japanese expansionist policies on the continent: "It is not a question of ambition, but a matter of necessity, that Japan should become a great power on the Asiatic continent. Should she fail in that, there is but one thing for her—national death." Arguing from both biology and history, Okuma stated that from the most remote past the Japanese and the Koreans were more or less together.[22] William T. Ellis of the *Philadelphia Press*, who visited Korea during the period, listed numerous complaints against Japanese policy in

Korea: first, "the imprisonment and humiliation of the King"; second, the substitution of Japanese for Korean authority; and third, the conduct of the Japanese toward the Koreans.[23] The January 1906 issue of *World Today* printed some specific Korean complaints: The Japanese were not only taking their government from them "by a force," but were also virtually confiscating all commercial privileges of any great value; the land along the new railways and near large inland cities was confiscated under "the pretext of the military necessity"; and the country was rapidly filling with Japanese coolies.[24] These words must have reached at least some Americans, even though not a large enough number to have an impact at a policy-making level.

Between September 1905, the end of the Russo-Japanese War, and August 1910, the month in which Japan annexed Korea, the Japanese absorption of Korea proceeded through three steps: transfer of the authority for the administration of external affairs from Korea to Japan through the November 1905 treaty; transfer of the authority for the administration of internal affairs through the treaty of July 1907; and finally, annexation, which took place in August 1910. The July 1907 treaty was important as a step toward the completion of Japan's Korean project; and the summer of 1907, another memorable season in Korea, can be compared with the fall of 1895 and the fall of 1905. Three major events occurred during this summer that shook the minds of Koreans and disturbed, in one way or another, some of the foreigners involved in Korean affairs: The Hague mission of late June and early July, the abdication of the emperor on July 20, and the Korean-Japanese treaty of July 24.

The first of these important events—the sending of the Korean mission to The Hague conference—occurred during the summer. Emperor Kojong had the wishful thought that, if the European powers learned the truth about the reality of the Korean situation, they would sympathize with Korea and would do something for the poor nation. When he heard about the conference to be held at The Hague, he decided to send a three-man mission (Yi Hyo-sŏl, Yi Chun, and Yi Wi-chong). The three, who were successful in slipping out of the country, arrived in The Hague in late June and tried to talk to the chairman of the conference—a Russian—and the delegates from the United States and the other major powers, but they failed to gain a hearing. The three did their best, reaching small groups of audiences in the city through speeches given to clubs and making contacts with the news media in the city, but the mission failed and one of the three committed suicide on July 14.[25] Two of the emperor's three emissaries later came to the United States and tried to see Roosevelt; this venture also failed.[26] A separate but parallel one-man mission was carried out by Homer B. Hulbert in The Hague and the United States. Hulbert had no better luck than the three-man team in The Hague, but he was more effective in his homeland in carrying out his mission, appealing to the American public through newspaper articles and talks before civic groups. His talk to the Chamber of Commerce in San Francisco eventually resulted in a letter from Senator Frank P. Flint of California and Secretary Root's response. In his speech to the San Francisco organization, Hulbert pointed out the atrocities committed by the Japanese in Korea, the danger of the closing of the Korean door to American goods, and the danger of the abrogation of the American-Korean treaty of 1882, which would result in increasing the tariff rate from 7 percent to 40–50 percent. Root responded by indicating that the government was not considering the abrogation of the treaty and that most of the American export goods to Korea had gone through Japan in the past and thus had paid a double tariff.[27] Korea in 1907 might best be equated with a drowning man grasping at straws. The tragedy was that the more he tried the deeper he was drawn into the water.

Two other events soon followed. The Hague mission gave the Japanese a golden opportunity to execute the advancement of their Korean project. Itō, who probably had known of the mission from the beginning but who, as a European correspondent surmised, kept silent purposely, took the first step by suggesting to Hayashi Tadasu, the foreign minister, in Tokyo that the Japanese government take advantage of the incident and seize Korea's internal administrative machinery. He further suggested that the cabinet make a decision and send him instructions. Five days later Hayashi telegraphed to Itō Prime Minister Saionji Kimmochi's message: The Privy Council had decided, and imperial approval had been given, to take advantage of the incident and to take over the internal administration of Korea. The message also indicated that Itō, not the Tokyo government, would work out the details for the execution of this policy. A note attached to the message sketched alternatives regarding some details, including the abdication of the Korean emperor.[28] Once the policy was established, its execution was not a problem. Itō, a man of intergrity and resources, would not dirty his own hands; a direct threat to the emperor, a sense of fear created by the news of the coming of the Japanese foreign minister, and the giving of ideas about a certain action to some of the members of the cabinet who were ready to do practically anything for the Japanese were sufficient; the rest was worked out by the Koreans themselves. The angry emperor told his unworthy ministers that he was occupying the throne by right of inheritance from his ancestors and that his subjects had no authority to advise his dethronement, much less to carry it out with the support of foreigners. Nevertheless, he did not see any other choice at this point, and on July 19 he delegated his governing powers to the crown prince, an act that was mistaken, probably purposely, by the Japanese government as an abdication. According to the erroneous interpretation of the Japanese authorities, not the wish of the emperor himself, the abdication ceremony was carried out the next day; the new emperor took the empty seat, and the Japanese took the real power.[29] The codification of the change took place immediately: the Korean prime minister signed the seven-article treaty, which had been prepared by Itō, Hayashi, and Hasegawa and which transferred legislative and judicial power as well as the executive authority from the Korean government to the resident general.[30] On the last day of July, in a final institutional change, the Korean army was formally disbanded.[31]

Sammons in Seoul did not do much beyond observing the developments in Korea and reporting on them to the American ambassador in Tokyo and the State Department.[32] When the emperor's emissary approached him to hear his view about the coming of the Japanese foreign minister, which was a source of worry for the Korean ruling circle, Sammons responded coldly, saying simply that he had no information on the matter and that he was "not authorized to enter into any discussion in such matters," an attitude similar to that of the American representatives in Seoul in the latter part of the 1890s and 1900s.[33] Three days later, in the midst of the crisis, came a rumor that the Korean emperor had tried to leave his palace and that he might seek asylum in one of the foreign consulates, probably the American or Russian. When Sammons received an inquiry from the Japanese authorities in Seoul by way of "mutual friends" about what he would do if the emperor sought asylum in the American compound, the American representative answered that he would notify Marquis Itō in such an emergency.[34] There is no doubt that he would have done exactly that if the crisis had come; Sammons was as realistic as Allen was. Washington showed no great reaction to the changes in Korea. The Roosevelt administration certainly would not take any action on behalf of the Koreans; and if there was any view in the minds of the leaders of the nation, it was not expressed.

The news media were even more loud and eloquent than usual. Many papers in the United States carried detailed reports about the changes in Seoul, and many of them expressed clearly their views.

The *New York Times* editorially responded to the news of Kojong's abdication by saying that he was well advised to lay aside the shadow of his imperial pretensions after the substance had been taken away from him. Although usually favorable to the Japanese, it was somewhat critical when the new treaty was announced: "It is the extinction of Korean nationality at which Japan is aiming." "Japan's interference," the same editorial continued, "had neither the fact nor the pretense of any altruistic motive. It was simply business."[35] The *New York Tribune* rejoiced at hearing the news from the Orient: "As a bone of international contention we may bid farewell to Korea. As a protectorate of Japan we may welcome it to a large measure of the prosperity and progress which Japan herself enjoys."[36] After the signing of the treaty, the same paper declared that Korea failed to survive because it had been conspicuously unfit.[37] The *New York Evening Post* was one of the few American newspapers that tried to understand the real position of the Koreans and that demonstrated, more than once, its sympathy with the people. In its July 25 issue, the paper editorially said in reference to the "righteous army" activity: "The obstinacy with which they have resisted the Japanese advance, themselves without an efficient leader, or an army, or any other resource but the hope of possible foreign interference, would show that there is good material among them which an efficient government might mold into something like a real nation, as Great Britain has done with the Egyptian felaheen."[38] The changes in Korea drew much attention from magazines in the United States. Some articles expressed favorable views on the Japanese actions in Korea,[39] while a few showed sympathy for the Koreans.[40] Many magazines took a middle road, expressing some sympathy toward the Koreans while maintaining the hope for good works on the part of the Japanese in the future. "It is impossible," a typical article of this category began, "not to feel sympathy for Korea, however one may also believe that in the end the iron hand of Japan will be for the benefit of that unhappy country."[41]

Korea in 1907 was a nation completely isolated from all nations. "The Emperor of Korea is without a friend among the governments of Europe," the London correspondent of the *New York Times* succinctly described Korea's standing in Europe.[42] The Japanese government was still somewhat sensitive to the reactions of the Western powers, and the Foreign Ministry received the views of the major European countries from its representatives. Komura Jutaro in London observed that the British thought the change was the work of the Japanese, but considered that the Korean emperor had brought the disaster on himself and therefore did not criticize the Japanese actions at all.[43] Both the Russians and the French took the change as a part of a natural process inherited from the past; neither of them criticized the Japanese actions.[44] The Germans took the Korean changes as part of a logical process and did not show any surprise or sympathy for the Koreans. The *Vossische Zeitung* even declared that the whole affair reduced itself to the question "whether the Emperor would lose with his own crown also his life, or if he would get off with sufficient pocket money to live in future."[45] The Austrians also received the news quietly.[46]

In terms of communication, consciousness, and participation—communication theory as a basis for the concept of the nation—there was no such entity as a nation in Korea in the early twentieth century. What existed were more than ten million individuals—they should be considered more as a family—under an opprosssive and corrupt bureaucracy. The unproductive and cruel *yangban* (gentry) class was always upon them; and to the average commoner, the emperor and his family meant very little. However, when the Korean people realized that the position and even the life of the emperor and the royal family were endangered by the Japanese—a foreign people—they began to feel a pain—a rise of national consciousness. The five-year period between 1905 and 1910, especially the three years after the memorable summer of 1907, was significant in the history of Korean nationalism. National consciousness began to awaken in the hearts of many common people in Korea, a consciousness quite different from that of the 1890s. That nationalism was more an intellectual and elite movement; this sense of patriotism was more wide-spread and began to be expressed in violence because the Koreans felt the pressure of helplessness, desperation, and fear. In concrete form, this violence showed itself in armed resistance against the Japanese authorities and in the assassination of persons considered enemies of the nation. Soon after the November 1905 treaty, the "Righteous Army" began to emerge; it grew slowly through 1906 and then much more rapidly in the following three years. According to one record, more than 40,000 Koreans were involved in 323 engagements against police and army units in 1907, and more than 3,629 of them were killed; during the first six months of the following year, 548,079 were involved in 795 engagements with a loss of 7,079 lives; in 1909 the movement recorded a participation of 25,763 in as many as 898 engagements; casualties reached 2,374.[47] There may be some miscalculation in these figures, but they show the magnitude of the armed struggle by the Koreans against the well-organized Japanese police force and army units that covered the peninsula. Harassed greatly by the armed resistance of the Koreans, the Japanese used a firm hand in Korea, and by the summer of 1909, they declared that Itō had been successful. Sammons interpreted Itō's leaving his Korean position as evidence of this success.[48] The most notable assassinations were those of Durham W. Stevens in the spring of 1908 and Itō Hirobumi in the fall of the following year. Stevens was an American who served the Japanese authorities in Korea, taking charge of the external affairs of the country, and his frank pro-Japanese utterances in San Francisco became a direct cause of death; Itō was assassinated in Manchuria after he had left his position in Korea.[49] Thus, even though the Righteous Army was proportionally small, it managed a significant resistance. Sammons reported its activities, together with his view on them, to Washington.[50]

During this three-year period, Sammons' view of his position in Seoul remained about the same: semidiplomatic.[51] The general posture of the American government—realistic cooperation with the Japanese authorities in Korea—continued during this period, a policy succinctly described in late 1907 by Ambassador Thomas J. O'Brien in Tokyo, who was much involved in the process of America's Korean policy making and its execution during this period, as one of giving Japan "a free hand in Korea."[52] Two years later his view was the same: "The United States raised no hand against the protectorate in Korea and is not likely to do so. . . . Meantime it would be to the advantage of all concerned if citizens of the United States residing in that country should maintain an attitude of indifference to the methods and purposes of the protectorate."[53] Some Koreans, probably not a small number, who were encouraged by some of the Americans, mostly the missionaries, still had a special feeling toward the Americans; and their disappointment, which came from an apparent lack of sympathy in most Americans, irritated Sammons and his staff. The story of the coming of the White Fleet will serve as a typical case. When the Koreans heard that the White Fleet was approaching Far Eastern waters, some of them thought that it was coming to Korea to help them against the Japanese, and great disappointment followed when this dream was not realized.[54] In general, by maintaining an attitude of caution and conciliation, Sammons and the others in the Seoul position performed their job well during this period.

As the American government retreated more and more from any political involvement, it advanced in nonpolitical matters, probably as a compensation, and those involved in Korean affairs in Seoul, Washington, and Tokyo were very active during the five-year period, especially in the last three years. American interests, both in the material and spiritual domains, reached their peak during this period, although a decline began before the end of the period. Among the various economic interests, the most important was mining. Toward the end of this period, in 1909, the Americans owned fourteen mines, a small figure in relative terms—only five percent—but in terms of importance, quite significant.[55] Sammons proudly said in the summer of 1908 that the America-owned mines represented "almost the entire active mineral exploitation of Korea."[56] Several problems or concerns developed in this sector of American interests during this period. The first major concern to arise was the promulgation of the new mining regulations, which became effective on September 15, 1906. These regulations had their positive aspects, as the Americans did not hesitate to point out, for they created order out of a very chaotic situation by giving clearly stated legal protection and, above all, by encouraging the foreigners in the mining business—probably because of a lack of adequate Japanese capital resources.[57] Because of certain governmental controls in the regulations, however, especially the government's right to revoke permission for mining operations, the regulations also had a negative impact on the foreign concession holders, including the Americans.[58]

The case of the Kapsan copper mine points out not only the degree of involvement of both governments but also the position of the State Department regarding American interests in Korea. The copper mine concession, which was the only one of its kind in Korea, was obtained by two American citizens—Henry Collbran and Harry Bostwick—during the Russo-Japanese War, on February 15, 1904; mainly because of inadequate documentation, the Japanese denied the legal basis of the concession. After much communication, both intra- and international, the case was finally resolved in June 1908 through a compromise, a political settlement.[59] The most significant part of the case was the very high degree of interest Root and others in the State Department took in the case.[60] Three minor cases involving mining concessions were resolved in 1908 and in the following year.[61] These cases were handled without too much difficulty, largely because of the great interest shown by the American authorities and because of the wise tactics of trying "to ensure a fair, and conciliatory attitude."[62]

The Americans had a considerable amount of trade and other economic interests in Korea during this period in addition to mining interests. The United States occupied fourth place in Korea's foreign trade, after Japan, which took more than two-thirds of the total foreign trade, China, and England.[63] One of the American enterprises in Korea, of which the Americans were very proud, was the Seoul waterworks, one of the best of its kind in the Far East; construction, begun in the fall of 1906, was completed about two years later, and the waterworks provided the residents of Seoul with a daily supply of 4,000,000 gallons of water.[64] Finally, we note the sale of the property of the American-Korean Seoul Electric Company, which was concluded in the summer of 1909. The electric power plant and the electric streetcar were enterprises of the company, which was one of the oldest and most established American enterprises in Korea. When they were sold to the Japanese (for $1,200,000), the Koreans showed much anger and resentment, feelings similar to those showed when James R. Morse sold his Seoul-Inchon railway concession to the Japanese.[65]

Thus, even though the Americans, through their "inexhaustible patience" and "judicious and tireless pressure," did their best to protect their economic interests in Korea after 1905, one enterprise after another was sold to the Japanese; by the summer of 1909, the only American enterprise left in Korea was mining.[66] Allen was telling his audiences in the United States in 1910: "Go over there now and what will you find? Korea is Japanese and the American is all but eliminated."[67]

Along with mining, an important American interest in Korea was missionary work. Not only because of the magnitude and degree of success and importance, but also because of certain elements almost inherently involved in this area, this domain demanded more attention and energy from both Sammons and Itō. The special element involved in the missionary work was its emotional content: these men and women who had come to Korea to save the Korean people's souls also cared about the welfare of the people, and they naturally shared the happiness and sorrows of the Koreans. When the missionaries saw the Koreans suffering in the hands of the Japanese, they naturally sympathized, and many of them became involved in Korean politics. Businessmen, whose main interest in Korea was making money, simply sold their enterprises and left Korea when the situation became impossible; but the missionaries, who were involved emotionally in the life of the Koreans, could not just walk away. However, because of the understanding of the problem and the caution exercised on both the American and the Japanese sides, the problem was handled successfully.

By all accounts, Korea was a very successful field for American missionary work.[68] As life became more painful for the Koreans, missionary opportunities increased.[69] The increase in evangelical work was great, and sociocultural work was even more successful.

On the cultural side, the greatest of the mission work occurred in education: a Japanese source listed 2 seminaries, 22 middle schools, and 508 elementary schools educating more than 13,000 Korean students in 1907; by the end of 1909; there were 829 missionary schools in Korea, more than one-third of the total number of private schools in the country.[70] The importance of these schools was much greater than the numbers indicated: the work gave new hope to many Koreans. Itō paid special attention to the educational work of the missionaries, and he adopted and carried out rather firmly a policy of mutual noninterference: as long as the missionaries did not interfere with the Japanese in Korea, the Japanese authorities would not interfere with them, but under no circumstances would the Japanese tolerate any interference in Korean political affairs.[71] In addition to Japanese cooperation, the successful handling of missionary problems was possible because of the caution and effort of the missionaries themselves,[72] the skillful handling of the American representatives in Seoul,[73] and the guidance and support of the people in Washington.[74]

The three-year period after the summer of 1907 in Korea did not draw much attention from the American news media. The small amount of news on the Korean situation was mixed: the *New York Times*, usually optimistic about the Japanese in Korea, praised "the material welfare of the general population of Korea"; the *New York Evening Post*, however, was critical of the Japanese achievement in Korea and said, in reference to the killing of some one thousand members of the Ilchinhoe, a pro-Japanese Korean group who did the dirty work for the Japanese: "That the supposedly spiritless and cowardly Korean should venture to challenge the might of victorious Japan only shows how far the most 'inferior' of nations will go in defense of its right to work out its own destinies."[75] *Outlook* and a number of other magazines published mostly either pro-Japanese or neutral articles.[76] The January 11, 1908, issue of *Harper's Weekly* gave Itō an opportunity to defend Japanese policy in Korea: "As a result of war," the Japanese statesman wrote, "we have come to see the conditions and situations which are prevailing today. These are not what the Koreans had paid for. Simply, it is the natural outcome of the life of weak that cannot cope against the strong."[77] A better defense of imperialism could hardly be found.

When the last step in the Japanese take-over of Korea came in the summer of 1910, nothing material was left to be changed; the only change that took place through the annexation was a change of form. The treaty, the instrument of the annexation, was signed by the Korean prime minister and the resident general on August 22, and its promulgation was made seven days later.[78] Thus independence of an ancient nation ended quietly. The cession, however, was not as "complete" as the two emperors intended in the treaty; the assimilation was far from complete, and the annexation turned out to be only temporary.

The Americans took these changes in Korea as quietly as they had those on the two previous occasions, in 1905 and 1907. President Taft, when he later reported to the Congress, said the treaty annexing Korea to the empire of Japan marked "the final step in a process of control of the ancient empire by her powerful neighbor."[79] In his communication to George D. Scidmore, the new consul general, Ambassador O'Brien simply pointed out that the change would result in the ending of the Korean treaties with the powers and the end of consular jurisdiction.[80] Following instructions from Washington, however, O'Brien later made an inquiry to the Japanese government concerning the economic and judicial effect of the annexation.[81]

The European powers raised somewhat more serious questions on the same two issues—the economic issue of how soon the new tariffs would be applied in Korea and whether the judicial institutions in Korea were good enough for the powers to drop immediately their consular jurisdiction—than the American government had done. The British government pursued the economic question persistently, and Japan agreed to continue the old tariff rate in Korea for ten more years.[82] The British government also expressed its "surprise" because the annexation came earlier than it thought it would, but otherwise the European governments, including the British, accepted the annexation as a logical, natural process and took it quietly.[83]

The American newspapers in general viewed the annexation of Korea as a logical step;[84] some of them, nevertheless, showed some sympathy toward the Koreans.[85] Most of the magazines in the United States were either mildly pro-Japanese or neutral on the changes in Korea. The writings by James S. Gale, Arthur J. Brown, and William E. Griffis, who well understood Korean affairs, belonged to this category.[86] "The annexation of Korea is simply the formal recognition of an existing fact, for Japan has absolutely ruled the country ever since the close of the Russo-Japanese War," Brown wrote. He continued: "There was indeed an ostensible Korean Government, but it merely registered the decision of the Japanese 'Residents.' The domination of the foreign country was inevitable."[87] This was a standard expression of many authors. The sense of inevitability, logical outcome, and natural process prevailed among them.[88]

"It would be hard to imagine anything more peaceful than the appearance of Seoul at the present moment." The description of a *London Times* correspondent continues: "The capital of what ten days ago was the Empire of Korea and is now the Japanese province of Chosen lies flooded with September sunshine, surrounded by a guarding ring of beautiful, if barren, hills."[89] One who observed the demise of the ancient kingdom could not help feeling sorry. The question remains: Was there any possibility that the United States, which did not, or could not, raise its hand for the Koreans in 1905 and 1907, would have raised its hand in 1910 on behalf of the Koreans? Certainly not. "It is time for the Korean people to cease looking for aid from outside. It will never come." These words, which were written in 1907 by another correspondent who knew well the Korean situation, were still pertinent as a reprimand for the Koreans in 1910.[90]

8 CONCLUSION

Looking back at the more than half century of American-Korean relations, which began with the arrival of shipwrecked American seamen on the Korean shore in the middle of the nineteenth century and ended with the withdrawal of the legation and the closing of the Korean door after the annexation of Korea by Japan in the early part of the following century, one cannot help concluding that the relationship between the two nations was an unhappy, even a tragic one. When two quite different nations like the United States and Korea have contact, problems are perhaps inevitable. Nonetheless, the unhappy nature of this bilateral relationship in the early years cannot be denied; this outcome needs to be clarified, and the bases for it sought out.

Excluding the early years, when contact was minimal, involving only a few shipwrecked American seamen and a few Koreans, we find there were at least forty-four years of relatively intensive contact between the two nations from 1866 to 1910, including the twenty-eight years of formal diplomatic relations from 1882. For a better understanding of the nature of this bilateral relationship, these forty-four years can be divided into three periods: the sixteen-year period from 1866 to 1882; the twelve-year period from 1882 to 1894; and the final sixteen years from 1884 to 1910.

The first sixteen-year period began with the 1866 *General Sherman* affair, a violent contact in which three Americans, two Englishmen, and nineteen Asiatics were killed and the American-owned ship was burned by the Koreans. This incident was followed by frustration on the American side through the 1858 Febiger and the 1867 Shufeldt fact-finding missions in Korean waters. This series of pretreaty encounters ended with the 1871 Low-Rodgers expedition, the first military conflict in which a large part of the Asiatic Squadron of the United States was involved; more than 350 human lives were lost, including those of three Americans. The last ten years of this period were eventless, a time of stalemate. During this period the American side took the initiative for opening the relationship, and the Koreans responded with rejection.

The period between 1882 and 1894 was a time of amicable relations. The period began with the making of the treaty of 1882. This resulted from the American need to protect its shipwrecked seamen and a hope for trade, the Korean leaders' realization of the need to bring in American influence in their efforts to maintain national independence, and the Chinese desire for deployment of American influence as a counterforce against Japanese influence on the peninsula. The coming of the first American minister, Lucius H. Foote, to Seoul was a joyous occasion for the Korean government; and his successors—especially George C. Foulk, Hugh A. Dinsmore, and Augustine Heard—were equally understanding and capable; all served both nations well. During this period the Americans also welcomed two missions from Korea—the 1883–1884 Min mission and 1887–1888 Pak mission. This was the time when the American government established its basic policy toward Korea—strict neutrality and absolute noninvolvement. Mainly because of the favorable outlook and the disposition of the Americans who were involved in American-Korean diplomatic relations in Washington and Seoul, this period was pleasant and congenial. The period ended with the beginning of the Sino-Japanese War, which would be damaging to Korea. The United States tried to prevent the war by offering its good offices. This offer did not bring any fruit, but it was a demonstration of U.S. good will toward Korea.

The last period was one of unpleasantness and rejection. This time, a reversal of roles took place: Korea anxiously approached the United States, and the latter rejected its advances. Throughout the whole period the main American policy toward Korea—strict neutrality and absolute nonintervention—remained firm; however, diplomacy between the two nations gradually deteriorated. Under Richard Olney, who succeeded Walter Q. Gresham in the spring of 1895, the neutrality and nonintervention policy was more strictly enforced in Seoul. The four-and-a-half-year period of the McKinley administration was a transition to further deterioration, with the bilateral relationship reaching its lowest point during the first four years of the Roosevelt administration. Roosevelt's cooperation with the Japanese reached the level of collaboration through his role in the making of the Portsmouth peace treaty, the handling of the Taft-Katsura Memorandum, and the hasty withdrawal of the American legation in Seoul. An observer even gets the impression that he had departed from the traditional neutrality and nonintervention policy in Korea.

Thus, American-Korean diplomatic relations went from the violent beginning through the pleasant middle period and to the final unpleasant period. Whether the congenial middle period was normal and the two other periods abnormal or the reverse is arguable, although the latter seems closer to the real situation. An important question is, then, Why was the first half century of American-Korean relationship such an unhappy one?

Like other bilateral relationships, the American-Korean one had two groups of underlying factors: the relatively constant, structural factors and the circumstantial, functional factors. An attempt will be made here to explore the causal factors of this bilateral relationship by putting together these two groups of factors, which have already been discussed.

As we have noted, the constant factors can be divided into seven categories: economic, missionary, security, historical, cultural, geographical and image. Of the seven categories, the first three belong to the hard core of national interests; the rest may be considered as peripheral. The economic factor, which was directly tied to the objectives of the United States in opening the "Hermit Kingdom," was definitely one of the most important categories. The significant fact regarding the economic factor was that the Korean share of American trade and investment was very small—0.02 percent— while the American share of Korean trade and investment—especially the latter—was relatively large. The missionary interest showed a similar phenomenon: the Korean share of total American missionary work—at 0.05 percent in 1898 somewhat bigger than the level of trade—was qualitatively important, but still small, whereas the American share of the missionary activities in Korea was great. Regarding the third factor, security, after 1898, when the United States became an Asian power through the acquisition of the Philippines, the United States became sensitive to its security interests in the region, and maintaining the balance of power became important, especially to Theodore Roosevelt, in maintaining U.S. security in the region. The maintenance of the balance of power was also very important for the independence of Korea. However, while the Koreans wanted the United States to render them assistance in maintaining the balance of power and the independence of Korea, the United States did not see any security interest in Korea and even thought that Korea was a hindrance to its maintenance of balance of power in the Far East.

The historical meaning of the opening of Korea in 1882 was also quite different for the two countries. Korea's strategic location made its opening desirable to the Americans; but because trade was minimal, the opening was not really significant to the Americans. The Korean situation was quite different. The Koreans were reluctant to open their country to a Western power; but once the door was open, the United States became important, and the event has always been remembered as an important historical landmark. The cultural factor, too, operated differently in the two countries. Cultural difference created a certain amount of common attraction for the two nations, but the differences had opposite effects: Korea was simply another backward Oriental nation to the Americans, whereas to the Koreans, especially to the king and a few of his advisers, the United States was very attractive as the representative of Western culture. Geographically speaking, under normal circumstances a large distance is a negative factor for the development of a close relationship between nations. In the Korean-American bilateral relationship this was certainly the case for the Americans, but the Koreans found the United States even more attractive for being so far away, because the great distance made the Americans look less dangerous and more beneficial. Finally, there was a similar difference in the image each nation had of the other; the American image of Korea changed, in general, from poor to worse, while the Korean image of America was in general much more favorable, with some fluctuations.

Thus, we find that with regard to all seven of the constant, structural factors there were great differences between the two countries. The asymmetrical nature of the constant factors seems to have been significant for the unhappy relations that occurred. To a certain extent, differences can have a positive effect in international affairs, but under normal circumstances, differences such as in this case make a satisfactory international relationship impossible.

The circumstantial or functional factors can be divided into two categories: the conditions that developed and the personalities that were involved in policy making in the two countries during the period. The Japanese policy toward Korea during this time was a significant factor for American-Korean relations. The destruction of the balance-of-power system through the elimination of both China and Russia by Japan in two wars at the turn of the century and the transformation of the system into one of one-power domination was fatal to the existence of Korea as a sovereign state. There was, however, another side to this conditional factor: as important as what the Japanese succeeded in doing was what the Koreans failed to do. There were many reasons for the Koreans' failure to move faster than they did in the three decades after 1882 in their modernization efforts; but, whatever the reasons were, they failed to move quickly to modernize, and this failure had a great impact upon their position in the period. The backwardness, slowness, and above all, weakness of Korea were all serious factors in dealing with the two regional powers—China and Japan—and in conducting diplomacy with the

United States. It is possible that, if the Koreans had changed faster in the 1880s and the following decade, American-Korean relations in the forty-four-year period would have been quite different.

Whatever the basic factors and circumstances may be, policy outcome depends on the men who make the policy. Thus, the policy makers are an important factor for any piece of foreign policy-making. A survey of the personalities involved in policy making on both sides shows considerable differences in the different periods. The American foreign policy-making apparatus during the pretreaty-making period was dominated by men like William H. Seward and Hamilton Fish, who held a vigorous and expansionist outlook; on the Korean side, the Taewŏn'gun, the king's father, who controlled Korean politics during this period with an iron hand, held firmly to the exclusion policy. During the middle period, Chester Alan Arthur, Frederick T. Frelinghuysen, Grover Cleveland, and Walter Q. Gresham—all very traditional and thoughtful persons—filled the policy-making positions in Washington; in Seoul, the real ruling force behind the king was the queen, who was capable, shrewd, and, above all, favored a policy opposite to that of her father-in-law, the Taewŏn'gun. She advocated the open-door policy toward the Western powers. After a group of figures who occupied a transitional period—Richard Olney, William McKinley, John Sherman, and William R. Day—Theodore Roosevelt and his advisers, who can be characterized as modern and realistic men, controlled American policy toward Korea; the person who controlled policy on the Korean side—King Kojong—was a strong contrast; he was definitely not a person able to handle the crises that occurred at this time. Probably all of these personalities were, in a sense, products of their times; but it is evident that personality was an important factor for particular characteristics of American-Korean relations.

Thus, the unhappy American-Korean relationship during the first half of the century seems to have resulted from several relatively constant factors, a number of circumstances or conditions in the region, and the different personalities responsible for the relationship. Could the relationship between the two countries have developed otherwise? Probably not. Like all other historical events, the particular nature of the American-Korean relationship during this period seems to have been inevitable: with the given constant and historical factors, it could not have been otherwise.

ABBREVIATIONS

FRUS	*Foreign Relations of the United States*
KOM	*Kuhan'guk oekyomunsŏ* (Diplomatic documents of old Korea)
MT	Meiji-Taisho
NA	National Archives
NGB	*Nihon gaiko bunsho* (Japanese diplomatic documents)
NYT Index	*New York Times Index*
rg	record group

NOTES

INTRODUCTION

1. Frelinghuysen to Foote, March 17, 1883, Instructions, Korea (file microfilm copies of records in the National Archives, no. 77, reel no. 109; hereafter cited as microfilm, NA, m77 r109).

2. Treasury Dept., *Foreign Commerce and Navigation* (1893–1894), p. xxxi; ibid. (1894–1895), p. xxxiii; Dept. of Commerce and Labor, *Foreign Commerce and Navigation* (1908), pp. 46–47.

3. Dept. of State, *Commercial Relations* (1895–1896), pp. LXX, 16.

4. Residency General, *The Third Annual Report, 1909–1910* (Seoul: Residency general, n.d.), p. 101; Dept. of Commerce and Labor, *Foreign Commerce and Navigation* (1908), pp. 46–47.

5. Allen to Hay, February 2, 1902, Despatches, Korea (microfilm, NA, m134 r11); Dept. of State, *Commercial Relations* (1896–1897), vol. 1, p. 1086; ibid. (1902), p. 1060; Dept. of State, *Consular Reports*, vol. 57 (1898), pp. 565, 567; *New York Times*, January 16, 1904, 2:1.

6. See Treasury Dept. and Dept. of Commerce and Labor, *Foreign Commerce and Navigation*, for 1894 and 1905.

7. Kirkland, *Industry Comes of Age*, vol. 6, p. 81.

8. Sill to Olney, August 15, 1896, Despatches, Korea (microfilm, NA, m134 r12); Allen to Hay, June 1, 1904, ibid. (r21); Allen to Morse, June 24, 1895, Allen papers; Allen to Hunt, July 25, 1902, ibid.; "Narrative of Enterprise," ibid.; Residency General, *Annual Report, 1908–1909* (Seoul, Residency General, n.d.), p. 147; ibid. (1910–1911), p. 200.

9. Sill to Olney, April 16, 1896, Despatches, Korea (microfilm, NA, m134 r14); Allen to Hay, November 18, 1899; April 29, 1901, ibid. (r15, r17).

10. Sill to Sherman, February 15, 1898, ibid. (r14); Allen to Hay, November 18, 1899; April 29, 1901, ibid. (r15, r17).

11. Allen to Hay, November 18, 1899, ibid. (r15).

12. Allen to Hay, February 2, 1903, ibid. (r19); Henry Collbran, "Seoul Waterworks," Allen papers.

13. Allen to Rockhill, January 30, 1898, Rockhill papers.

14. Allen to Rockhill, February 28, 1901, ibid.

15. "Report on the Trade of Korea for the Year 1904 and Abstract for the Years, 1895–1905," Allen papers.

16. *Missionary Review of the World* 12 (1889): 312; 13 (1890): 295; 16 (1893): 658; 28 (1905): 328; 31 (1908): 94.

17. Ibid., New Series 16 (1898): 958.

18. Sammons to Assistant Secretary of State, June 16, 1908, Seoul Consular Documents (NA, record group 84; hereafter rg); Horace G. Underwood,

"Twenty Years of Missionary Work in Korea," *Missionary Review of the World*, New Series 19 (1906): 375.

19. *Missionary Review of the World* 12 (1899): 72–73; *Boston Transcript*, December 13, 1905, 2:3.

20. *Boston Transcript*, December 13, 1905, 2:3.

21. *Missionary Review of the World*, New Series 14 (1901): 66–67.

22. *Missionary Review of the World*, 11 (1888): 313, 397; ibid. 13 (1890): 295.

23. Ibid., New Series 14 (1901): 76.

24. Yi Hyŏn-chong, "Kuhanmal sŏkue chongkyoŭi p'okyo sanghang," *Idae sawŏn* 9 (1970): 29.

25. Ibid., p. 25.

26. Paik, *History of Protestant Missions*, pp. 97–98, 110–112, 229.

27. Allen to Hay, November 28, 1902; November 21, 1904, Despatches, Korea (microfilm, NA, m134 r19). See also Clark, *Avison of Korea*.

28. Paik, *History of Protestant Missions*, pp. 114–115, 230; Yi, "Kuhanmal sŏkue chonggyoŭi p'okyo sanghang," p. 29.

29. Paik, *History of Protestant Missions*, pp. 112–113.

30. Ibid., pp. 236–238. See also Sands, *Undiplomatic Memoirs*, pp. 48, 91.

31. Allen to Hay, February 2, 1903, Despatches, Korea (microfilm, NA, m134 r19).

32. See Morgenthau, *Politics among Nations*, p. 161.

33. Almond, "Public Opinion and National Security Policy," p. 376; Rosenau, *National Leadership and Foreign Policy*, p. 3. See also Rosenau's *Public Opinion and Foreign Policy*.

34. *New York Times Index* (1851–1885) (hereafter *NYT Index*) (New York: New York Times, 1962–1966), *Poole's Index to Periodical Literature* (1802–1881) (New York: Peter Smith, 1938), pt. 1, pp. 301–302.

35. *NYT Index* (1886–1889, 1890–1893); *Poole's Index* (1882–1896).

36. *NYT Index* (1894–1898).

37. *Poole's Index* (1882–1896).

38. *NYT Index* (1894–1898, 1899–1905); *Poole's Index* (1892–1902); *Readers' Guide to Periodical Literature* (1900–1904) (Minneapolis, Minn.: Wilson, 1905).

39. *NYT Index* (1899–1905); *Readers' Guide* (1900–1909).

40. *NYT Index* (1905–1910); *Readers' Guide* (1905–1914).

41. For the structure of the image system see Scott, "Psychological and Social Correlates of International Image," p. 72; and Deutsch and Merritt, "Effects of Events on National and International Image," p. 133.

42. "Korea: What Shall We do with Her?" *Galaxy* 13 (1892): 303–313; Frank C. Carpenter, "The Koreans at Home," *Cosmopolitan* 6 (1888–1889): 381–396; Charles Chaille-Long, "Art and the Monastery in Korea," ibid. 10 (1890–1891): 73–80; J. B. Bernadou, "Korea and the Koreans," *National Geographic Magazine* 2 (1890): 231–242.

43. William E. Griffis, "Jack and the Giant in Korea," *Outlook* 50 (1894): 212–213; "Korea and Her Bosses," *Harper's Weekly* 39 (1895): 1244; "Korea, the Pigmy Empire," *Overland Monthly* 39 (1902): 945–954; Arthur J. Brown, "Unhappy Korea," *Century* 46 (1904): 147–150; James S. Gale, "Unconscious Korea," *Outlook* 96 (1910): 494.

44. Kennan, "Land of Morning Calm," pp. 363–369; "Capital of Korea," pp. 464–472.

45. Itō Hirobumi, "Japanese Policy in Korea," *Harper's Weekly* 52 (1908): 27; Ōkuma Shigenobu, "Japan's Policy in Korea," *Forum* 37 (1906): 571–580; Kennan, "Korea: A Degenerate State," pp. 307–315; William E. Griffis, "Japan's Absorption of Korea," *North American Review* 192 (1910): 409–416, 516–526; James S. Gale, "Unconscious Korea," *Outlook* 96 (1910): 494–497; Willard Straight, "American Legation at Seoul," *Putnam's Magazine* 1 (1906): 131–137.

46. Samuel MacClintock, "The Passing of Korea," *World Today* 13 (1907): 939–946; A. Maurice Low, "Japan Absorbs Korea," *Forum* 39 (1907): 166–170; "Japan Virtually Annexed Korea," *Harper's Weekly* 51 (1907): 1155; "Crisis in Korea," *Outlook* 86 (1907): 626–627.

47. Kennan, "Japanese in Korea," pp. 609–616; idem, "What Japan Has Done in Korea," pp. 669–673; Arthur J. Brown, "Japanese in Korea," *Outlook* 96 (1910): 591–595.

48. Roosevelt to Hay, January 28, 1905, in Morison et al., eds., *Letters*, vol. 4, p. 1112.

49. For more detailed discussion of the subject see Chay, "American Image of Korea," in Koo and Suh, eds., *Korea and the United States*, pp. 53–76.

50. For a detailed discussion about the role of these people see Ham P'yong-ch'oon, "Korean Perceptions of America," in Ku et al., *Han'gukkwa Mikuk*, pp. 39–52.

51. See *Kojong sidaesa*, vol. 2, pp. 183–186, 190, 225, 227, 231, 241, 242, 253, 261.

CHAPTER 1

1. Griffis, *Corea, the Hermit Nation*, p. 502.

2. *Ilsŏngnok*, December 15, 17, 3rd year, Ch'ŏlchong.

3. *Pipyŏnsa tamnok*, June 2, 12, July 2, 6th year, Ch'ŏlchong.

4. *Kojong silnok*, August 17, 2nd year, Kojong; *Kojong sidaesa*, vol. 1, p. 151.

5. *Sŭngjŏn'gwŏn ilki*, February 25, 3rd year, Kojong; *Ilsŏngnok*, February 25, 3rd year, Kojong; *Kojong silnok*, February 25, 3rd year, Kojong; *Kojong sidaesa*, vol. 1, p. 192.

6. Wells Williams to William H. Seward, October 24, 1866, Despatches, China (microfilm, NA, m92 r24); *Kojong sidaesa*, vol. 1, p. 215.

7. Anson Burlingame to William H. Seward, December 15, 1866, Despatches, China (microfilm, NA, m92 r24); Robert W. Shufeldt to Henry H. Bell, January 8, 1867, Shufeldt papers.

8. Williams to William H. Seward, October 24, 1866, Despatches, China (microfilm, NA, m92 r24); William H. Seward to Burlingame, February 23, 1867, Instructions, China (microfilm, NA, m77 r38).

9. George F. Seward to William H. Seward, October 14, 1868, Consular Despatches, Shanghai (microfilm, NA, m112 r9).

10. See William H. Seward to George F. Seward, June 27, 1868, Consular

Instructions, China (microfilm, NA, rg59). Secretary Seward called the case a "painful mystery" in 1868, two years after the incident. See also Drake, *Empire of the Seas*, pp. 96–98.

11. For both sides of the story see Burlingame to William H. Seward, December 15, 1866, Despatches, China (microfilm, NA, m92 r24); Meadows and Company to Burlingame, October 27, 1866, enclosure in ibid.; E. I. Sanford to William H. Seward, December 31, 1866, Consular Despatches, Chefoo (microfilm, NA, m102, r2); *Kojong sidaesa*, vol. 1, pp. 221–230; *Kojong silnok*, July 5, 12, 13, 15, 16, 18, 3rd year, Kojong; *Pipyŏnsa tamnok*, July 5, 12, 13, 16, 25, 3rd year, Kojong; *Sŭngjŏn'gwŏn ilki*, July 5, 12, 13, 16, 22, 23, 25, 27, 3rd year, Kojong.

12. See also Robert W. Shufeldt to the Korean King, May 4, 1880, enclosure no. 2 in John Bingham to William M. Evarts, Despatches, Japan, May 3, 1880 (microfilm, NA, m133 r42).

13. *Sŭngjŏn'gwŏn ilki*, July 5, 12, 13, 16, 3rd year, Kojong; *Kojong silnok*, July 5, 12, 13, 16, 3rd year, Kojong; *Pipyŏngsa tamnok*, July 5, 12, 13, 16, 3rd year, Kojong. Also see *Tongmun ŭiko*, vol. 3, p. 2490.

14. For critical views of the incident, see the letter of the Korean king (Kojong) in Shufeldt to the Korean King, May 4, 1880, enclosure no. 2 in Bingham to Evarts, May 31, 1880, Despatches, Japan (microfilm, NA, m133 r42); Swartout, "Cultural Conflict," pp. 140–144; Cable, *United States–Korean Relations*, p. 11; Tyler Dennett, "Seward's Far Eastern Policy," *American Historical Review* 28 (1922): 59; S. J. Whitewell, "Britons in Korea," *Transactions of the Korean Branch of the Royal Asiatic Society* 41 (1964): 8; Kim Wŏn-mo, *Kŭndae Han-Mi kyosŏpsa* pp. 162–163.

15. Williams to William H. Seward, October 24, 1866, Despatches, China (microfilm, NA, m92 r24); Kim, *Kŭndae Han-Mi kyosŏpsa*, p. 160.

16. Burlingame to William H. Seward, December 15, 1866, Despatches (microfilm, NA, m92 r24); C. T. Sanford to William H. Seward, December 31, 1866, Consular Despatches, Chefoo (microfilm, NA, m102 r1).

17. William H. Seward to Burlingame, February 23, 1867, Despatches, China (microfilm, NA, m61 r38).

18. Bell to Welles, November 30, December 12, 1866, Squadron Letters, Asiatic (microfilm, NA, m89 r251).

19. Bell to Welles, December 14, 27, 1866, ibid.

20. Bell to Welles, December 12, 1866, ibid.

21. Shufeldt to Bell, January 8, 9, 19, 1867, Shufeldt papers; Logbooks (NA, rg24). For a summary report of the mission see Shufeldt to Bell, January 30, 1867, enclosure in Bell to Welles, February 16, 1867, Squadron Letters, Asiatic (microfilm, NA, m89 r252). See also *Kojong sidaesa*, vol. 1, p. 316; *Sŭngjŏn'gwŏn ilki*, December 27, 28, 3rd year, Kojong.

22. Shufeldt to the Korean King, January 24, 1867; Shufeldt to the official of Chang Yŏn, January 24, 1867, enclosures in Bell to Welles, February 16, 1867, Squadron Letters, Asiatic (microfilm, NA, m89 r252).

23. Han Chi-yong to Shufeldt, December 1866, enclosure in Stephen C. Rowan to Welles, July 24, 1868, Squadron Letters, Asiatic (microfilm, NA, m89 r253). See also Drake, *Empire of the Seas*, pp. 100–108.

24. Bell to Welles, February 16, 1867, Squadron Letters, Asiatic (microfilm, NA, m89 r252).

25. Ibid.

26. *Kojong sidaesa*, vol. 1, pp. 289-290; Burlingame to William H. Seward, January 31, 1867, Despatches, China (microfilm, NA, m92 r25).

27. Burlingame to William H. Seward, January 31, 1867, Despatches, China (microfilm, NA, m92 r25).

28. Dennett, "Seward's Far Eastern Policy," pp. 54-58.

29. Ibid., p. 59.

30. Bell to Welles, December 12, 1866, Squadron Letters, Asiatic (microfilm, NA, m89 r251); William H. Seward to Burlingame, February 23, 1867, Instructions, China (microfilm, NA, m61 r38); William H. Seward to Welles, April 14, 1868, Domestic Letters, State Department (microfilm, NA, m40 r64).

31. Sanford to William H. Seward, December 31, 1866, Consular Despatches, Chefoo (microfilm, NA, m102 r1); Bell to Welles, December 30, 1866, Squadron Letters, Asiatic (microfilm, NA, m89 r252). See also William H. Seward to Welles, April 14, 1868, Domestic Letters, State Department (microfilm, NA, m40 r64).

32. J. R. Goldsborough to John C. Febiger, February 8, 1868, Squadron Letters, Asiatic (microfilm, NA, m89 r252).

33. For a detailed report of the mission see Febiger to Rowan, May 29, 1868, enclosure in Rowan to Welles, July 24, 1868, Squadron Letters, Asiatic (microfilm, NA, m89 r253); Logbook (NA, rg24); *Kojong sidaesa*, vol. 1, p. 390.

34. *Report of the Secretary of Navy, 1868* (Washington D.C.: Government Printing Office, 1868), p. xiv. See also Low to Fish, July 6, 1871, Despatches, China (microfilm, NA, m92 r31); George F. Seward to William H. Seward, May 25, 1868, Consular Despatches, Shanghai (microfilm, NA, m112 r9).

35. *Sŭngjŏn'gwŏn ilki*, December 27, 28, 3rd year, Kojong.

36. For a description of the expedition see George F. Seward to William H. Seward, July 13, 1868, Consular Despatches, Shanghai (NA, m112 r9); *Kojong sidaesa*, vol. 1, pp. 388-392; Swartout, "Cultural Conflict," pp. 146-148.

37. Low to Fish, July 6, 1871, Despatches, China (microfilm, NA, m92 r31).

38. Williams to William H. Seward, August 5, 1868, Despatches, China (microfilm, NA, m92 r25); Sŏ, *Kŭktong kukche chŏngch'isa*, vol. 1, p. 231; Ch'oe, *Roles of the Taewŏn'gun*, pp. 112-114; Swartout, "Cultural Conflict," pp. 146-148.

39. Bell to Welles, December 14, 1866, Squadron Letters, Asiatic (microfilm, NA, m89 r251).

40. George F. Seward to William H. Seward, April 24, 1868, enclosure in Fish to Low, April 20, 1870, Diplomatic Instructions, China, Exec. Doc., House, 41st Cong., 1st sess. (1870), pt. 1, no. 1, pp. 336-337.

41. Fish to Low, April 20, 1870, ibid.

42. Fish to Low, April 20, 1870, Dept. of State, *Foreign Relations of the United States* (hereafter *FRUS*) (1870), pp. 334-335.

43. Report of Rear Admiral John Rodgers, June 3, 1871, U.S. Congress, House, "Annual Report of the Secretary of Navy, 1871," Exec. Docs., 42nd Cong., 2nd sess., pt. 3, no. 1, appendix 18, p. 275; Fish to Low, April 20, 1870, Dept. of State, *FRUS* (1871), p. 335; Low to Fish, April 20, 25, May 13, 1871, Despatches, China (microfilm, NA, m92 r31).

44. Paullin, *Diplomatic-Negotiations*, p. 288.

45. Low to Fish, May 31, 1871, Despatches, China, Dept. of State, *FRUS* (1871), p. 117.

46. For a detailed description of the expedition see report of Rear Admiral Rodgers, June 3, 1871, "Annual Report of the Secretary of Navy, 1871," pp. 275-309; Low to Fish, June 2, 1871, Dept. of State, *FRUS* (1871), pp. 121-124; *Kojong sidaesa*, vol. 1, p. 557; Schley, *Forty-five Years*, pp. 83-85.

47. Chŏng (Ki-wŏn) to the American Mission, June 6, 1871; American reply to the Korean communication of June 3, 1871; Drew to Chŏng, June 7, 1871, enclosures in Low to Fish, June 20, 1871, Dept. of State, *FRUS* (1871), pp. 133-134, 135.

48. Chŏng to American Mission, June 6, 1871, ibid.

49. Low to Fish, June 20, 1871, ibid., p. 122; American reply to the Korean communication of June 3, 1871; Drew to Chŏng, June 7, 1871, enclosures in Low to Fish, June 20, 1871, ibid., pp. 131, 135; Report of Rear Admiral John Rodgers, June 3, 1871, "Annual Report of the Secretary of Navy, 1871," p. 277.

50. Order to Commander H. C. Blake, June 9, 1871, "Annual Report of the Secretary of Navy, 1871," p. 285.

51. For a detailed account of the expedition see Report of Rear Admiral John Rodgers with enclosures, July 5, 1871, "Annual Report of the Secretary of Navy, 1871," pp. 279-313; Schley, *Forty-five Years*, pp. 83-96; *Kojong sidaesa*, vol. 1, pp. 560-573; *Kojong silnok*, April 24, 8th year, Kojong.

52. Drew to Chŏng, June 13, 1871; Yi to Drew, June 15, 1871, enclosures in Low to Fish, June 20, 1871, Dept. of State, *FRUS* (1871), p. 137.

53. Yi to the American Minister, June 11, 1871, ibid., pp. 137-138; *Tongmun ŭiko*, vol. 3, p. 2494.

54. Drew to Yi, June 15, 1871, enclosure in Low to Fish, June 20, 1871, Dept. of State, *FRUS* (1871), pp. 138-140. Every communication from Yi was under the instructions of the Korean government, *Kojong sidaesa*, vol. 1, pp. 578-579.

55. Yi to Drew, June 17, 1871; Drew to Yi, June 18, 1871, enclosures in Low to Fish, June 20, 1871, Dept. of State, *FRUS* (1871), pp. 140-141.

56. Drew to Yi, July 2, 1871, enclosure in Low to Fish, July 6, ibid., pp. 148-149.

57. Low to Fish, July 6, 1871, ibid., p. 144. For a scholarly consensus see Dennett, *Americans in Eastern Asia*, p. 453; Sŏ, *Kŭk-tong kukche chŏngchi'sa*, vol. 1, p. 218; Pak, *Kŭndae Han-Mi oekyosa*, p. 150; Okuhira, *Chōsen*, p. 14; Kim Wŏn-mo, *Kŭndae Han-Mi kyosŏpsa*, pp. 235-371; Cable, *United States-Korean Relations*, p. 109. For the Rose expedition see Kim Wŏn-mo,

"Rose hamdaeŭi naech'imkwa Yang Hŏn-chuŭi hangchŏn (1866)" (The expedition of the Rose Fleet and Yang Hŏn-chu's resistance), *Tongyanghak* (Tongyanghak Yŏn'guso, Dankuk University), 13 (1983): 173–218.

58. *Kojong silnok*, April 10, 19th year, Kojong; *Kojong sidaesa*, vol. 1, pp. 556–557. Kersten, *Naval Aristocracy*, p. 146; Johnson, *Far China Station*, pp. 154–169.

59. See *Kojong silnok*, April 10, 11, 12, 13, 8th year, Kojong; *Sŭngjŏn'gwŏn ilki*, April 10, 11, 12, 13, 8th year, Kojong; *Pipyŏnsa tamnok*, April 10, 12, 8th year, Kojong. *Kojong silnok* indicates that the survey expedition was made without prior approval.

60. The king made clear this point in his letter to the Chinese Board of Rites, enclosure in Low to Fish, November 23, 1871, Despatches, China (microfilm, NA, m92 r32).

61. George F. Seward to Fish, November 20, 1871, Despatches, China (microfilm, NA, m92 r44); Shufeldt to R. W. Thompson, October 13, 1880, misc. docs., State Department (microfilm, NA, m179 r576).

62. Fish to Low, September 20, 1871, Instructions, China, Dept. of State, *FRUS* (1871), p. 153.

63. *Kojong sidaesa*, vol. 1, pp. 574, 576–577; *Sŭngjŏn'gwŏn ilki*, April 25, 8th year, Kojong; *Kojong silnok*, April 25, 29, 8th year, Kojong.

64. Shufeldt to R. W. Thompson, October 13, 1880, enclosure in Thompson to Evarts, December 14, 1880, misc. docs., State Department (microfilm, NA, m179 r576). See also *New York Times*, January 23, 1872, 2:5–6.

65. Bell to Welles, December 14, 1866, Squadron Letters, Asiatic (microfilm, NA, m89 r251); Shufeldt to Bell, January 30, 1867, enclosure in Bell to Welles, February 16, 1867, ibid. (r252); Shufeldt to King Kojong, May 4, 1880, enclosure in Bingham to Evarts, May 21, 1880, Despatches, Japan (microfilm, NA, m133 r42).

66. See Ch'oe, *Roles of the Taewŏn'gun*, pp. xv, 32–133; Palais, *Politics and Policy*, pp. 58–195.

67. Shufeldt to Bell, January 30, 1867, enclosure in Bell to Welles, February 16, 1867, Squadron Letters, Asiatic (microfilm, NA, m89 r252).

68. Low to Fish, May 13, June 2, 1871, Despatches, China (microfilm, NA, m92 r31).

69. Low to Fish, June 20, 1871, Despatches, China, Dept. of State, *FRUS* (1871), p. 127.

70. *Kojong silnok*, April 20, 8th year, Kojong. On the issue of cultural conflict, see Swartout, "Cultural Conflict," pp. 117–169.

CHAPTER 2

1. Dennett, *Americans in Eastern Asia*, p. 450.
2. Paullin, *Diplomatic Negotiations*, p. 470.
3. Okuhira has interesting observations; see Okuhira, *Chōsen*, pp. 1–15.
4. Dennett, *Americans in Eastern Asia*, pp. 129–134, 246; Tansill, *Foreign Policy*, p. 414.

5. U.S. Congress, House, no. 138, 28th Cong., 2nd sess., pp. 1–2.

6. George F. Seward to William H. Seward, April 24, 1868, Consular Despatches, Shanghai (microfilm, NA, m112 r9).

7. William H. Seward to George F. Seward, June 27, 1868, Consular Instructions (NA, rg59).

8. George F. Seward to William H. Seward, July 3, 1868, Consular Despatches, Shanghai (microfilm, NA, m112 r9).

9. William H. Seward to George F. Seward, July 22, 1868, Consular Instructions (NA, rg59).

10. U.S. Congress, *Congressional Record*, 45th Cong., 2nd sess., pp. 2324, 2589, 2599–3601.

11. Thompson to Shufeldt, October 29, 1878, enclosure in Thompson to Evarts, October 30, 1878, Domestic File, State Department (microfilm, NA, m40 r523). See also Evarts to Thompson, November 9, 1878, ibid., (r87).

12. Log USS *Ticonderoga*, Navy (NA, rg24). For a detailed account see Drake, *Empire of the Seas*, pp. 238–252.

13. Shufeldt to Bingham, February 14, 1880, enclosure in Bingham to Evarts, March 20, 1880, Despatches, Japan, NA.

14. Ibid.

15. Evarts to Bingham, April 1, 1880. Instructions, Japan, NA; Bingham to Shufeldt, March 12, 1880, enclosure in Bingham to Evarts, March 20, 1880, Despatches, Japan, NA.

16. Bingham to Inouye, March 12, 1880, enclosure in Bingham to Evarts, March 20, 1880, Despatches, Japan, NA.

17. Inouye to Bingham, April 7, 1880, enclosure in Bingham to Evarts, May 6, 1880, ibid.

18. Inouye to Kondo Masuki, April 20, 1880, enclosure in Bingham to Shufeldt, April 20, 1880, Shufeldt papers; Inouye to Kondo, April 20, 1880, enclosure in Wooyeno to Bingham, April 20, 1880, *Nihon gaiko bunsho* (hereafter *NGB*), vol. 13, p. 437.

19. Kondo to Shufeldt, May 6, 1880, Subject File, Korea, Shufeldt papers; "Journal of F. A. Miller," May 3–6, 1880, ibid.; *Kojong silnok*, April 10, May 18, 17th year, Kojong.

20. Shufeldt to Korean King, May 4, 1880, enclosure in Bingham to Evarts, May 31, 1880, Despatches, Japan, NA.

21. For the process see "Journal of F. A. Miller," May 7–26, 1880, Shufeldt papers. See also Inouye to Sanjo Sanetomi (Japanese prime minister), May 24, 1880, *NGB*, vol. 13, p. 442.

22. Bingham to Shufeldt, May 27, 1880, Subject File, Korea, Shufeldt papers; Inouye to Bingham, May 29, 1880, enclosure in Bingham to Evarts, May 31, 1880, Despatches, Japan, NA. See also Inouye to Yun, May 29, 1880, ibid.

23. Inouye to Kondo, May 27, 1880, *NGB*, vol. 13, pp. 443–444.

24. Kondo to Inouye, June 10, 1880, enclosure in Bingham to Shufeldt, July 12, 1880, Shufeldt papers.

25. Kondo to Inouye, July 31, 1880, *NGB*, vol. 13, pp. 448–449.

26. Wooyeno to Bingham, August 4, 1880, enclosure in Bingham to Shu-

feldt, August 6, 1880; Bingham to Shufeldt, August 6, 1880; Shufeldt to Bingham, August 17, 1880, Shufeldt papers.

27. Yun to Inouye, June (July) 1880, enclosure in Bingham to Shufeldt, August 6, 1880, Subject File, ibid.; Yun to Inouye, June (July) 1880, enclosure in Wooyeno to Bingham, August 4, 1880, *NGB*, vol. 13, pp. 448–449.

28. Shufeldt to Bingham, August 17, 1880, Subject File, Korea, Shufeldt papers.

29. Bingham to Shufeldt, September 7, 1880, enclosure in Bingham to Evarts, September 14, 1880, Despatches, Japan, NA.

30. Bingham to Inouye, September 11, 1880, ibid.

31. Bingham to Shufeldt, September 7, 1880, ibid. See Deuchler, *Confucian Gentlemen*, p. 111.

32. Inouye to Bingham, September 17, 1880, enclosure in Bingham to Evarts, January 5, 1880, Despatches, Japan, NA.

33. Shufeldt to Mary A. Shufeldt, June 11, July 22, 1880, Shufeldt papers.

34. See, for the development, Shufeldt to Mary A. Shufeldt, July 1, September 9, 1880, Shufeldt papers; U.S. Commission, Chefoo, to Evarts, August 28, 1880, Despatches, China, NA; Shufeldt to Thompson, August 30, 1880, enclosure in Thompson to Evarts, October 21, 1880, Miscellaneous, State Department (microfilm, NA, m179 r572).

35. Robert W. Shufeldt to Mary A. Shufeldt, May 30, 1880, Shufeldt papers.

36. Shufeldt to Thompson, October 13, 1880, Miscellaneous, State Department (microfilm, NA, m179 r576).

37. Jones, "Foreign Diplomacy in Korea," p. 204; Chien, *Opening of Korea*, p. 76. See also Deuchler, *Confucian Gentlemen*, pp. 112–113.

38. Inouye to Bingham, April 7, 1880, enclosure in Bingham to Evarts, May 6, 1880, Despatches, Japan, NA; Inouye to Bingham, September 17, 1880, enclosure in Bingham to Evarts, January 5, 1881, ibid. See also Drake, *Empire of the Seas*, pp. 244, 250–251.

39. Shufeldt to Thompson, August 17, 1880, enclosure in William J. Jeffert to Evarts, October 23, 1880, Miscellaneous, State Department (microfilm, NA, m179 r572).

40. Thompson to Evarts, June 30, 1880, Miscellaneous, State Department (microfilm, NA, m179 r565). See also Robert Wilson Shufeldt to Mary A. Shufeldt, June 11, July 22, 1880, Shufeldt papers.

41. *Kojong sidaesa*, vol. 2, pp. 183–189; Pak, *Mikukŭi kaekuk chŏngch'aek*, p. 155. See a discussion in Deuchler, *Confucian Gentlemen*, pp. 90–92.

42. Inouye to Bingham, September 18, 1880, enclosure in Bingham to Evarts, January 5, 1881, Despatches, Japan, NA.

43. Shufeldt to Bingham, February 14, 1880, enclosure in Bingham to Evarts, March 20, 1880, ibid.

44. *New York Times*, June 21, 1880, 4:5.

45. Blaine to William H. Hunt, March 15, 1881, Miscellaneous, State Department (microfilm, NA, m40 r93); Hunt to Blaine, March 18, 1881, Miscellaneous, State Department (microfilm, NA, m179 r582). For Frederick C.

Drake's account of the Shufeldt mission see Drake, *Empire of the Seas*, pp. 257-304.

46. Blaine to Shufeldt, May 9, 1881, Instructions, China, NA. See also Blaine to Angell, May 9, 1881, ibid.

47. Shufeldt to Blaine, July 1, 1881, Despatches, China, NA.

48. Angell to Shufeldt, August 12, 1881, Shufeldt papers.

49. Angell to Blaine, October 13, 1881, Despatches, China, NA; Angell to Shufeldt, October 14, 1881, Shufeldt papers.

50. Henry Shufeldt to Robert W. Shufeldt, December 1, 1881, Shufeldt papers. See also Drake, *Empire of the Seas*, pp. 267-272.

51. Tel., Chester Holcombe to Shufeldt, December 19, 1881, Despatches, China, NA. The telegram reached Shufeldt on December 21.

52. Pak, *Mikukŭi kaekuk chŏngch'aek*, p. 139. See Key-hiuk Kim, *Last Phase*. See also Deuchler, *Confucian Gentlemen*, pp. 86-92.

53. Bingham to Blaine, June 20, 1881, Despatches, Japan, NA; Angell to Blaine, July 16, 1881, Despatches, China, NA.

54. For the Korean side of the story see *Sŭngjon'gwŏn ilki*, December 14, 18th year, Kojong; *Kojong silnok*, July 19, 16th year, Kojong; February 14, 16, 18th year, Kojong; *Jongjŏng yŏnp'yo*, pp. 120-124; *Maech'ŏn yarok*, vol. 1, pp. 150-151; Pak, *Mikukŭi kaekuk chŏngch'aek*, pp. 139, 140, 150, 154-157, 184-191. See also Deuchler, *Confucian Gentlemen*, pp. 104-106.

55. Tel., Frelinghuysen to Holcombe, January 7, 1882, Instructions, China, NA.

56. Blaine to Shufeldt, November 14, 1881, ibid.

57. Frelinghuysen to Shufeldt, January 1, 1882, ibid.; Shufeldt to Frelinghuysen, March 11, 1882, Despatches, China, NA.

58. Shufeldt to Frelinghuysen, January 23, 1882, ibid.; Blaine to William Hung (Secretary of Navy), November 17, 1881, Domestic File, State Department (microfilm, NA, m40 r94).

59. Shufeldt to Li, January 23, 1882, enclosure in Shufeldt to Frelinghuysen, March 11, 1882, Despatches, China, NA.

60. *Ŭmch'ŏngsa*, pp. 26-55; *Kojong sidaesa*, vol. 2, pp. 283-284, 295-296, 301-302; Pak, *Mikukŭi kaekuk chŏngch'aek*, pp. 189-197.

61. Holcombe to Frelinghuysen, May 29, 1882, Despatches, China, NA.

62. Shufeldt to Frelinghuysen, March 11, 1882, ibid. For the negotiation process see also Drake, *Empire of the Seas*, pp. 282-295.

63. Shufeldt to Frelinghuysen, April 10, 1882, Despatches, China, NA; *Ŭmch'ŏngsa*, pp. 51-55; Pak, *Mikukŭi kaekuk chŏngch'aek*, pp. 169-173.

64. Shufeldt to Frelinghuysen, March 30, 1882, Despatches, China, NA.

65. Shufeldt to Li, April 4, 1882, enclosure in Shufeldt to Frelinghuysen, April 10, 1882, ibid.

66. Shufeldt to Frelinghuysen, April 10, 1882, ibid.

67. Tel., Shufeldt to Frelinghuysen, April 12, 1882, ibid.

68. Shufeldt to Frelinghuysen, April 28, 1882, ibid.

69. Ibid.

70. Shufeldt to Holcombe, May 6, 1882, enclosure in Holcombe to Frelinghuysen, May 16, 1882, ibid.

71. Jones, "Foreign Diplomacy," p. 282.

72. Shufeldt to Holcombe, May 6, 1882, enclosure in Holcombe to Shufeldt, May 16, 1882, Despatches, China, NA.

73. Shufeldt to Frelinghuysen, April 28, 1882; Shufeldt to Holcombe, May 6, 1882, ibid.

74. *Jongjŏng yŏnp'yo*, pp. 125–130.

75. Shufeldt to Frelinghuysen, August 23, 1882, Despatches, China, NA; *Ch'ŏng'kuk mundap*, pp. 6, 18.

76. Shufeldt to Frelinghuysen, May 29, June 8, 1882, Despatches, China, NA; P. H. Cooper to Clitz, May 30, 1882, enclosure in Clitz to Hunt, June 5, 1882, Squadron Letters, Asiatic (microfilm, NA, m89 r268); Shufeldt to Clitz, June 5, 1882, enclosure in Clitz to H. E. Chandler, June 14, 1882, ibid. *Kojong sidaesa*, vol. 2, pp. 304, 307–318.

77. Frelinghuysen to John Russell Young, January 16, 22, 1883, Instructions, China, NA.

78. Bingham to Frelinghuysen, November 13, 29, 1882, Despatches, Japan, NA.

79. Bingham to Frelinghuysen, August 19, 1882, ibid.; Young to Frelinghuysen, December 26, 1882, Despatches, China, NA.

80. Frelinghuysen to Young, January 16, 22, 1883, Instructions, China, NA.

81. Foote to Frelinghuysen, Despatches, Korea, NA; *Kojong silnok*, April 13, 20th year, Kojong; *Kojong sidaesa*, vol. 2, pp. 438–439.

82. *U.S. Statutes at Large* vol. 23, pp. 720–725.

83. Ibid., vol. 8, p. 75.

84. Ibid., vol. 11, pp. 597–598, 723–724; vol. 8, pp. 572–605; vol. 12, pp. 1023–1030.

85. Chung, ed., *Korean Treaties*, pp. 133–163.

86. Jones, "Foreign Diplomacy," p. 289; Hagan, *American Gunboat Diplomacy*, p. 10.

87. See the two instructions: Blaine to Shufeldt, November 14, 1881; Frelinghuysen to Shufeldt, January 6, 1882, Instructions, China, NA. See also Drake, *Empire of the Seas*, pp. 303–304, 335–336.

88. Robert W. Shufeldt to Mary A. Shufeldt, April 28, 1880, Shufeldt papers. For general discussion on the motivation, see Kersten, *Naval Aristocracy*, pp. 187–267.

89. Bingham to Blaine, June 20, 1882, Despatches, Japan, NA; Holcombe to Blaine, December 12, 1881, Despatches, China, NA; Shufeldt to Frelinghuysen, January 23, 1882, Despatches, China, NA. See Deuchler, *Confucian Gentlemen*, pp. 86, 114.

90. Chien, *Opening of Korea*, p. 92. See also Kim, *Last Phase*, p. 276. The author traces the Chinese interest in the opening of Korea back to late 1876. For discussions of the Chinese motives see also Drake, *Empire of the Seas*, pp. 299–303, and Kim and Kim, *Korea*, pp. 27–28. On Li's motive see Hunt, *Special Relationship*, pp. 128–130.

91. *Kojong sidaesa*, vol. 2, pp. 183–186. See also Kim and Kim, *Korea and the Politics of Imperialism*, p. 28.

92. Shufeldt to Thompson, October 13, 1880, enclosure in Thompson to Evarts, December 14, 1880, Miscellaneous, State Department (microfilm, NA, m179 r576). See also Deuchler, *Confucian Gentlemen*, pp. 219–228 for Korea's reform effort.

93. Okuhira, *Chōsen kaikoku*, p. 166; Jae Souk Sohn, "The United States and the Opening of Korea," *Koreana Quarterly*, 7 (1965): 57. See also Hunt, *Special Relationship*, pp. 130–132.

94. Dennett, *Roosevelt and the Russo-Japanese War*, pp. 103–104; Bridgham, "American Policy toward Korean Independence," p. 19; Okuhira, *Chōsen kaikoku*, p. 181. See Hagan, *American Gunboat Diplomacy*, p. 10: the author calls the opening of Korea by Commodore Shufeldt "one of the most vivid examples in a well-established pattern of global gunboat diplomacy"; Drake, *Empire of the Seas*, p. 10; Kim and Kim, *Korea*, pp. 29–30.

95. Hunter (Acting Secretary of State) to Shufeldt, September 6, 1882, Instructions, China, NA.

96. Dept. of State, *FRUS* (1884), pp. vii–viii. For his retirement, life, and death see Drake, *Empire of the Seas*, pp. 324–333.

97. Robert W. Shufeldt to Mary A. Shufeldt, May 20, 1882, Shufeldt papers.

CHAPTER 3

1. Inouye to Bingham, August 1, 1882, enclosure in Bingham to Frelinghuysen, August 2, 1882, Despatches, Japan, NA; Yi Sŏn-kŭn, *Han'guksa*, pp. 462–479. See also Kim and Kim, *Korea*, pp. 33–40, for a description of the event; and Conroy, *Japanese Seizure*, pp. 101–106.

2. Tel., Young to Frelinghuysen, July 30, 1882, Despatches, China, NA.

3. Tel., Frelinghuysen to Young, August 2, 1882, Instructions, China, NA.

4. Young to Cotton, August 7, 1882, enclosure in Young to Frelinghuysen, August 19, 1882, Despatches, China, NA.

5. Young to Frelinghuysen, October 2, 1882, ibid.

6. Cotton to Young, August 29, 1882, enclosure in ibid.

7. Frelinghuysen to Bingham, September 20, 1882, Instructions, Japan, NA.

8. For the details of the Japanese moves and terms of the treaty see Bingham to Frelinghuysen, November 20, 1882, Despatches, Japan, NA; and Yi Sŏn-kŭn, *Han'guksa*, pp. 494–504, 518–524.

9. *Jongjŏng yŏnp'yo*, p. 136; Yi Sŏn-kŭn, *Han'guksa*, pp. 489–494, 498–500, 504–517.

10. For a somewhat similar view see Jones, "Foreign Diplomacy," p. 337. See also Deuchler, *Confucian Gentlemen*, p. 147.

11. Allen Johnson et al., eds., *Dictionary of American Biography*, 22 vols. (New York: Scribner's Sons, 1928–1958), vol. 6, pp. 501–502; Frelinghuysen to Foote, March 17, 1882, Frelinghuysen papers (Library of Congress, Washington, D.C.); Yur-Bok Lee, *Diplomatic Relations*, p. 52.

12. Foote to Frelinghuysen, May 24, 25, 1883, Despatches, Korea (microfilm, NA, m134 r1); *Kojong sidaesa*, vol. 2, pp. 438–439; *New York Times*, July 19, 1883, 3:1–3.

13. See the enclosures in Foote to Frelinghuysen, May 25, 1883, Despatches, Korea (microfilm, NA, m134 r1).

14. Frelinghuysen to Foote, March 9, 17, 1883, Instructions, Korea (microfilm, NA, m77 r109).

15. Frelinghuysen to William H. Hunt, December 28, 1883, Instructions, Russia (microfilm, NA, m77 r138); Frelinghuysen to Levi P. Morton, January 8, 1883, Instructions, France (microfilm, NA, m77 r60).

16. Foote to Frelinghuysen, May 1, 24, October 23, 1883, Despatches, Korea (microfilm, NA, m134 r1); John Davis to Foote, October 6, 1883, Instructions, Korea (microfilm, NA, m77 r109); Frelinghuysen to Foote, December 24, 1883, Instructions, Korea (microfilm, NA, m77 r109).

17. Foote to Frelinghuysen, December 18, 1883; July 26, 31, September 4, 1884, Despatches, Korea (microfilm, m134 r1).

18. Foote to Frelinghuysen, September 1, 1884, ibid.

19. Chandler to Frelinghuysen, March 16, 1883, Misc. Corresp., State Department (microfilm, NA, m179 r627); Foote to Frelinghuysen, May 25, 1883, Despatches, Korea (microfilm, NA, m134 r1). See also John L. Davis to Foote, January 9, 1884, Navy Corresp., Seoul Legation Papers (NA, rg84).

20. S. Cotton to Foote, May 27, 1883, Navy Corresp., Seoul Legation Papers (NA, rg84). For some of the survey activities see Fred C. Bohm and Robert W. Swartout, Jr., eds., *Naval Surgeon in Yi Korea: The Journal of George W. Woods*, Korea Research Monograph 10 (Berkeley, Calif.: Institute of East Asian Studies, University of California, Berkeley, 1984), pp. 23–108.

21. Bingham to Frelinghuysen, April 20, 1883, Despatches, Japan, NA.

22. Davis to Chandler, May 28, 1883, Domestic File, State Department (microfilm, NA, m40 r98); Chandler to Frelinghuysen, May 31, 1883, Misc. Corresp., State Department (microfilm, NA, m179 r631); Foote to Frelinghuysen, July 19, 1883, Domestic File, State Department (microfilm, NA, m40 r99); Chandler to Frelinghuysen, September 17, 1883, Misc. Corresp., State Department (microfilm, NA, m179 r638).

23. Foulk to Cho Peung Ho, December 24, 1884, Seoul Legation Note to Korean Foreign Office (NA, rg84).

24. Chien, *Opening of Korea*, p. 134. See also Wright, "Adaptation of Ch'ing Diplomacy," pp. 380–381.

25. Chien, *Opening of Korea*, p. 198; Nelson has a similar view in his *Korea and the Old Order*, p. 164. See also Yur-Bok Lee, *Diplomatic Relations*, p. 63; his view on the object of the change is also similar to Chien's. See also Deuchler, *Confucian Gentlemen*, p. 227.

26. Frelinghuysen to Young, August 4, 1882, Instructions, China, NA.

27. Ibid., January 22, 1883.

28. Frelinghuysen to Foote, March 17, 1883, Instructions, Korea (microfilm, NA, m77 r109).

29. Holcombe's memorandum on the convention, enclosure in Young to Frelinghuysen, December 26, 1882, Despatches, China, NA; *Kojong sidaesa*, vol. 2, pp. 370–378.

30. Frelinghuysen to Foote, March 17, 1883, Instructions, Korea (microfilm, NA, m77 r109).

31. Chien, *Opening of Korea*, p. 121; Jones, "Foreign Diplomacy," p. 343.

32. Young to Frelinghuysen, March 21, August 6, 1883, Despatches, China, NA; Foote to Frelinghuysen, June 30, October 30, November 10, 1883, Despatches, Korea (microfilm, NA, m134 r1).

33. Foote to Frelinghuysen, January 17, May 28, July 18, September 10, October 7, November 11, 1884, Despatches, Korea (microfilm, NA, m134 r1).

34. Foote to Frelinghuysen, October 19, 1883; April 8, September 3, 17, November 15, 1884, ibid. (r1–2). Also see Lee Kwang-nin (Yi Kwang-nin), *Han'guk kaehwasa yŏn'gu* (A study of the enlightenment in Korea) (Seoul: Ilchogak, 1969), pp. 159–189; Donald M. Bishop, "Shared Failure: American Military Advisors in Korea, 1888–1896," *Transactions of the Royal Society, Korea Branch* 58 (1983): 53–76.

35. Frelinghuysen to Foote, November 6, 1884, Instructions, Korea (microfilm, NA, m77 r109).

36. Foote to Frelinghuysen, October 19, April 8, September 3, November 15, 1884, Despatches, Korea (microfilm, NA, m134 r1–2). Also see Swartout, *Mandarins, Gunboats, and Power Politics*, pp. 42–44.

37. Frelinghuysen to Foote, September 18, 1883, Instructions, Korea (microfilm, NA, m77 r109).

38. Foote to Frelinghuysen, July 13, 1883, Despatches, Korea (microfilm, NA, m134 r1).

39. Foote to Frelinghuysen, July 13, 1883; June 17, 1884, ibid.; Frelinghuysen to Foote, August 30, 1883, Instructions, Korea (microfilm, NA, m77 r109).

40. Frelinghuysen's instruction to Foote of October 16, 1883, is a good summary of the mission's schedule, Instructions, Korea (microfilm, NA, m77 r109). See also *New York Times*, September 19, 1883, 8:3; *New York Tribune*, September 18, 1883, 8:1.

41. Foote to Frelinghuysen, June 17, 1884, Despatches, Korea (microfilm, NA, m134 r1).

42. Foulk to Chandler, enclosure in Chandler to Frelinghuysen, August 5, 1884, Misc. Corresp., State Department (microfilm, NA, m179 r659). See also Kim Wŏn-mo, "Kyŏnmi Sajŏl Hong Yŏng-sik pokmŏng mundapki" (Report of Hong Yŏng-sik, an emissary to the United States) *Sahakchi* 15 (1981): 183–230. See also idem, "Choson bobingsaŭi Miguksahaeng (1883) yŏn'gu" (A study of the Korean mission to the United States [1883]), *Tongbang hakchi* 49 (December 1985): 33–87, 50 (March 1986): 333–381.

43. Yi Sŏn-kŭn, *Han'guksa*, pp. 565–588, 595–605. See also Cook, *Korea's 1884 Incident*, pp. 102–218, for the story from Kim Ok'kyun's side.

44. Kim Ok-kyun, *Kapsin ilki*, pp. 121–122; Yun, *Yun Ch'i-ho ilki*, vol. 1, p. 274.

45. Foote to Frelinghuysen, December 5, 1884, Despatches, Korea (microfilm, NA, m134 r1); Yun, *Yun Chi-ho ilki*, vol. 1, pp. 276–286; Yi Sŏn-kŭn, *Han'guksa*, p. 662. See also Deuchler, *Confucian Gentlemen*, pp. 205–212; Kim and Kim, *Korea*, pp. 41–51; Conroy, *Japanese Seizure*, pp. 139–158.

46. Bingham to Frelinghuysen, January 23, 1885, Despatches, Japan, NA; *Kuhan'guk oekyomunsŏ* (Diplomatic documents of old Korea) (hereafter KOM) (Seoul: Koryŏ taeha'ckyo ch'ulp'anpu, 1965–1973), vol. 1, pp. 205–206;

Yi Sön-kŭn, *Han'guksa*, pp. 672–682. See also Kim and Kim, *Korea*, pp. 52–53, Conroy, *Japanese Seizure*, p. 171–174.

47. Chien, *Opening of Korea*, p. 168; Tsiang, "Sino-Japanese Diplomatic Relations," p. 87; Yi Sön-kŭn, *Han'guksa*, pp. 682–693. See also Deuchler, *Confucian Gentlemen*, pp. 212–214.

48. Richard B. Hubbard to Bayard, December 18, 1885, Despatches, Japan, NA. See also Deuchler, *Confucian Gentlemen*, p. 216; Kim and Kim, *Korea*, pp. 53–58.

49. Foote to Frelinghuysen, December 17, 19, 27, 1884, Despatches, Korea (microfilm, NA, m134 r1–2).

50. Foote to Frelinghuysen, December 17, 1884, ibid. (r2); Yun, *Yun Ch'i-ho ilki*, vol. 1, pp. 290–298.

51. Davis to Chandler, December 13, 1884, enclosure in Chandler to Frelinghuysen, January 15, 1885, Misc. Corresp., State Department (microfilm, NA, m179 r667).

52. Frelinghuysen to Foote, July 14, 1884, Instructions, Korea (microfilm, NA, m77 r109); Foote to Frelinghuysen, September 17, 1885, Despatches, Korea (microfilm, NA, m134 r1).

53. Frelinghuysen to Bingham, January 7, 1885, Instructions, Japan, NA; Johnson et al., eds., *Dictionary of American Biography*, vol. 6, p. 501.

54. Dennett, "Early American Policy," p. 93.

55. Ibid., p. 96; Jones, "Foreign Diplomacy," p. 512; Reordan, "Role of George Clayton Foulk," p. 280.

56. Bingham to Bayard, June 1, 1885, Despatches, Japan, NA.

57. Foulk to Bayard, July 22, 1885, Despatches, Korea (microfilm, NA, m134 r2).

58. Foulk to Bayard, November 25, 1885, ibid.

59. Foulk to Bayard, October 14, 15, 20, 1885, ibid.

60. Foulk to Bayard, April 28, 1886, ibid.; Charles Denby to Bayard, December 3, 8, 1885, Despatches, China, NA.

61. Denby to Bayard, October 12, 18, 1885, Despatches, China, NA; Denby to Foulk, January 6, 1886, Misc. Corresp., Seoul Legation, (NA, rg84).

62. Bayard to Denby, November 16, December 9, 1885, Instructions, China, NA.

63. Chandler to Frelinghuysen, November 3, 1883, Misc. Corresp., State Department (microfilm, NA, m179 r641).

64. Frelinghuysen to Foulk, November 12, 1883, Instructions, Korea (microfilm, NA, m77 r109).

65. Foulk to Bayard, November 25, 1885; September 24, 1886; William M. Parker to Bayard, June 13, 1886, Despatches, Korea (microfilm, NA, m134 r3).

66. Johnson et al., eds., *Dictionary of American Biography*, vol. 6, p. 559.

67. Foulk to Bayard, September 24, 1886, Despatches, Korea (microfilm, NA, m134 r3); Pollard, "American Relations with Korea," p. 444.

68. Foulk to William W. Rockhill, enclosure in Rockhill to Bayard, January 3, 1887, Despatches, Korea (microfilm, NA, m134 r4); Rockhill to Kim Yun Sik, January 11, 1887, enclosure in Rockhill to Bayard, January 24, 1887, ibid.

69. For the defense see Foulk to Kim Yun Sik, January 11, 1887; Rockhill to Kim Yun Sik, December 31, 1886; January 8, 1887, Seoul Legation Note to Korean Government (NA, rg84); Rockhill to Kim Yun Sik, January 11, 1887, enclosure in Rockhill to Bayard, January 24, 1887, Despatches, Korea (microfilm, NA, m134 r4); Dinsmore to Kim Yun Sik, May 2, 10, 1887, Seoul Legation Note to Korean Government (NA, rg84); Dinsmore to Yuan Shih-kai, May 26, 1887, enclosure in Dinsmore to Bayard, May 30, 1887, Despatches, Korea (microfilm, NA, m134 r4). For the process of the recall see Kim Yun Sik to Dinsmore, May 8, 1887, Korean Note to Seoul Legation (NA, rg84); Dinsmore to Bayard, May 9, 1887, Despatches, Korea (microfilm, NA, m134 r4); Shu Cheon Pon (Chinese minister in Washington) to Bayard, June 8, 1887; Bayard to Shu, June 16, 1887, enclosures in Bayard to William C. Whitney (Navy Secretary), June 17, 1887, Naval Record Collection (NA, rg45); Bayard to Dinsmore, June 7, 23, 1887, Instructions, Korea (microfilm, NA, m77 r109).

70. Foulk to Bayard, November 25, 1885, Despatches, Korea (microfilm, NA, m134 r3).

71. Bayard to Foulk, March 31, 1886, Instructions, Korea (microfilm, NA, m77 r109); Bayard to Whitney, November 1, 1887, Domestic File, State Department (microfilm, NA, m40 r108).

72. Bayard to Whitney, November 19, 1887, Domestic File, State Department (microfilm, NA, m40 r108).

73. Dinsmore to Bayard, June 25, 1887, Despatches, Korea (microfilm, NA, m134 r4); Dennett, "Early American Policy," pp. 86, 101; Chong-sik Lee, *Diplomatic Relations*, p. 182; Jones, "Foreign Diplomacy," p. 505; Reordan, "Role of George Clayton Foulk," pp. 276, 286.

74. Noble, "Korean Mission to the United States," p. 20; Johnson et al., eds., *Dictionary of American Biography*, vol. 6, pp. 559–560; Donald M. Bishop, "Policy and Personality in Early Korean-American Relations: The Case of George Clayton Foulk," in Nahm, ed., *United States and Korea*, pp. 27–63.

75. Foulk to Frelinghuysen, March 5, 1885, Despatches, Korea (microfilm, NA, m134 r2); Bayard to Foulk, July 15, 1885, Instructions, Korea (microfilm, NA, m77 r109); Foulk to Bayard, June 3, 1886, Despatches, Korea (microfilm, NA, m134 r3); Harrington, *God, Mammon and the Japanese*, p. 55.

76. Bayard to Parker, May 5, 1886, Instructions, Korea (microfilm, NA, m77 r109); Parker to Bayard, July 6, 1886, Despatches, Korea (microfilm, NA, m134 r3).

77. Foulk to Frelinghuysen, March 12, 1885; Foulk to Bayard, April 28, May 9, 13, 15, 16, 20, June 18, 1885, Despatches, Korea (microfilm, NA, m134 r2); Foulk to Bayard, December 9, 1885; November 3, 4, 6, 1886, ibid. (r3); Rockhill to Bayard, February 13, 1887; Dinsmore to Bayard, June 29, 1887, ibid. (r4).

78. Foulk to Bayard, May 9, 16, June 18, July 22, August 16, 1885, ibid. (r2).

79. Foulk to Bayard, May 25, September 10, November 17, 1885; February 26, 1886, ibid. (r3). See also Swartout, *Mandarins, Gunboats, and Power Politics*, pp. 42–44, 56–58.

80. Bayard to Foulk, March 19, September 22, 1885, Instructions, Korea (microfilm, NA, m77 r109).

81. Bayard to Foulk, August 19, 1885, February 20, 1886, ibid.

82. For a similar characterization, see Dennett, "Early American Policy," p. 96; Jones, "Foreign Diplomacy," p. 512; Reordan, "The Role of George Clayton Foulk," p. 280.

83. Foulk to Bayard, May 19, 1885, Despatches, Korea (microfilm, NA, m134 r2); Foulk to Kim Yun Sik, May 20, June 26, 1885, Seoul Legation Note to Korean Foreign Office (NA, rg84). For the friction between the secretaries of state and American representatives in Seoul see Swartout, "United States Ministers to Korea, pp. 29–40.

84. Kim Wŏn-mo, "Yŏn Se-keŭi Hanbando anboch'aek (1886)" (Yuan Shih-kai's security policy for the Korean peninsula), Tongyanghak 16 (supplement) (1986): 227–261; Yur-Bok Lee, Korean Legation; Swartout, Mandarins, Gunboats, and Power Politics, pp. 23–152.

85. Reordan, "Role of George Clayton Foulk," p. 276.

86. Dinsmore to Bayard, May 3, 1887, Despatches, Korea (microfilm, NA, m134 r4).

87. Dinsmore to Bayard, May 27, 1887, ibid.

88. Kojong sidaesa, vol, 2, p. 941; Yi Sŏn-kŭn, Han'guksa, p. 843.

89. Dinsmore to Bayard, August 20, 1887, Despatches, Korea (microfilm, NA, m134 r4); Pak Chung Yang to Dinsmore, September 16, 1887, KOM, vol. 10, p. 316.

90. Dinsmore to Bayard, October 15, 1887, Despatches, Korea (microfilm, NA, m134 r4); Dinsmore to Yuan, September 27, 1887, Misc. Corresp., Seoul Legation Papers (NA, rg84).

91. Yuan to Korean Foreign Office, September 23, 1887, and n.d., enclosure in Dinsmore to Bayard, September 30, 1887 Despatches, Korea (microfilm, NA, m134 r4).

92. Tel., Dinsmore to Bayard, September 30, 1887, ibid.

93. Dinsmore to Bayard, November 11, 1887, ibid.; Kojong sidaesa, vol. 2, p. 942.

94. Dinsmore to Yuan, September 27, 1887, Misc. Corresp., Seoul Legation Papers (NA, rg84).

95. Dinsmore to Yuan, October 1, 1887, enclosure in Dinsmore to Bayard, October 1, 1887, Despatches, Korea (microfilm, NA, m134 r4).

96. Yuan to Dinsmore, October 3, 1887, enclosure in Dinsmore to Bayard, October 4, 1887, ibid.

97. Dinsmore to Yuan, October 7, 1887, ibid.

98. Yuan to Dinsmore, October 10, 1887, enclosure in Dinsmore to Bayard, October 15, 1887, ibid.

99. Dinsmore to Yuan, October 12, 1887, enclosure in Dinsmore to Bayard, October 12, 1887, ibid.

100. Yuan to Dinsmore, October 14, 1887, enclosure in Dinsmore to Bayard, October 14, 1887, ibid.

101. Dinsmore to Bayard, October 5, 1887, ibid.

102. Tel., Bayard to Denby, October 6, 1887, Instructions, China, NA. See also Bayard to Denby, October 7, 1887, ibid.

103. Tsungli yamen to Denby, October 26, 1887, enclosure in Denby to Bayard, October 27, 1887, Despatches, China, NA; Yuan to Dinsmore, October 12, 1887, enclosure in Dinsmore to Bayard, November 11, 1887, Despatches, Korea (microfilm, NA, m134 r4).

104. Denby to Bayard, October 27, 1887, Despatches, China, NA; Dinsmore to Bayard, November 11, 1887, Despatches, Korea (microfilm, NA, m134 r4).

105. Yuan to Cho, October 21, 1887, *KOM*, vol. 8, p. 382; Yuan to Dinsmore, October 21, 1887, enclosure in Dinsmore to Bayard, November 11, 1887, Despatches, Korea (microfilm, NA, m134 r4).

106. Dinsmore to Bayard, November 17, 1887, Despatches, Korea (microfilm, NA, m134 r4).

107. Yuan to Dinsmore, October 21, 1887, enclosure in Dinsmore to Bayard, November 11, 1887, ibid.

108. *Kojong sidaesa*, vol. 2, p. 942.

109. Yuan to Cho, November 8, 1887, *KOM*, vol. 8, p. 384.

110. Ibid.; Dinsmore to Bayard, November 17, 1887, Despatches, Korea (microfilm, NA, m134 r4).

111. Bayard to Dinsmore, January 26, 1888, Instructions, Korea (microfilm, NA, m77 r109); Chang Yen Hoon to Bayard, January 9, 1888, Notes from Chinese Legation to State Department, NA.

112. Bayard to Dinsmore, January 26, 1888, Instructions, Korea (microfilm, NA, m77 r109).

113. *Kojong sidaesa*, vol. 2, p. 957.

114. Yuan to Cho, January 13, 14 (2 notes), 15 (2 notes), 1888, *KOM*, vol. 8, pp. 396, 398, 399–400.

115. Cho to Yuan, January 17, 1888 ibid., p. 400.

116. Statement of Pak to the President, January 17, 1888; Statement from the President to Pak, January 17, 1888, Notes from Korean Legation to State Department (microfilm, NA, m166 r1). See also Pak to Bayard, January 18, 1888, ibid.; *New York Times*, January 18, 1888, 10:4.

117. Yuan to Cho, November 11, 1888; March 2, August 20, 27, 31, September 3, 5, 1889, *KOM*, vol. 8, pp. 492, 522, 584, 587, 589, 591, 592–595; Dinsmore to Blaine, December 10, 24, 1888, Despatches, Korea (microfilm, NA, m134 r5). See the recent studies on the Pak mission: Swartout, *Mandarins, Gunboats, and Power Politics*, pp. 88–95; Yur-Bok Lee, *Korean Legation*.

118. For the Korean side see Dinsmore to Bayard, October 15, 1887, Despatches, Korea (microfilm, NA, m134 r4); Translation of the Korean King's memorial to Chinese Government, enclosure in Denby to Bayard, December 9, 1887, Despatches, China NA. For the Chinese side see Yuan to Korean Foreign Office, September 23, 1887, enclosure in Dinsmore to Bayard, September 30, 1887, Despatches, Korea (microfilm, NA, m134 r4); Tsungli yamen to Denby, October 26, 1887, enclosure in Denby to Bayard, October 27, 1887, Despatches, China, NA; Chang Yen Hoon to Bayard, January 9, 1887, Notes from Chinese Legation to State Department, NA; Bayard to Dinsmore, January 26, 1888, Instructions, China (microfilm, m77 r109).

119. Dinsmore to Bayard, October 25, 1887, Despatches, Korea (microfilm, NA, m134 r4).

120. Bayard to Denby, November 4, 1887, Instructions, China, NA.

121. *New York Times*, January 17, 1890, 4:2.

122. Wharton to Heard, April 25, 1890, Instructions, Korea (microfilm, NA, m77 r109); Wharton to Denby, June 27, 1890, Instructions, China, NA.

123. Blaine to Chaille-Long, March 15, 1889, Instructions, Korea (microfilm, NA, m77 r109).

124. Denby to Blaine, December 9, 1889, Despatches, China, NA; Blaine to Denby, June 27, 1890, Instructions, China, NA.

125. Heard to Blaine, June 3, 1890, Despatches, Korea (microfilm, NA, m134 r6); *New York Times*, August 18, 1890, 1:1.

126. Heard to Blaine, October 15, 1890, Despatches, Korea (microfilm, NA, m134 r7).

127. Dinsmore to Blaine, February 1, 1890; Heard to Blaine, June 8, 1890; Yuan to Heard, December 24, 1890, enclosure in Heard to Blaine, January 22, 1890, ibid. (r6).

128. Blaine to Heard, March 20, 1890; Gresham to Horace N. Allen, November 21, 1893, Instructions, Korea (microfilm, NA, m77 r109).

129. Dinsmore to Bayard, April 13, June 21, 25, 1887; February 7, 1888, Despatches, Korea (microfilm, NA, m134 r4); Bayard to Dinsmore, March 21, 1888, Instructions, Korea (microfilm, NA, m77 r109). See also Swartout, *Mandarins, Gunboats, and Power Politics*, pp. 104–123; Yur-Bok Lee, *Diplomatic Relations*, pp. 119, 163, 171.

130. Andrew D. White to Bayard, April 1, 1885, Application File, State Department, NA; Heard to Blaine, July 10, 1890; June 22, 1891, Despatches, Korea (microfilm, NA, m134 r6, r8).

131. Heard to Blaine, October 21, 1890, Despatches, Korea (microfilm, NA, m134 r7).

132. James D. Porter to Dinsmore, August 9, 1887, Instructions, Korea (microfilm, NA, m77 r109); Dinsmore to Bayard, October 1, 1887; November 30, 1888, Despatches, Korea (microfilm, NA, m134 r4, r5).

133. Tel., Chandler to Whitney, June 22, 1888, Naval Area File (microfilm, NA, m625 r350); Dinsmore to Bayard, July 1, 1888, Despatches, Korea (microfilm, m134 r5); Beard to Blaine, June 7, October 15, 1890, ibid. (r6, r7); Min Chong Mok to Heard, October 15, 1890, *KOM*, vol. 10, p. 527.

134. Heard to Wharton, December 31, 1892, Seoul Consul Despatches, Consul Series 36 (microfilm, NA, m167 r1).

135. Allen to Gresham, October 26, 1893, ibid., Series 50; Allen to Gresham, November 20, 1893, Despatches, Korea (microfilm, NA, m134 r10). For Townsends's activities in Korea, see Cook, *Pioneer American Businessman in Korea*.

136. Dinsmore to Bayard, February 7, 1888, Despatches, Korea (microfilm, NA, m134 r5).

137. Dinsmore to Bayard, April 21, 1888, ibid.; Circular to All American Missionary Residents in Korea, May 3, 1888, Misc. Corresp., Seoul Legation Papers (NA, rg84).

138. Blaine to Dinsmore, May 1, 1889, Instructions, Korea (microfilm, NA, m77 r109); Dinsmore to Min Chong Mok, November 22, 1889; Heard to Min, May 31, 1892, Notes to Korean Foreign Office, Seoul Legation Papers

(NA, rg84); Gresham to Allen, February 5, 1894, Instructions, Korea (microfilm, NA, m77 r109).

139. Heard to Blaine, January 5, October 30, 1890; January 26, 1891, Despatches, Korea (microfilm, NA, m134 r7). For the role of American advisers in Korea, see Young I. Lew, "American Advisers in Korea, 1885-1894: Anatomy of Failure," in Nahm, *United States and Korea*, pp. 64-90.

140. Dinsmore to Cho Pyŏng Sik, April 10, 1888, Legation Note to Korean Foreign Office (NA, rg84); Dinsmore to Blaine, September 25, 1889, Despatches, Korea (microfilm, NA, m134 r6); Heard to Blaine, March 2, 1891, ibid. (r7). See Jones, "Foreign Diplomacy," p. 490; Bishop, "Shared Failure," pp. 53-76.

141. Nam Chung Chul to Joseph R. Herod, August 27, 1893, enclosure in Allen to Gresham, September 6, 1893; Allen to Gresham, September 6, October 16, 1893, Despatches, Korea (microfilm, NA, m134 r10); Gresham to Ye Sung Soo, November 22, 1893, Notes to Korean Legation, State Department (microfilm, NA, m99 r68).

142. Heard to Blaine, May 28, December 17, 1891, Despatches, Korea (microfilm, NA, m134 r7); Allen to Gresham, October 16, 1893, February 12, 1894, ibid. (r10). For the role of American teachers in Korea, see Yi Kwangnin, *Han'guk kaehwasa yŏn'gu*, pp. 99-106.

143. Heard to Blaine, June 3, 1891, Despatches, Korea (microfilm, NA, m134 r8).

144. Park Chung Yang to Bayard, July 16, 1888, Notes from Korean Legation (microfilm, NA, m166 r1); Dinsmore to Bayard, January 21, 1889, Despatches, Korea (microfilm, NA, m134 r5); Heard to Gresham, March 21, 1893, ibid. (r9); Allen to Gresham, September 28, 1893, ibid. (r10).

145. Frelinghuysen to Foote, March 18, 1883, Instructions, Korea (microfilm, NA, m77 r109); Frelinghuysen to Young, April 11, 1883; John Davis to Young, April 26, 1883, Instructions, China, NA.

146. Bayard to Foulk, September 22, 1885; Blaine to Long, March 15, 1889, Instructions, Korea (microfilm, NA, m77 r109).

147. Denby to Bayard, October 12, 28, 1885; February 6, 1886, Despatches, China, NA; Bayard to Denby, November 16, 1885, Instructions, China, NA.

148. Bayard to Foulk, September 22, 1885, Instructions, Korea (microfilm, NA, m77 r109).

149. Frelinghuysen to Foote, March 17, 1883; Blaine to Dinsmore, May 7, 1889, ibid.

CHAPTER 4

1. See Kaplan, *System and Process*, pp. 22-36, esp. p. 22, in which Kaplan points out that at least five powers are necessary to maintain a stable balance-of-power system.

2. See Liska, *International Equilibrium*, pp. 36-39. See also Morgenthau, *Politics among Nations*, 4th ed., p. 171.

3. Memoir of the conversation between Gresham and Tateno, July 7, 1894, Note from Japanese Legation to Department of State (microfilm, NA, 163, r5). See also Maki, *Japanese Imperialism*, p. 195; Iriye, *Pacific Estrange-*

ment, p. 80; Tanin and Yohan, *Militarism and Fascism*, p. 37; Yanaga, *Japan since Perry*, p. 331; Ro, "Power Politics in Korea," p. 191.

4. *New York Times*, August 1, 1894, 4:4; November 8, 1894, 4:2; William E. Griffis, "Jack and the Giant in Korea," *Outlook* 50 (1894): 213.

5. *Tonghakran kirok*. See also Kim and Kim, *Korea*, pp. 75–79; Conroy, *Japanese Seizure*, pp. 229–241; Chong-sik Lee, *Politics of Korean Nationalism*, pp. 19–33.

6. *Maech'ŏn yarok*, pp. 130–133; *Kojong sidaesa*, vol. 3, pp. 438–443.

7. Denby to Gresham, June 9, 1894, Despatches, China, NA; Yuan to Cho, June 3, 1894, *KOM*, vol. 9, p. 311; *Kojong sidaesa*, vol. 3, pp. 443–445.

8. Wang to Mutsu, June 6, 1894, enclosure in Otori to Cho, June 28, 1894, *KOM*, vol. 2, pp. 651–652; Denby to Gresham, June 9, 1894, Despatches, China, NA; *Maech'ŏn yarok*, p. 135; *Kojong sidaesa*, vol. 3, p. 446.

9. Dun to Gresham, July 15, 1894, Despatches, Japan, NA. See also Sugimura to Cho, June 9, 1894, *KOM*, vol. 2, pp. 632–633.

10. Cho to Sugimura, June 8, 10, 11, 1894, *KOM*, vol. 2, pp. 632, 634.

11. *North China Daily News*, June 20, 1894, enclosure in Denby to Gresham, July 5, 1894, Despatches, China, NA. For a similar view, see also Lensen, *Balance of Intrigue*, vol. 1, pp. 149–150.

12. Mutsu to Otori, June 22, 1894, Japanese Penetration of Korea, (microfilm, Hoover, no. 2). For the Japanese side, see Conroy, *Japanese Seizure*, pp. 239–245, 261.

13. Uhl to Ye, June 22, 1894, Notes from Department of State to Foreign Legations in the United States, 1834–1905, Korea, Persia, and Siam (microfilm, NA, m99 r68).

14. Tel., Gresham to Sill, June 22, 1894, Instructions, Korea (microfilm, NA, m77 r109).

15. Cho to Sill, June 24, 1894, *KOM*, vol. 9, p. 35; Cho to Celus Gardner, June 24, 1894, ibid., vol. 13, p. 547; Cho to Karl Ivanovich Weber, June 24, 1894, ibid., vol. 15, pp. 558–559. See also Lensen, *Balance of Intrigue*, vol. 1, p. 147.

16. Sill, Paul de Kehberg, Lefevre, C. T. Gardeus to Otori and Yuan, June 25, 1894, enclosure in Sill to Cho, July 3, 1894, *KOM*, vol. 11, pp. 38–39.

17. Otori to Sill and others, June 25, 1894; Yuan to Sill and others, June 25, 1894, Misc. Corresp., Seoul Legation (NA, rg84).

18. Sill to Otori, July 9, 1894; Otori to Sill, July 10, 1894, ibid.

19. On the reform issue see Otori to Kojong, June 27, 1894, *KOM*, vol. 2, p. 650; Otori to Cho, June 28, 19, July 3, 1894, ibid., pp. 661–662. For the dependency issue see Otori to Cho, June 28, 29, July 3, 1894, ibid., pp. 661, 665, 660–661; Cho to Otori, June 30, 1894, ibid., 656–657. For a discussion on the reform see Kim and Kim, *Korea*, pp. 81–83; Conroy, *Japanese Seizure*, pp. 245–252.

20. The Palace [Seoul] to Yi, June 28, 1894, Notes form Korean Legation to Department of State (microfilm, NA, m166).

21. Tel., Gresham to Dun, June 29, 1894, Instructions, Japan, NA.

22. Tel., Dun to Gresham, July 3, 1894, Despatches, Japan, NA. See also Dun to Gresham, July 13, 1894, ibid.

23. N.d. [July 1894], Notes from Korean Legation (microfilm, NA, m166).

24. Yi to Gresham, July 5, 1894, ibid.

25. Tel., Gresham to Dun, July 7, 1894, Instructions, Japan (microfilm, NA, m77 r107).

26. Dun to Mutsu, July 8, 1894, NGB, vol. 27, pt. 2, p. 296; Mutsu to Dun, July 9, 1894, ibid., pp. 297–298; tel., Dun to Gresham, July 10, 1894, Despatches, Japan (microfilm, NA, m133 r67).

27. See Dulebohn, Foreign Policy, p. 12.

28. Richardson, ed., Messages and Papers, vol. 11, p. 4886. See also Dulebohn, Foreign Policy, pp. 5–6, 10; Nevins, Grover Cleveland, p. 560; May, Imperial Diplomacy, p. 35.

29. Dulebohn, Foreign Policy, pp. 42, 91. See also Williams, Mr. Cleveland, pp. 3–4, 23, 56; Nevins, Grover Cleveland, p. 560; May, Imperial Diplomacy, p. 37.

30. Richardson, ed., Messages and Papers, vol. 18, p. 5957.

31. Gresham to Palmer, January 15, 1894, Gresham papers.

32. Gresham to Cooper, February 5, 1894, ibid.

33. Gresham, Life, vol. 1, p. vii. See also Montgomery Schuyler, "Walter Q. Gresham," in Bemis, ed., American Secretaries of State, vol. 8, p. 263.

34. Memorandum, July 7, 1894, Notes from Japanese Legation (microfilm, NA, m163 r5).

35. Dennett, "American 'Good Offices' in Asia," pp. 18–20.

36. New York Herald, July 19, 1894, 8:3.

37. New York Daily Tribune, July 19, 1894, 6:2.

38. New York Herald, July 21, 1894, 6:2.

39. George F. Parker, Recollection of Grover Cleveland (New York: Century 1909), pp. 359, 376.

40. Gresham to Bayard, July 20, 1894, Dept. of State, FRUS (1894), appendix 1, p. 30; Denby to Gresham, July 6, 1894, Despatches, China, NA.

41. Tel., Denby to Gresham, July 8, 1894, Despatches, China, NA; tels., Li to Yang, July 12, 15, 1894, Notes from Chinese Legation to Department of State, NA.

42. Sill to Dun, July 26, 1894, enclosure in Dun to Gresham, August 6, 1894, Despatches, Japan, NA; tel., Denby to Gresham, July 28, 1894, Despatches, China, NA.

43. Sill to Dun, July 26, 1894, enclosure in Dun to Gresham, August 6, 1894, Despatches, Japan, NA; Cho to Lefevre, July 23, 1894, KOM, vol. 19, p. 228; Cho to Weber, July 23, 1894, ibid., vol. 17, pp. 297–298; Cho to Krien, July 23, 1894, ibid., vol. 15, pp. 559–560; Otori to Cho, July 23, 1894, ibid., vol. 2, p. 685; Kojong sidaesa, vol. 3, pp. 487–488.

44. Sill to Gresham, July 18, 1894, Despatches, Korea (microfilm, NA, m134 r11).

45. Gresham to Dun, July 31, 1894, Instructions, Japan (microfilm, NA, m133 r67).

46. Gresham to Denby, November 24, 1894, Dept. of State, FRUS (1894), appendix 1, p. 38.

47. Tel., Kurino to Mutsu, October 21, 1894, NGB, vol. 27, pt. 2, pp. 483, 490–491.

48. Kurino to Mutsu, November 8, 1894, ibid., pp. 491–493.

49. William E. Goschen to Gresham, October 6, 1894, Notes from British Legation to Department of State (microfilm, NA, m50 r124).

50. Gresham to Goschen, October 12, 1894, Notes to Foreign Legation from Department of State (microfilm, NA, m99 r51).

51. Goschen to Gresham, October 14, 1894, Notes from British Legation to Department of State (microfilm, NA, m50 r124).

52. Mutsu to Suematsu Kanezumi, August 20, 1894, Japanese Penetration of Korea (microfilm, Hoover, no. 2). See Mutsu to Otori, August 9, 21, 1894, ibid. See also Lensen, *Balance of Intrigue*, vol. 1, p. 259.

53. Mutsu to Itō, October 8, 1894, Japanese Penetration of Korea (microfilm, Hoover, no. 16).

54. Mutsu to Itō, October 17, 1894, ibid.

55. Denby to Gresham, November 3, 1894, Despatches, China, NA; Gresham to Dun, November 6, 1894, Dept. of State, *FRUS* (1894), appendix 1, p. 76; tel., Dun to Gresham, November 14, 15, 16, 17, 1894. Despatches, Japan, NA.

56. Tel., Dun to Gresham, November 17, 1894, ibid.

57. Sill to Skerett, May 4, June 1, 1894, Misc. Corresp., Seoul Legation (NA, rg84).

58. Gresham to Herbert, June 1, 1894, Navy Area File (microfilm, m625 r355); W. McAdoo to Gresham, June 1, 1894, Misc. Corresp., Department of State (microfilm, NA, m179 r890); Skerett to Herbert, June 3, 1894, Navy Area File (microfilm, NA, m625 r355).

59. Sill to Skerett, May 4, 1894, Naval Corresp., Seoul Legation (NA, rg84); Sill to George W. Coffin, December 4, 1894, enclosure in Coffin to Carpenter, December 5, 1894, Navy Area File (microfilm, NA, m625 r356).

60. Sill to Skerett, June 27, 1894, Navy Area File (microfilm, NA, m624/5 r355); Sill to B. F. Day, July 25, 1895, enclosure in McAdoo to Gresham, September 12, 1894, ibid. (m179 r897); C. C. Carpenter to Sill, September 6, 1894, enclosure in Carpenter to Herbert, October 4, 1894, ibid. (m625 r356); Carpenter to Herbert, July 6, 1895, enclosure in McAdoo to Olney, August 1, 1895, Misc. Corresp., Department of State (microfilm, NA, m179 r918).

61. Sill to Skerett, May 4, 1894, Misc. Corresp., Seoul Legation (NA, rg84); Gresham to Herbert, June 1, 1894, Navy Area File (microfilm, NA, m625 r355).

62. Sill to Skerett, June 26, 1894, enclosure in Skerett to Herbert, July 2, 1894, Navy Area File (microfilm, NA, m625 r355).

63. Skerett to Herbert, June 16, 1894; Carpenter to Herbert, June 16, 1894, ibid.

64. Skerett to Herbert, June 16, 1894, ibid.

65. Day to Sill, July 31, 1894, enclosure in Day to Herbert, August 7, 1894, ibid.; Sill to Day, August 1, 1894, Misc. Corresp., Seoul Legation (NA, rg84); Day to Sill, August 3, 1894, enclosure in Day to Carpenter, August 7, 1894, Navy Area File (microfilm, m625 r355); Carpenter to Herbert, April 13, 1895, ibid.

66. The following list is to give an idea of the intensity of the reform measures: R. Greathouse to Sill, August 1, 2, 11, 13, 14, 15, 16, 17, 20, 1894, Misc. Corresp., Seoul Legation (NA, rg84); *Kojong sidaesa*, vol. 3, p. 462

(June 26, 1894); vol. 3, p. 463 (June 27, 1894); vol. 3, pp. 469–470 (July 3, 1894); vol. 3, p. 471 (July 7, 1894); vol. 3, p. 475 (July 11, 1894); vol. 3, pp. 481–482 (July 16, 1894); vol 3, pp. 487–488 (July 23, 1894); vol 3, p. 489 (July 24, 1894); vol. 3, pp. 496–508 (July 30, 1894); vol. 3, p. 510 (August 1, 1894); vol. 3, pp. 511–512 (August 2, 1894); vol. 3, pp. 512–513 (August 3, 1894); vol. 3, pp. 513–514 (August 4, 1894); vol. 3, pp. 514–515 (August 8, 1894); vol. 3, pp. 518–519 (August 10, 1894); vol. 3, pp. 519–521 (August 11, 1894); vol. 3, pp. 521–525 (August 12, 1894); vol. 3, pp. 526–549 (August 14, 1894); vol. 3, pp. 551–556 (August 16, 1894); vol. 3, pp. 557–561 (August 17, 1894); vol. 3, pp. 567–576 (August 21, 1894); vol. 3, pp. 578–579 (August 26, 1894); vol. 3, pp. 582–583 (August 28, 1894); vol. 3, pp. 588–589 (September 4, 1894); vol. 3, p. 590 (September 9, 1894); vol. 3, pp. 593–594 (September 13, 1894); vol. 3, pp. 594–595 (September 15, 1894); vol. 3, pp. 615–616 (October 9, 1894); vol. 3, pp. 652–653 (November 10, 1894); vol. 3, pp. 676–679 (December 17, 1894); vol. 3, pp. 694–695 (January 6, 1895); vol. 3, pp. 695–699 (January 7, 1895); vol. 3, pp. 731–736 (April 3, 1895).

67. Sill to Gresham, July 18, 1894, Despatches, Korea (microfilm, NA, m134 r11).

68. *New York Daily Tribune*, July 21, 1894, 6:2.

69. *NYT Index* (1880–1905); *Poole's Index*, (1882–1902); *Readers' Guide* (1900–1904).

70. *New York Times*, December 30, 1894, 4:3.

71. Ibid., November 8, 1894, 4:2. See also ibid., August 1, 1894, 4:4; April 13, 1895, 4:2–3; *New York Tribune*, August 26, 1894, 6:2; Griffis, "Jack and the Giant," p. 213; Heard et al., "China and Japan in Korea," pp. 307–308.

72. *New York Daily Tribune*, October 1, 1894, 6:3.

73. Ibid., August 4, 1894, 6:2. See also Heard et al., "China and Japan in Korea," p. 300; Arthur H. Lee, "Korean Notes," *Harper's Weekly* 38 (1894): 1134.

74. Tel., Denby to Dun, November 22, 1894, enclosure in Dun to Gresham, November 28, 1894, Despatches, Japan, NA.

75. Dun to Gresham, February 2, 1894, ibid.

76. Tel., Dun to Denby, December 30, 1894, enclosure in Dun to Gresham, January 7, 1895, ibid. For the process of the communication see Denby to Dun, tel., November 22, 1894, enclosure in Dun to Gresham, November 28, 1894; tel., Denby to Dun, November 30, 1894, enclosure in Dun to Gresham, December 7, 1894; tel., Dun to Denby, December 2, 1894, enclosure in Dun to Gresham; tel., Denby to Dun, December 12, 1894, enclosure in Dun to Gresham, December 20, 1894; tel., Dun to Denby, December 18, 1894, enclosure in Dun to Gresham, December 20, 1894; tel., Denby to Dun, December 20, 1894, enclosure in Dun to Gresham, December 28, 1894; tel., Dun to Denby, December 26, 1894, enclosure in Dun to Gresham, December 28, 1894; tel., Denby to Dun, December 29, 1894, enclosure in Dun to Gresham, January 7, 1895; tel., Denby to Dun, December 31, 1894, enclosure in Dun to Gresham, January 7, 1895, ibid.

77. Inouye Kaoru to Kim Yun-sik, April 21, 1895, *KOM*, vol. 3, pp. 236–237; tel., Dun to Gresham, April 17, 1895, Despatches, Japan, NA.

78. *New York Times*, April 11, 1895, 4:4.

79. Ibid., April 18, 1895, 4:4.

80. Gardner to Sill, June 24, 1894, Misc. Corresp., Seoul Legation (NA, rg84).

CHAPTER 5

1. Langer, *Diplomacy of Imperialism*, vol. 1, pp. 178, 182–184. For the Russian side of the story, see Lensen, *Balance of Intrigue*, vol. 1, pp. 256–264, 291–292, 298, 300.

2. Langer, *Diplomacy of Imperialism*, vol. 1, pp. 179, 185–186. See also Clifton R. Breckenridge to Gresham, April 24, 1895, Despatches, Russia (microfilm, NA, m35 r46).

3. Tel., Mutsu to Kurino, March 19, 1895, *NGB*, vol, 28, pt. 1, p. 715.

4. Tel., Kurino to Mutsu, March 20, 1895, ibid., pp. 715–716.

5. Tel., Kurino to Mutsu, March 25, 1895, ibid., p. 720.

6. Tel., Hayashi to Mutsu, April 23, 1895, ibid., pt. 2, pp. 17–18; tel., Dun to Gresham, April 24, 1895, Despatches, Japan (microfilm, NA, m35 r46).

7. Kurino to Mutsu, May 7, 1895, *NGB*, vol. 28, pt. 1, pp. 89–92.

8. Langer, *Diplomacy of Imperialism*, vol. 1, p. 186.

9. Dun to Gresham, May 9, 1895, Despatches, Japan, NA.

10. Uchida to Saionji, November 15, 1895, *NGB*, vol. 28, pt. 1, pp. 552–561. This report made by the Japanese consul is the best description of the incident.

11. Dun to Olney, February 6, 1896, Despatches, Japan (microfilm, NA, m134 r69); tel., Saionji to Komura, January 22, 1896, Japanese Penetration of Korea (microfilm, Hoover, r3), folder 38, pp. 27–28; *Korean Repository*, 3 (1896): 124–125.

12. Allen to Olney, October 11, 1895, Despatches, Korea (microfilm, NA, m134 r12); Sill to Cramm, November 11, 1895, Sill papers; tel., Miura to Saionji, October 8, 1895; Saionji to Miura, October 11, 1895, Japanese Penetration of Korea (microfilm, Hoover, no. 3), folder 38; Underwood, *Underwood of Korea*, pp. 147–148; Bishop, *Korea and Her Neighbors*, vol. 2, pp. 73–74.

13. Allen to Olney, October 10, 14, 1895, Despatches, Korea (microfilm, NA, m134 r12).

14. Allen to Kim Yun Sik, October 12, 1895, Note from American Legation to Korean Foreign Office (NA, rg84); Dun to Olney, November 15, 1895, Despatches, Japan, NA.

15. Olney to Sill, November 21, 1895, Instructions, Korea (microfilm, NA, m77 r109); tel., Saionji to Kurino and others, November 15, 1895, *NGB*, vol. 28, pt. 1, pp. 585–586.

16. Sill to Olney, November 15, 1895, Despatches, Korea (microfilm, NA, m134 r12); tel., Saionji to Kurino and others, November 15, 1895, *NGB*, vol. 28, pt. 1, pp. 585–586.

17. Tel., Olney to Sill, November 20, 1895, Instructions, Korea (microfilm, NA, m77 r109).

18. Tel., Olney to Sill, December 2, 1895, ibid.

19. Tels., Dun to Olney, October 9, 12, 14, 1895, Despatches, Japan, NA.
20. Tel., Dun to Olney, October 12, 1895; Dun to Olney, October 9, 17, 19, 1895, ibid.
21. See tel., Dun to Olney, October 12, 1895; Dun to Olney, October 17, 19, 1895, ibid. See also Olney to Bonsal, November 11, 18, 1895, Instructions, Japan (microfilm, NA, m61 r107).
22. Tel., Dun to Olney, October 14, 1895, Despatches, Japan, NA.
23. Allen to Everett, November 5, 1895, Allen papers.
24. Sill to Olney, October 26, 1895, Despatches, Korea (microfilm, NA, m134 r12).
25. Dun to Olney, November 4, 1895, Despatches, Japan, NA.
26. Dun to Olney, October 9, 12, 17, 1894, ibid.; note from Japanese legation to Department of State, November 2, 1895, NA.
27. Komura to Saionji, December 31, 1895, *NGB*, vol. 28, pt. 1, pp. 603–619.
28. Sill to Olney, December 3, 1895, Despatches, Korea (microfilm, NA, m134 r12); Allen to Rockhill, December 3, 1895, Allen papers.
29. Sill to Olney, December 3, 1895, Despatches, Korea (microfilm, NA, m134 r12).
30. Allen to Rockhill, January 25, 1896, Rockhill papers; Allen to Olney, February 5, 1896, Despatches, Korea (microfilm, NA, m134 r12); Allen to Inouye, February 7, 1896, Allen papers.
31. Tel., Komura to Saionji, November 28, 1895, *NGB*, vol. 28, pt. 1, pp. 591–592.
32. Kurino to Saionji, March 3, 1896, ibid., pp. 752–757.
33. See C. M. Knepper to William M. Folger, October 19, 1895, enclosure in W. McAdoo to Olney, November 27, 1895, Misc. Corresp., Department of State (microfilm, NA, m179 r926). Ensign Knepper, who stayed with the guard in Seoul, said that were half a dozen "important Korean refugees within the Legation."
34. Olney to Sill, December 31, 1895, Instructions, Korea (microfilm, NA, m77 r109).
35. Tel., Olney to Sill, January 10, 1896, ibid. Also see Olney to Sill, January 11, 1896, ibid.
36. Tel., Sill to Olney, January 13, 1896, Despatches, Korea (microfilm, NA, m134 r12).
37. Sill to Olney, January 20, 1896, ibid.
38. Ibid.
39. Tel., Nishi to Saionji, February 17, 1896, *NGB*, vol. 29, p. 729; Hitrovo to Saionji, February 19, 1896, ibid., p. 734; memorandum of Itō-Hitrovo conversation, March 5, 1896, ibid., pp. 761–762.
40. Kurino to Saionji, February 13, 1896, *NGB*, vol. 28, pp. 683–688. For the Russian side of the story, see Lensen, *Balance of Intrigue*, vol. 2, pp. 580–588.
41. H. A. Herbert to Olney, February 6, 1896, Misc. Corresp., Department of State (microfilm, NA, m179 r931).
42. McAdoo to Olney, October 12, 1895, ibid. (r923); Herbert to Olney, February 6, 1896, ibid.

43. J. V. McNair to Herbert, February 24, 1896, Navy Area File (microfilm, NA, m625 r360).

44. McNair to Herbert, July 8, 1896, enclosure in Herbert to Olney, July 29, 1896, Misc. Corresp., Department of State, (microfilm, NA, m179 r945).

45. McNair to Herbert, August 14, 1896; February 6, 1897, Navy Area File (microfilm, NA, m625 r361).

46. Knepper to Folger, October 19, 1895, enclosure in McAdoo to Olney, November 27, 1895, Misc. Corresp., Department of State (microfilm, NA, m179 r926); C. H. Stockton to Herbert, November 4, 1895, Navy Area File (microfilm, NA, m625 r360); McNair to Herbert, June 25, 1896, ibid. (r361).

47. See the text in Rockhill, ed., *Treaties*, pp. 431–432. See also Lensen, *Balance of Intrigue*, vol. 2, pp. 592–596, for Russian's caution and moderation.

48. Allen to Wilson, March 11, 1896, Allen papers; Sakamoto, *Yamagata Aritomo*, p. 551; Romanov, *Russia in Manchuria*, p. 106; Langer, *Diplomacy of Imperialism*, vol. 1, p. 407. See also Lensen, *Balance of Intrigue*, vol. 2, pp. 603–635, 848.

49. Sill to Olney, July 17, 1896, Despatches, Korea (microfilm, NA, m134 r13); Sill to Cramm, December 26, 1895, Sill papers; Allen to Morse, February 11, November 17, 1896; Allen to Hunt, November 27, 1896; Allen to Wilson, February 18, 1897, Allen papers. See also Weems, ed., *Hulbert's History*, vol. 2, pp. 307, 310.

50. Sill to Uhl, August 15, 1895, Consular Despatches, Seoul (microfilm, NA, m167 r1).

51. Sill to Rockhill, April 16, 1896, Japanese Penetration of Korea (microfilm, Hoover), folder 33.

52. *NYT Index* (1894–1898), pp. 508, 627, 710, 739, 820; *Poole's Index* (1892–1896), pp. 133–134; ibid. (1897–1902), p. 319.

53. See *Harper's Weekly*, 41 (1897): 728.

54. See, for the views of historians, May, *Imperial Diplomacy*, p. 114; McLean, *William Rufus Day*, p. 36; Lester B. Shippe and Royal B. Way, "William Rufus Day," in Bemis, eds., *American Secretaries of State*, vol. 9, p. 31.

55. Richardson, ed., *Messages and Papers*, vol. 14, p. 6241.

56. Speech at banquet at Ohio Society of New York, March 3, 1900, McKinley, *Speeches and Addresses*, p. 362. See also Leech, *In the Days of McKinley*, pp. 23, 26, 240; Glad, *McKinley, Bryan, and People*, p. 23.

57. Leech, *Days of McKinley*, pp. 100–101; Morgan, *McKinley and His America*, p. 254; Louis M. Sears, "John Sherman," in Bemis, ed., *American Secretaries of State*, vol. 9, pp. 3, 13; James R. Rhodes, *The McKinley and Roosevelt Administrations 1897–1909* (New York: MacMillan 1922), p. 312; Dawes, *McKinley Years*, p. 156; Burton, *John Sherman*, pp. 413–414; Dennett, *John Hay*, p. 197; May, *Imperial Diplomacy*, p. 114.

58. Dawes, *McKinley Years*, p. 156; Shippe and Way, "William Rufus Day," in Bemis, ed., *American Secretaries of State*, vol. 9, pp. 29–30; McLean, *William Rufus Day*, p. 32; May, *Imperial Diplomacy*, p. 114.

59. See Thayer, *Life and Letters of John Hay*, vol. 2, p. 339; Dawes,

McKinley Years, p. 238; Dennett, *John Hay*, pp. 441–443; Alfred L. P. Dennis, "John Hay," in Bemis, ed., *American Secretaries of State*, vol. 9, pp. 117–120.

60. *New York Times*, July 15, 1897, 2:4; Allen to Everett, September 17, 1896; Allen to Wilson, April 1, 1897; Allen to Foraker, September 14, 1896; Nash to Allen, July 17, 1896; Allen to McKinley, September 14, 1896, Allen papers.

61. Allen to Morse, April 15, 1896; Allen to Everett, January 30, 1897, Allen papers; Harrington, *God, Mammon and the Japanese*, pp. 75–80.

62. Allen to Collbran, July 21, 1900, Allen papers.

63. Allen to Weiper, December 20, 1903, Allen papers. See also tel., Allen to Hay, January 3, 1904, Despatches, Korea (microfilm, NA, m134 r20); Allen to Hunt, April 16, 21, 1900, Allen papers.

64. Tel., Allen to Hay, January 1, 1904, Despatches, Korea (microfilm, NA, m134 r20); Allen to Rittenhouse, January 20, 1903, Allen papers.

65. Allen to Hay, June 2, 1902, Despatches, Korea (microfilm, NA, m134 r18); Horace N. Allen to Horace E. and Maurice Allen, December 20, 1903, Allen papers.

66. Horace N. Allen to Horace E. and Maurice Allen, January 10, 1904, Allen papers; Allen to Rockhill, February 28, 1901, January 4, 1904, Rockhill papers.

67. Sherman to Allen, November 19, 1897, Instructions, Korea (microfilm, NA, m77 r109). See also Allen to Morse, October 22, 1897, Allen papers.

68. Ibid.

69. Allen to Sherman, September 13, 1897, Despatches, Korea (microfilm, NA, m134 r13).

70. Allen to Carpenter, September 10, 1897, Allen papers. See Lensen, *Balance of Intrigue*, vol. 2, pp. 240–249, on the Russian policy of caution and self-denial.

71. Allen to Sherman, October 14, 1897, Despatches, Korea (microfilm, NA, m134 r13); Allen to Wilson, October 11, 1897, Allen papers; Allen to Rockhill, October 11, 1897, Rockhill papers. For the impact of Russia's lease of Port Arthur upon its policy in Korea see Lensen, *Balance of Intrigue*, vol. 2, pp. 694–700, 849–851.

72. Allen to Sherman, May 26, 1898, Despatches, Korea (microfilm, NA, m134 r14). See also Allen to Sherman, December 27, 1897; February 2, March 19, 22, April 12, 1898, ibid. (r13, r14); Allen to Hay, May 31, 1898, ibid. (r14); Buck to Hay, May 10, 1898, Despatches, Japan (microfilm, NA, m133 r71). For the Russian policy see Lensen, *Balance of Intrigue*, vol. 2, pp. 240–249.

73. Allen to Fassett, March 13, 1898, Allen papers.

74. Allen to Speer, June 5, 1898, ibid.

75. Allen to Sherman, October 5, 1897, Despatches, Korea (microfilm, NA, m134 r13).

76. Allen to Sherman, October 1, 1897, ibid. See also Allen to Morse, October 3, 1897; Allen to Wilson, October 11, 1897; Allen to Everett, October 12, 1897; Allen Diary, October 14, 1897, Allen papers.

77. Allen to Sherman, October 6, 1897, Despatches, Korea (microfilm, NA, m134 r13).

78. Allen to Sherman, October 16, 1897, ibid.

79. Allen to Hunt, January 10, 1898; see also Allen to Rockhill, January 30, 1898, Allen papers.

80. Sherman to Allen, November 19, 1897, Instructions, Korea (microfilm, NA, m77 r109).

81. Allen to Sherman, November 11, 1897. Despatches, Korea (microfilm, NA, m134 r13).

82. Allen to Sherman, February 2, 1898, ibid. (r14).

83. Allen to Sherman, October 3, December 27, 1897; March 8, 1898, ibid. (r13, 14).

84. For the history of the club see *Korean Repository* 4 (1897): 486; 5 (1898): 281–287; Weems, eds., Hulbert's *History*, vol. 2, pp. 307–308; Chongsik Lee, *Korean Nationalism*, pp. 61–69.

85. Allen to Sherman, November 13, 1897, Despatches, Korea (microfilm, NA, m134 r13).

86. Allen to Day, October 13, 1898, ibid. (r15).

87. Allen to Sherman, April 27, 1898, ibid., (r14).

88. Allen to Day, October 13, 1898; Allen to Hay, November 14, 1898, ibid. (r15).

89. Allen to Day, October 27, 1898, ibid. (r13); Hioki to Aoki, November 8, 1898, *NGB*, vol. 31, pt. 2, p. 402.

90. Allen to Day, August 4, 1898; Allen to Hay, November 14, 1898, Despatches, Korea (microfilm, NA, m134 r14); tel., Kato to Aoki, December 31, 1898, *NGB*, vol. 31, pt. 2, p. 448.

91. Allen to Hay, May 31, 1902, Despatches, Korea (microfilm, NA, m134 r18).

92. The change of the title occurred in the fall of 1897: Allen to Sherman, October 5, 1897, ibid. (r13).

93. Allen to Hay, November 18, 1898, ibid. (r15).

94. Ibid.

95. Allen to Speet, June 5, 1898, Allen papers.

96. Allen to Hay, November 18, 1899, Despatches, Korea (microfilm, NA, m134 r15). See also Allen to Rockhill, October 20, 1899, Rockhill papers.

97. Allen to Rockhill, March 13, 1901, Rockhill papers. See also Allen to Day, October 20, 1898, Despatches, Korea (microfilm, NA, m134 r15); Buck to Hay, October 3, 1900, Despatches, Japan (microfilm, NA, m133 r74); Allen to Hunt, November 18, 1900, Allen papers.

98. Tel., Aoki to Komura, July 30, 1900, *KGB*, vol. 33, p. 700.

99. Allen to Morse, January 5, 1899, Allen papers.

100. Allen to Hay, November 18, 1899, Despatches, Korea (microfilm, NA, m134 r15).

101. Allen to Hay, August 25, September 25, 1900, ibid. (r16).

102. Allen to Hay, August 25, 1900, ibid. See Allen to Hunt, July 29, 1900, Allen papers.

103. Allen to Hay, October 20, 1900, Despatches, Korea (microfilm, NA, m134 r16).

104. Allen to Hay, October 2, 1900, ibid. See also Allen to Fassett, November 3, 1900, Allen papers.

105. Aoki to Hayashi, September 14, 1900, Archives, Japanese Ministry of Foreign Affairs (microfilm, Library of Congress, Meiji-Taisho [hereafter MT] 60), 1, 4, 1, 30:16.

106. Russian Minister [Rosen] to Kato, January 7, 1901, NGB, vol. 34, p. 521. See also Gubbins to Lansdowne, March 13, 1901, Gooch and Temperley, eds., British Documents, vol. 2, p. 45.

107. Tel., Kato to Chinda, January 17, 1901, NGB, vol. 34, pp. 526-528; tel., Chinda to Kato, January 23, 1901, ibid., pp. 529-530.

108. Buck to Hay, October 3, 1900, Despatches, Japan (microfilm, NA, m133 r74).

109. Allen to Hay, October 11, 1900, Despatches, Korea (microfilm, NA, m134 r16). See also Allen to Fassett, November 3, 1900, Allen papers.

110. Allen to Hay, September 10, 1900, Despatches, Korea (microfilm, NA, m134 r16).

111. Allen to Hay, October 2, 1900, ibid.

112. Allen to Morgan, October 30, 1902, Allen papers.

113. Tel., Mutsu to Nabejima, May 15, 1895, NGB, vol. 28, pt. 1, pp. 412-413.

114. See tel., Komura to Kato, January 12, 1901, Archives, Japanese Ministry of Foreign Affairs (microfilm, MT 60), 1, 4, 1, 30:3709; Itō, ed., Chōsen kaiko siryo, vol. 2, pp. 178-191.

115. See Allen to Sherman, February 15, 1898, Despatches, Korea (microfilm, NA, m134 r14); Allen to Hay, June 6, 1900, ibid. (116); Allen to Carpenter, August 23, 1900; "Seoul Water Works," prepared by Henry Collbran, Allen papers.

116. Allen to Hunt, April 21, 25, May 14, 1900; Allen to Fassett, May 20, 1900, Allen papers.

117. Allen to Sherman, December 1, 1897; Allen to Day, June 24, 1898, Despatches, Korea (microfilm, NA, m134 r14); Allen to Fassett, May 17, 1898, Allen papers.

118. For involvement of missionaries in local politics see Allen to Sherman, October 16, 1897, Despatches, Korea (microfilm, NA, m134 413); Allen to Ellingwood, October 15, 1897, January 7, 1898, Allen papers.

119. Sill to Gresham, May 15, 1897, Despatches, Korea (microfilm, NA, m134 r13).

120. Allen to Hunt, June 21, 1902; Allen to Morse, December 3, 1902, Allen papers.

121. Allen to Hay, May 31, 1902, Despatches, Korea (microfilm, NA, m134 r18); Allen to Durham W. Stevens, September 2, 1902; Allen to Buck, September 13, 1902, Allen papers.

122. Allen to Morse, December 3, 1902, Allen papers.

123. Allen to Wilson, December 16, 1902, ibid.

124. Allen to Hay, August 5, 1902, Despatches, Korea (microfilm, NA, m134 r18).

125. Allen to Sperry, September 25, 1904, Allen papers. See also tel., Matsunichi to Chief of Staff, November 21, 1903, Archives, Japanese Ministry of Foreign Affairs (microfilm, MT 41), 1, 2, 1, 17:5.

126. Allen to Collbran, December 30, 1903; Allen to Morgan, September 2, 1902, Allen papers.

127. Hay to Eddy, June 7, 1904, Hay papers; Chang, *Anglo-Japanese Alliance*, p. 111; Gelber, *Anglo-American Friendship*, p. 14. See also Nash, *Russo-Japanese War*, pp. 124–142.

128. Tel., Hayashi to Komura, January 15, 1902, *NGB*, vol. 35, pp. 1–3; Gooch and Temperley, eds., *British Documents*, vol. 2, p. 116.

129. See Komura's statement of December 7, 1901, before a group of senior Japanese statemen, *KGB*, vol. 34, p. 38; Lansdowne to Whitehead, July 31, 1901, Gooch and Temperley, eds., *British Documents*, vol. 2, p. 91; Pooley, ed., *Secret Memoirs*, p. 64; Langer, *Diplomacy of Imperialism*, vol. 2, p. 760.

130. Hayashi to Komura, May 6, 1902, *NGB*, vol. 35, p. 89. See also Chang, *Anglo-Japanese Alliance*, p. 259; Lansdowne to C. MacDonald, October 29, 1901, Gooch and Temperley, eds., *British Documents*, vol. 2, p. 98.

131. Hayashi to Komura, May 6, 1902, *NGB*, vol. 35, p. 89.

132. *New York Times*, July 26, 1902, 8:2.

133. Lansdowne to J. N. Jordan, February 15, 1902, Gooch and Temperley, eds., *British Documents*, vol. 2, p. 129. See also *Times* (London), April 9, 1902, 12:1.

134. Tel., Aoki and Hayashi, September 14, 1902, *NGB*, vol. 34, p. 523.

135. Buck to Hay, August 15, 1902, Despatches, Japan (microfilm, NA, m133 r76).

136. Tel., Takahira to Komura, October 16, 1902, *NGB*, vol. 35, pp. 397–398, 434; Takahira to Komura, October 17, 1904, ibid., pp. 404–407.

137. Takahira to Komura, November 24, 1902, *NGB*, vol. 35, p. 416.

138. Takahira to Komura, October 17, 1902, ibid., p. 405.

139. Takahira to Komura, November 24, 1902, ibid., p. 416.

140. Allen to Morgan, October 29, 1902, Allen papers.

141. Harrington, *God, Mammon and the Japanese*, p. 32.

142. Allen Diary, September 30, 1903; Allen to Morse, February 27, 1904; Allen to Everett, November 10, 1904; Allen to Foraker, April 23, 1905, Allen papers.

143. See Harrington, *God, Mammon and the Japanese*, p. 316.

CHAPTER 6

1. Roosevelt to Spring Rice, September 27, 1904, Roosevelt papers (LC).

2. Roosevelt to Spring Rice, May 13, 1905, ibid.

3. Roosevelt to Hay, July 26, 1904, ibid.

4. Roosevelt to Meyer, December 26, 1904, Morison et al., eds., *Letters*, vol. 4, p. 1029; Roosevelt to Spring Rice, December 27, 1904, Roosevelt papers (LC).

5. Roosevelt to Lodge, June 16, 1905, Morison et al., eds., *Letters*, vol. 2, p. 1230. For balance of power as an important concept in Roosevelt's Far Eastern policy, see Harbaugh, *Power and Responsibility*, pp. 273, 277; Beale, *Roosevelt*, pp. 270–272; Dennett, *Roosevelt and the Russo-Japanese War*, pp. 4, 154.

6. Richardson, ed., *Messages and Papers*, vol. 6, p. 7230.

7. Foster R. Dulles recognizes a constant "interplay between selfish national interest and ethical purpose" in Roosevelt. Dulles, *Imperial Years*, pp. 30–31.

8. See ibid.

9. Richardson, ed., *Messages and Papers*, vol. 16, p. 6931. For similar remarks see his speech, Richmond, Virginia, October 8, 1905, Roosevelt papers (LC).

10. Roosevelt to Spring Rice, June 13, 1904, Morison et al., eds. *Letters*, vol. 4, p. 832.

11. Roosevelt to Hay, September 2, 1904, ibid.

12. Roosevelt to Spring Rice, November 19, 1900, Roosevelt papers (LC); Roosevelt to Rockhill, August 29, 1900, Rockhill papers.

13. See Roosevelt to Grant, March 4, 1905, Morison et al., eds., *Letters*, vol. 4, p. 1140; Roosevelt to Kennan, May 6, 1905, ibid., p. 1169.

14. Roosevelt to Rockhill, August 29, 1905, Rockhill papers.

15. Roosevelt to Kennan, January 6, 1905, Roosevelt papers (LC). See also Roosevelt to Kennan, April 15, 1902; March 23, 30, 1904; May 6, 1905; Roosevelt to Gamble, February 15, 1904, Roosevelt papers (LC). Roosevelt to Kermit Roosevelt, June 9, 1906, Roosevelt papers, Houghton Library; Loeb to Kennan, January 1, 1904; Loeb to Hay, November 14, 1904, Roosevelt papers (LC).

16. See Roosevelt to Kaneko, March 31, April 23, 1904; May 31, 1905; Kaneko to Roosevelt, July 19, 1905, Roosevelt papers (LC).

17. Roosevelt to Meyer, December 26, 1904, Morison et al., eds., *Letters*, vol. 4, p. 1080.

18. Roosevelt to Spring Rice, March 19, 1904, ibid., p. 760.

19. Roosevelt to Meyer, February 6, 1905, Roosevelt papers (LC). Roosevelt scholars, especially Beale, pay special attention to Roosevelt's affectionate feelings toward Japan. Beale, *Roosevelt*, pp. 264–265; Pringle, *Roosevelt*, p. 264. For his fear of the Japanese see Beale, *Roosevelt*, pp. 269–270; Dulles, *Imperial Years*, p. 267.

20. Roosevelt to Rockhill, August 29, 1905, Rockhill papers. See also Roosevelt to Spring Rice, December 27, 1904, Roosevelt papers (LC).

21. Allen thought Roosevelt learned about Korea from conversations with and writings of Brown. Allen to Brown, July 25, 1902, Allen papers.

22. Roosevelt to Hay, January 28, 1905, Morison et al., eds., *Letters*, vol. 4, p. 1112.

23. Roosevelt to Meyer, February 5, 1905, Roosevelt papers.

24. Dennett, *Roosevelt and the Russo-Japanese War*, pp. 7, 10, 33–38, 336; Dennett, *John Hay*, p. 198; Dulles, *Imperial Years*, pp. 105, 238.

25. Dennett, *John Hay*, p. 403.

26. There was no official communication between the president and Hay from March 6 to June 19, which was followed by the last letter of the following day, Roosevelt papers (LC).

27. Roosevelt to Kermit Roosevelt, March 20, 1905, Roosevelt papers (LC).

28. Hay to Allen, November 17, 1904, Allen papers.

29. Leopold, *Elihu Root*, pp. 50–51; Jessup, *Elihu Root*, vol. 2, p. 4.

30. Root to Lodge, February 26, 1916, cited in Jessup, *Elihu Root*, vol. 2, p. 6.

31. See Roosevelt to Rockhill, February 17, 1896, Rockhill papers; Hay to Roosevelt, July 17, 1903; Adee to Hay, September 23, 1903, Hay papers; Hay to Rockhill, March 7, 1905, Rockhill papers; Hay Diary, June 29, 1904; March 14, 1905, Hay papers.

32. Allen to Morgan, September 2, 1902; March 6, 1903; Allen Diary, September 30, 1903, Allen papers.

33. Rockhill to Allen, February 29, 1904, Rockhill papers.

34. Rockhill to Kennan, November 21, 1905, Kennan papers.

35. Allen to Hay, October 12, 1901, Despatches, Korea, NA.

36. *New York Times*, August 15, 1903, 6:1.

37. White, *Diplomacy*, pp. 95–131, 351–358; tel., Kurino to Komura, November 15, 22, 1903, *NGB*, vol. 36, pt. 1, pp. 31–33; Asakawa, *Russo-Japanese War*, pp. 1–64; Romanov, *Russia in Manchuria*, p. 12; Yakontoff, *Russia and the Soviet Union*, p. 65.

38. See White, *Diplomacy*, pp. 351–358. For the process of the Russo-Japanese negotiations see Nash, *Russo-Japanese War*, pp. 192–221.

39. Dept. of State, *FRUS* (1905), pp. 32–35.

40. Roosevelt to Spring Rice, March 19, 1904, Roosevelt papers (LC).

41. Tel., Hay to Allen, March 2, 1904, Instructions, Korea (microfilm, NA, m77 r109).

42. Hay to American representatives, February 20, 1904, Dept. of State, *FRUS* (1905), p. 3.

43. The Department of State sent at least seven notes to the Russian legation in Washington during the war on the subject of neutrality for China. See enclosure no. 2, Griscom to Hay, February 15, 1904, Despatches, Japan (microfilm, NA, m133 r78); Hay to Takahira, February 19, 1904, Notes to the Japanese Legation (microfilm, NA, m99 r67); Hay Diary, February 14, March 13, 1904, Hay papers.

44. Tel., Yi to Komura, January 21, 1904, *NGB*, vol. 37, pt. 1, pp. 310–311.

45. Cho to Hay, January 22, 1904, Notes from the Korean Legation (microfilm, NA, m166).

46. Hay to Allen, March 4, 1904, Instructions, Korea (microfilm, NA, m77 r109).

47. Allen to Hay, May 4, September 30, 1904, Despatches, Korea, NA.

48. Allen to Hay, February 11, 1904; January 6, 12, March 31, 1905, Des-

patches, Korea (microfilm, NA, m134 r20); Allen to Gunzburg, January 25, 1905, Allen papers.

49. Allen to Frank H. Beverly, June 7, 1904, Allen papers.

50. Allen to Georgia, July 10, 1904; Allen to Townsend, May 30, 1905, Allen papers; Allen to Hay, March 17, 1905, Despatches, Korea (microfilm, NA, m134 r22).

51. Allen to Morgan, March 2, 1904, Allen papers.

52. Allen to Townsend, May 15, 1904; Allen to Horace E. and Maurice Allen, March 9, 1905, ibid.

53. Allen to Hay, January 2, 21, February 21, March 8, 1904; January 19, 1905, Despatches, Korea (microfilm, NA, m134 r22).

54. Allen to Hay, October 25, 1904, ibid. (r21).

55. Allen to Hay, October 25, 1904, ibid.

56. Rockhill, ed., *Treaties*, p. 441.

57. Carnegie Endowment, ed., *Korea*, p. 37. For the Japanese imperialistic ambition in Korea see Iriye, *Pacific Estrangement*, p. 93.

58. Tel., Hay to Allen, February 23, 1904, Instructions, Korea (microfilm, NA, m77 r109).

59. Tel., Komura to Takahira, February 25, 1904, Dept. of State, *FRUS* (1904), p. 437.

60. Takahira to Hay, August 30, 1904, Notes from the Japanese Legation (microfilm, NA, m163 r8); Hay to Takahira, September 2, 1904, Notes to the Japanese Legation (microfilm, NA, m99 r67).

61. Tel., Allen to Hay, February 21, 1904, Despatches, Korea (microfilm, NA, m134 r20).

62. Tel., Allen to Hay, February 24, 1904, ibid.

63. Tel., Hayashi to Komura, February 29, 1904, *NGB*, vol. 37, pt. I, p. 349.

64. Dept. of State, *FRUS* (1904), pp. 437–440.

65. Dennett, "Secret Pact," pp. 15–21; Beale, *Roosevelt*, p. 235; Griswold, *Far Eastern Policy*, pp. 125–126.

66. Esthus, "Taft-Katsura Agreement," pp. 45–51; idem, *Roosevelt and Japan*, pp. 266–286.

67. See Chay, "Taft-Katsura Memorandum," pp. 321–326, esp. pp. 322–324. See also Ro, "Power Politics in Korea," p. 147.

68. Tel., Taft to Root, July 29, 1905, Roosevelt papers (LC).

69. Roosevelt to Taft, July 31, 1905, Roosevelt papers (LC); tel., Taft to Katsura, August 7, 1905, Taft papers.

70. Chay, "Taft-Katsura Memorandum," p. 326.

71. Roosevelt to Spring Rice, November 1, 1905, Morison et al., eds., *Letters*, vol. 5, p. 61.

72. Carnegie Endowment, ed., *Korea*, p. 404.

73. For the Japanese motivation in the treaty see the third article in the secret section of the Japanese proposal of May 26, 1905, in Gooch and Temperley, eds., *British Documents*, vol. 4, p. 129. See also tel., MacDonald to Lansdowne, May 29, 1905, ibid., p. 133; MacDonald to Lansdowne, June 29, 1905, ibid., pp. 141–143; Lansdowne to MacDonald, May 10, July 1, 1905, ibid., pp. 128, 144.

74. Roosevelt to Reid, September 16, 1905, Morison et al., eds., *Letters*, vol. 5, p. 29; Roosevelt to Spring Rice, November 11, 1905, Note from the Japanese Legation (microfilm, NA, m163 r9).

75. Roosevelt to Spring Rice, November 1, 1905, Morison et al., eds., *Letters*, vol. 5, p. 61.

76. Root to Bryce, September 27, 1905, Root papers.

77. *Washington Times*, September 27, 1905, 6:1; September 28, 1905, 6:1.

78. *New York Times*, September 28, 1905, 8:1. See also ibid., August 27, 1905, 6:1.

79. Ibid., September 5, 1905, 6:1; September 9, 1905, 8:4; September 28, 1905, 8:1.

80. *Boston Evening Transcript*, September 29, 1905, 8:3. For the process of the treaty making see Eugene P. Trani, *The Treaty of Portsmouth: An Adventure in American Diplomacy* (Lexington, Ky.: University of Kentucky Press, 1969).

81. See White, *Diplomacy*, pp. 242–309.

82. See ibid., pp. 249, 269–270, 359.

83. Enclosure, Takahira to Root, November 23, 1905, Notes from the Japanese Legation (microfilm, NA, m163 r9).

84. Allen to Morgan, February 26, 1904; Allen to Harper, April 8, 1905; Allen to Min, November 30, 1905; Allen to Ye, November 30, 1905, Allen papers. See also Rockhill to Allen, June 30, 1905, ibid.

85. See Allen to Rittenhouse, May 25, 1905, ibid.

86. Hay Diary, January 22, 1905, Hay papers.

87. See Rockhill to Stevens, March 21, 1905, Rockhill papers.

88. Varg, *Open Door Diplomat*, p. 86; Brown, *Mastery of the Far East*, p. 200.

89. Croly, *Willard Straight*, p. 187.

90. Hulbert, *Passing of Korea*, p. 223.

91. Allen to Stevens, November 29, 1905, Allen papers. See also Allen to Everett, October 12, 1897, ibid.

92. Allen to Hay, March 7, 1905, Despatches, Korea (microfilm, NA, m134 r22).

93. Tel., Takahira to Katsura, November 11, 1905, *NGB*, vol. 38, pt. 1, p. 530.

94. Tel., Takahira to Katsura, November 23, 1905, ibid., p. 548.

95. Tel., Root to Morgan, November 24, 1905, Instructions, Korea (microfilm, NA, m77 r109); tel., Root to Griscom, November 24, 1905, Instructions, Japan, ibid. (r108).

96. Tel., Komura to Takahira, November 27, 1905, filed in the Notes from the Japanese Legation (microfilm, NA, m163 r9).

97. *Jiji*, November 3, 1905, enclosure no. 3, Buck to Root, November 30, 1905, Despatches, Japan (microfilm, NA, m133 r81).

98. Roosevelt to Spring Rice, August 8, 1900, Morison et al., eds., *Letters*, vol. 1, p. 1394.

99. Roosevelt to Hay, January 28, 1905, Roosevelt papers (LC).

100. Roosevelt to Meyer, February 5, 1905, ibid.

101. Roosevelt to Hay, February 6, 1905, Morison et al., eds., *Letters*, vol. 4, p. 1116.

102. Roosevelt to Taft, April 20, 1905, Roosevelt papers (LC).

103. Roosevelt to Spring Rice, June 16, 1905; Roosevelt to Meyer, July 18, 1905; Roosevelt to Strachey, July 27, 1905, ibid.

104. Rockhill to Allen, February 29, 1904, Rockhill papers.

105. Tel., Ogihara to Komura, October 20, 22, 27, 29, 1905, *NGB*, vol. 38, pt. 1, pp. 661-663.

106. Holstein, Memorandum, March 27, 1901, Dugdale, ed. and trans., *German Diplomatic Documents*, vol. 3, pp. 140-141.

107. The best accounts of the negotiations are "A Detailed Account of the Forced Treaty Negotiations"; Deldon to Bostwick, November 22, 1905, Allen papers. See also Morgan to Root, November 20, 1905, Despatches, Korea (microfilm, NA, m134 r22); Croly, *Willard Straight*, p. 178-185; tel., Hayashi to Katsura, November 18, 1905, *NGB*, vol. 38, pt. 1, p. 532.

108. The Korean foreign minister, Pak, was one of those working with this idea. Croly, *Willard Straight*, p. 181.

109. Allen Diary, June 1, 1903, Allen papers; Allen to Hay, March 8, 1904, Despatches, Korea, NA.

110. Esthus, *Roosevelt and Japan*, p. 98.

111. Cho to Needham, September 30, 1904, enclosure in Allen to Hay, September 30, 1904, Despatches, Korea (microfilm, NA, m134 r21); Needham to Cho, December 22, 1904, enclosure in Hayashi to Komura, June 15, 1905, *NGB*, vol. 38, pt. 1, pp. 655-656. See also tel., Hayashi to Komura, June 15, 1905, ibid., p. 654.

112. Allen to Hay, January 26, 28, 1905, Despatches, Korea (microfilm, NA, m134 r22); Allen to Hay, February 2, 1905, Allen papers. For the views on the good offices clause see Ro, "Power Politics in Korea," pp. 149-150; Pak Kwŏn-sang, "Han'gukŭi Mikuk insik" in Han'guk chŏngsinmunhwa yŏn'guwŏn and The Wilson Center, eds., *Reflections*, pp. 149-150.

113. Morgan to Root, July 20, 1905, Despatches, Korea (microfilm, NA, m134 r22). See also Loomis to Barnes, August 23, 1905, Roosevelt papers (LC).

114. Visiting cards of Rhee, Yoon, and Mrs. J. Ellen Foster of Washington, D.C., are preserved in Roosevelt papers (LC). See also tel., Hayashi to Katsura, July 14, 1905, *NGB*, vol. 38, pt. 1, pp. 656-657.

115. See tel., Hayashi to Katsura, July 14, 1905, *NGB*, vol. 38, pt. 1, p. 656; Hioki to Katsura, August 5, 1905, ibid., p. 659.

116. Morgan to Root, July 20, 1905, Roosevelt papers (LC).

117. See Roosevelt to Root, November 25, 1905, Morison et al., eds., *Letters*, vol. 5, p. 96.

118. Ibid.

119. Dennett, *Roosevelt and the Russo-Japanese War*, p. 305.

120. Morgan to Root, October 19, 1905, Despatches, Korea (microfilm, NA, m134 r22).

121. See tel., Ogihara to Komura, October 22, 1905, *NGB*, vol. 38, pt. 1, pp. 662-663; Stevens to Allen, October 26, 1905, Allen papers.

122. Tel., Takahira to Katsura, November 22, 1905, *NGB*, vol. 38, pt. I, pp. 667–668.

123. Allen to Wilson, December 13, 1905, Allen papers.

124. *New York Times*, December 13, 1905, 1:5; *New York Daily Tribune*, December 13, 1905, 3:2.

125. Min to Root, December 7, 1905; Adee, Memorandum, December 7, 1905, Notes from the Korean Legation (microfilm, NA, m166); Takahira to Katsura, December 8, 1905, *NGB*, vol. 38, pt. I, pp. 668–669.

126. Root to Min, December 19, 1905, Notes to the Korean Legation (microfilm, NA, m99).

127. Root to Hioki, December 21, 1905, enclosure in Hioki to Katsura, December 22, 1905, *NGB*, vol. 38, pt. I, pp. 674–675.

128. Allen to Choate, December 18, 1905, Allen papers. See also Allen to Bostwick, December 18, 1905; Wilson to Allen, December 22, 1905, ibid.

129. Allen to Bostwick, February 12, 1906, ibid.

130. Root to Jessup, September 30, 1930, cited in Jessup, *Elihu Root*, vol. 2, p. 62.

131. See Esthus, *Roosevelt and Japan*, p. 110. Esthus argues that the only alternative Roosevelt had was a "nonrecognition" policy, but the Korean alternatives in 1905 were either "protectorate or outright annexation."

132. McKenzie, *Korea's Fight*, p. 101.

133. Bridgham, "American Policy toward Korean Independence," pp. 138–139.

134. See Ro Kwang-hae and Robert T. Smith, "Theodore Roosevelt and the Korean Intervenion Question: An Analysis of a President's Defense," *Koreana Quarterly* 11 (1969): 88–89.

135. Roosevelt to Spring Rice, June 13, 1905, Morison et al., eds., *Letters*, vol. 4, pp. 831–832.

136. Roosevelt to Hull, March 16, 1905, ibid., p. 1141.

137. Deldon to Bostwick, November 22, 1905, Allen papers.

138. See tel., Morgan to Root, October 14, November 17, 18, 1905; Morgan to Root, October 19, November 20, 1905, Despatches, Korea (microfilm, NA, m134 r22).

139. Beale, *Roosevelt*, p. 38; Dulles, *Imperial Years*, p. 267; Dennett, *Roosevelt and the Russo-Japanese War*, p. 4.

140. Dennett, *Roosevelt and the Russo-Japanese War*, p. 308.

CHAPTER 7

1. *Times* (London), July 19, 1910, 6:3.

2. Pierce to Paddock, January 30, 1906; Hasegawa to Paddock, February 3, 1906, Seoul Consular Record (NA, rg84).

3. See the first and the third articles of the November 1905 treaty, enclosure in Hayashi to Pak, November 16, 1905, *KOM*, vol. 7, p. 815; *Kojong sidaesa*, vol. 6, pp. 379–380.

4. Pierce to Paddock, January 30, 1906, Seoul Consular Record (NA, rg84).

5. Wilson to Saionji, March 9, 1906, *NGB*, vol. 39, pt. 2, p. 4.

6. Saionji to Wilson, March 23, 1906, ibid., p. 86. See also Wilson to Root, March 28, 1906, Despatches, Japan, NA.

7. Tel., Hayashi to Aoki, June 9, 1906, *NGB*, vol. 39, pt. 2, p. 112.

8. Sammons to Wright, July 20, 1907, Seoul Consular Record (NA, rg84).

9. Wilson to Sammons, April 22, 1907, ibid.

10. Paddock to Bacon, February 26, 1906. Seoul Consular Despatches (microfilm, NA, m167 r2).

11. Hitaka to Tokudaiji, May 5, 1908, *NGB*, vol. 41, pt. 1, p. 486.

12. Rosen to Root, April 9, 1906, Notes from Russian Legation (microfilm, NA, m39 r12); tel., Chinda to Tsuruhara, April 9, 1906, Japanese Penetration of Korea, 1894–1910, folder no. 246; Chinda to Itō, April 20, 1906, ibid.; tel., Itō to Hayashi, May 19, 1906, *NGB*, vol. 39, pt. 2, p. 427; tel., Hayashi to Itō, June 23, 1906, Japanese Penetration of Korea, 1894–1910, folder no. 250.

13. See Frederick A. McKenzie, *The Tragedy of Korea* (London: Hodder and Stoughton, 1908), pp. 142, 143, 146. See also Conroy, *Japanese Seizure*, p. 340.

14. See Conroy, *Japanese Seizure*, pp. 339, 379.

15. Sammons, "Confidential Notes on the Korean Situation," July 1, 1907, Seoul Consular Record (NA, rg84).

16. Wilson to Sammons, April 22, 1907, ibid.

17. Wright to Root, August 1, 1906, Department of State, Numerical File (NA, rg59); Hayward to Assistant Secretary of State, September 24, 1906, Seoul Consular Record (NA, rg84).

18. Notes from the Japanese Legation, November 9, 1905 (microfilm, NA, m163 49).

19. *New York Times*, July 5, 1906, 1:6.

20. *New York Evening Post*, July 24, 1906, 2:3.

21. *New York Times*, December 7, 1906, 10:2.

22. Okuma Shigenobu, "Japan's Policy in Korea," *Forum* 37 (1906): 571.

23. William T. Ellis, "A Tragedy among the Nations," *Independent* 62 (1907): 959–965.

24. "The Japanese Seizure of Korea," *World Today*, 10 (1906): 78. See also Bryan J. Ingram, "Royal Prisoner of the Far East," *Harper's Weekly* 50 (1906): 1910.

25. For the story of the The Hague mission see Hayashi to Aoki, January 17, 1907, *NGB*, vol. 40, pt. 1, p. 425; Tsuruhara to Chinda, May 9, 1907, ibid., pp. 425–426; tel., Tsuzuki to Hayashi, June 29, 1907, ibid., pp. 428–429; July 2, 1907, ibid., p. 430; July 7, 1907, ibid., pp. 434–436; July 8, 1907, ibid., p. 436; July 9, 1907, ibid., pp. 437–439; July 16, 1907, ibid., pp. 439; September 5, 1907, ibid., p. 447; tel., Itō to Hayashi, July 3, 1907, ibid., pp. 430–431; Sato to Hayashi, July 3, 7, 1907, ibid., pp. 431, 433–436; tel., Hayashi to Itō, July 5, 1907, ibid., p. 443; tel., Hayashi to Tsuzuki, July 10, 1907, ibid., p. 438; tel., Chinda to Hayashi, July 10, 1907, ibid.; *Maech'on yarok*, pp. 210–211.

26. Ye and Chiyi to Roosevelt, August 2, 1907; Loeb to Adee, August 3, 1907, Department of State, Numerical File (NA, rg59).

27. Tsuruhara to Chinda, May 9, 1907, *NGB*, vol. 40, pt. 1, pp. 425–426;

tels., Tsuzuki to Hayashi, July 2, 11, 1907, ibid., pp. 430, 438–439; tel., Aoki to Hayashi, July 22, 24, 1907, ibid., pp. 440–446; Matsuhara to Hayashi, November 15, 1907, ibid., p. 448; *New York Tribune*, July 20, 1907, 1:5, 7:5; Hulbert to Los Angeles Chamber of Commerce, November 9, 1907, enclosure in Flint to Root, November 29, 1907; Root to Flint, December 7, 1907, Department of State, Numerical File (NA, rg59); *New York Times*, July 20, 1967, 2:3–4; July 22, 1907, 2:3–4.

28. Tel., Hayashi to Itō, July 12, 1907, *NGB*, vol. 40, pt. 1, pp. 455–456.

29. Tel., Itō to Chinda, July 19, 1907, *NGB*, vol. 40, pt. 1, pp. 464–466; *Maech'ŏn yarok*, pp. 421–422; *Sokŭmch'ŏngsa*, vol. 2, pp. 211–212; *Kojong sidaesa*, vol. 6, pp. 636–642. *Times* (London), July 19, 5:2; August 12, 1907, 1:3.

30. *Maech'ŏn yarok*, pp. 424–425; *Sokŭmch'ŏngsa*, vol. 2, pp. 213–214; *Kojong sidaesa*, vol. 6, pp. 649–670.

31. Tel., Itō to Chinda, July 28, 1907, *NGB*, vol. 40, pt. 1, pp. 505–506; *Kojong sidaesa*, vol. 6, p. 655.

32. Sammons to Wright, July 16, 19, 20, 25, 1907, Seoul Consular Record (NA, rg84); Sammons to Root, July 19, 1907, Department of State, Numerical File (NA, rg59); Sammons to Dodge, August 28, 1907, Seoul Consular Record (NA, rg84). See also tels., Wright to Root, July 17, 20, 25, 1907, Department of State, Numerical File (NA, rg59).

33. Sammons to Wright, July 16, 1907, Seoul Consular Record (NA, rg84).

34. Sammons to Wright, July 19, 1907, ibid.

35. *New York Times*, July 20, 1907, 6:3; July 25, 1907, 6:3.

36. *New York Tribune*, July 20, 1907, 6:2.

37. Ibid., July 26, 1907, 6:2.

38. *New York Evening Post*, July 25, 1907, 4:1.

39. E. F. Baldwin, "Korea and Japan at the Hague," *Outlook* 87 (1907): 26–28; G. H. Blakeslee, "Korea and Japan," ibid., pp. 503–504; "Justice to Korea," ibid., pp. 237–238; Edwin Maxy, "Example of National Suicide," *Forum* 39 (1907): 281–290.

40. Maurice Low, "Japan Absorbs Korea," *Forum* 39 (1907): 166–170; Samuel MacClintock, "The Passing of Korea," *World Today* 13 (1907): 939–946; We Chong Ye, "A Plea for Korea," *Independent* 63 (1907): 424–426; "The Alleged 'Looting' in Korea," *Review of Reviews* 36 (1907): 502–503.

41. "Civilization Perforce," *Independent* 63 (1907): 577–578. See also "The Abdication of the Emperor of Korea," ibid., pp. 183–184; "The Extinction of Korea," ibid., pp. 230–232; "Japanese Protectorate," *Outlook* 86 (1907): 709–710; "Crisis in Korea, 1907," ibid., pp. 626–627; "Hermit Kingdom virtually Annexed to Japan," *Harper's Weekly* 51 (1907): 1155.

42. *New York Times*, July 20, 1907, 2:3.

43. Tel., Komura to Hayashi, July 20, 1907, *NGB*, vol. 40, pt. 1, p. 475.

44. Tels., Motono to Hayashi, July 22, 1907, ibid., p. 484, 536; tel., Kurino to Hayashi, July 21, 1907, ibid., pp. 477–478.

45. Tels., Inoue Katsunosuke to Hayashi, July 18, 1907, *NGB*, vol. 40, pt. 1, p. 459. See also tels., Inoue to Hayashi, July 20, 21, 22, 27, 31, 1907, ibid., pp. 474, 478–480, 504, 516–519.

46. Tel., Uchida to Hayashi, July 21, 1907, *NGB*, vol. 40, pt. 1, p. 478. For the general reaction of the European countries see also "The Coup d'Etat in Seoul," *Living Age* 254 (1907): 438–440.

47. *Kojong sidaesa*, vol. 6, pp. 716, 758, 945. See Chong-sik Lee, *Politics of Korean Nationalism*, pp. 79–85.

48. Sammons to O'Brien, October 26, 28, 1907; June 26, 1909, Seoul Consular Record (NA, rg84).

49. Tel., Koike to Hayashi, March 23, 1908, *NGB*, vol. 41, pt. 1, p. 818; *Kojong sidaesa*, vol. 6, p. 899. For more information on Stevens see Andrew C. Nahm, "Durham White Stevens and the Japanese Annexation of Korea," in Nahm, ed., *United States and Korea*, pp. 110–136; Kim Wŏn-mo, "Seoulesŏŭi Stevenseŭi ch'inilwaegyohwaltong" (Stevens' pro-Japanese activities in Korea), *Hyangto Seoul* 46 (1988): 59–120; idem, "Chang In-hwanŭi Stevens sasalsakŏn yŏnku" (A study of Chang In-hwan's assassination of Stevens), *Tongyanghak* 18 (October 1988): 273–310.

50. Sammons to O'Brien, October 26, December 6, 1907; Sammons to Assistant Secretary of State, August 1, 1907; "Statement to Consul General at Seoul, Korea, by Korean 'Righteous' or 'Volunteer Army' Leader," n.d., Seoul Consular Record (NA, rg84).

51. Sammons to Carr, January 5, 1908, State Department Application File (NA, rg59); Sammons to Jay, July 17, 1909, Seoul Consular Record (NA, rg84).

52. O'Brien to Sammons, November 13, 1907, Seoul Consular Record (NA, rg84).

53. O'Brien to Gould, November 23, 1909, ibid.

54. Sammons to O'Brien, April 3, June 12, 1908; January 19, February 6, 1909, ibid.; O'Brien to Root, October 25, 1908, State Department, Numerical File (NA, rg59).

55. Governor General, *Annual Report, 1910–1911*, p. 200.

56. Sammons to Chapple, August 3, 1909, Seoul Consular Record (NA, rg84).

57. Itō to Hayashi, September 15, 1906, *NGB*, vol. 39, pt. 2, pp. 177–179; Sammons to Assistant Secretary of State, April 13, 1908; January 9, 1909, Seoul Consular Record (NA, rg84).

58. McKenzie, *Tragedy of Korea*, p. 242.

59. Tel., Kato to Hayashi, January 12, 1906, *NGB*, vol. 39, pt. 2, p. 165; tel., Hayashi to Kato, January 17, 1906, ibid., pp. 165–166; Sammons to Collbran, June 18, 1908, Seoul Consular Record (NA, rg84); tel., O'Brien to Root, June 18, 1908, State Department, Numerical File (NA, rg59).

60. Tel., Root to Wright, January 29, 1907; Root to Wright, May 18, 1907; Adee to Mckenney, June 27, 1907; Bacon to O'Brien, July 16, 1907; tel., Adee to Sammons, September 7, 1907; Adee to O'Brien, September 16, 1907; tel., Root to O'Brien, May 5, 1908; tel., Root to O'Brien, May 20, 1908; O'Brien to Root, June 27, 1908; Adee to Peter A. Jay, August 10, 1908, State Department, Numerical File (NA, rg59).

61. Paddock to Tsuruhara, December 1, 1906; "Forest Regulation (Unsan

District)," August 31, 1908; Sammons to O'Brien, February 4, 1908; Collbran to Sammons, July 14, 1909, enclosure in Sammons to Jay, August 2, 1909, Seoul Consular Record (NA, rg84).

62. Sammons to Messerve, November 18, 1907, ibid.

63. *Times* (London), August 30, 1910, 1:3. See also Wright to Root, June 27, 1907, State Department, Numerical File (NA, rg59).

64. Sammons to Assistant Secretary of State, September 3, 1908; January 9, 1909, Seoul Consular Record (NA, rg84).

65. Ogihara to Somi, June 25, 1909, Japanese Penetration of Korea (microfilm, Hoover, r12, frame 304, pp. 13–14); Sammons to O'Brien, June 8, July 31, 1909, Seoul Consular Record (NA, rg84).

66. Collbran to Sammons, July 14, 1909, enclosure in Sammons to Jay, August 2, 1909, Seoul Consular Record (NA, rg84).

67. Horace N. Allen, speech to Knife and Fork Club, Kansas City, 1910, Allen papers.

68. See *Times* (London), October 28, 1907, 4:1–4; A. H. Blackslee, "Missionary Opportunity in Korea," *Outlook* 87 (1907): 703.

69. Griffis, *Corea, the Hermit Nation*, p. 519.

70. Residency General, *Annual Report* (1908–1909), p. 151; ibid. (1909–1910), p. 153.

71. Wright to Root, June 27, 1907, State Department, Numerical File (NA, rg59); Sammons to Nabeshima, December 11, 1907, Sammons to O'Brien, February 24, 1909, Seoul Consular Record (NA, rg84); *Seoul Press*, July 17, 1909; Sammons to Jay, July 22, 1909, Seoul Consular Record (NA, rg84).

72. Harris to Roosevelt, July 30, 1907; Carr to Harris, September 5, 1907, State Department, Numerical File (NA, rg59); Sammons to O'Brien, February 13, 1909, Seoul Consular Record (NA, rg84).

73. Sammons to Smith, April 3, 1908; Sammons to O'Brien, April 3, 1908, Seoul Consular Record (NA, rg84).

74. Carr to Sammons, May 19, 1908; Wilson to O'Brien, April 8, 1909, State Department, Numerical File (NA, rg59); "Resolution by Methodist Conference," enclosure in Sammons to Jay, July 22, 1909, Seoul Consular Record (NA, rg84).

75. *New York Times*, October 30, 1908, 8:1–2; *New York Evening Post*, July 3, 1908, 4:2.

76. *Outlook* 88 (1908): 275–277, 762–763; 89 (1908): 873–874; 90 (1908): 562–563; 93 (1909): 10–11, 665–669; *Independent* 67 (1909): 1068–1070; *Dial* 45 (1908): 289–291; James S. Gale, "New Places of the Far East," *Outlook* 88 (1908): 275–277; "Claims of Korea," ibid. 88 (1908): 762–763; "Japanese in Korea," ibid. 89 (1908): 873–874; "Japan Establishes Law Court in Korea," ibid. 90 (1908): 562–563; "Control of the Military, Banking, Korea by Japan," ibid. 90 (1909): 10–11; Kennan, "Itō and Korea," ibid., pp. 665–669; William T. Ellis, "An Interview with Prince Itō," *Independent* 67 (1909): 1068–1070; Frederick A. Ogg, "The Tragedy of Korea," *Dial* 45 (1908): 289–291: Thomas F. Millard, "Japanese Immigration into Korea," *Annals of American Academy of Political and Social Science* 34 (1909): 403–409.

77. Itō Hirobumi, "Japanese Policy in Korea," *Harper's Weekly* 52 (1908): 27.

78. Chung, ed., *Korean Treaties*, pp. 225–226; *Kojong sidaesa*, vol. 6, pp. 113–115; *Sokŭmch'ŏngsa*, vol. 2, pp. 331–334.

79. Address to the Congress, December 6, 1910, Taft papers.

80. O'Brien to Scidmore, August 24, 1910, Seoul Consular Record (NA, rg84).

81. O'Brien to Komura, September 20, 1910; Komura to O'Brien, October 6, 1910, *NGB*, vol. 43, pt. 1, pp. 708–714.

82. Tel., Komura to Takaski, July 6, 1910, ibid., pp. 662–664; Greaty to MacDonald, July 14, August 25, 1910, Gooch and Temperley, eds., *British Documents*, vol. 8, pp. 489–490, 500–501; tel., Kurino to Komura, November 5, 1910, *NGB*, vol. 43, pt. 1, pp. 714–715; *Times* (London), August 25, 1910, 3:1–2.

83. MacDonald to Greaty, October 10, 1910, Gooch and Temperley, eds., *British Documents*, vol. 8, pp. 501–502; *Times* (London), August 25, 1910, 3:1–2; August 29, 1910, 5:4–5; tel., Kurino to Komura, November 5, 1910, *NGB*, vol. 43, pt. 1, pp. 714–715; tel., Chinda to Komura, August 24, 1910, ibid., pp. 695–696; tel., Hayashi to Komura, October 5, 1910, ibid., pp. 718–719; *Times* (London), August 25, 1910, 3:1–2.

84. *Boston Daily Globe*, August 26, 1910, 10:1, *Washington Evening Star*, August 30, 1910, 6:1.

85. *New York Evening Post*, August 18, 1910, 6:4–5; *New York Times*, August 26, 1910, 8:1–2; *San Francisco Chronicle*, August 23, 1910, 6:3.

86. William E. Griffis, "Japan's Absorption of Korea," *North American Review* 192 (1920): 516–526; Arthur J. Brown, "The Japanese in Korea," *Outlook* 96 (1910): 591–595; James S. Gale, "Unconscious Korea," *Outlook* 96 (1910): 494–467.

87. Brown, "Japanese in Korea," p. 591.

88. For a recent author's view see Ro, "Power Politics in Korea," pp. 191–192.

89. *Times* (London), October 11, 1910, 5:1. For recent authors' views see Hishida, *Japan*, pp. 169–170; Conroy, *Japanese Seizure*, pp. 377, 388; Ro, "Power Politics in Korea," p. 190.

90. *New York Times*, July 22, 1907, 7:1–2.

BIBLIOGRAPHY

PRIMARY SOURCES

Manuscript and Archival Collections

Allen, Horace N. Papers. New York Public Library. New York City.

Ch'ŏng'kuk mundap (Conversation with the Chinese). Seoul National University Library. Seoul.

Cleveland, Grover. Papers. Library of Congress. Washington, D.C.

Gresham, Walter G. Papers. Library of Congress. Washington, D.C.

Hay, John. Papers. Library of Congress. Washington, D.C.

Japan, Foreign Ministry Archives. Microfilm. Library of Congress. Washington, D.C.

Japanese Penetration of Korea, 1894–1910. Microfilm. Japanese Archives. Hoover Institution. Stanford, Calif.

Kennan, George. Papers. Library of Congress. Washington, D.C.

Pak Chŏng-yang. Haesang ilkich'o (Voyage diary). Seoul National University Library. Seoul.

Rockhill, William W. Papers. Houghton Library. Harvard University. Cambridge, Mass.

Roosevelt, Theodore. Papers. Houghton Library. Harvard University. Cambridge, Mass.

————. Papers. Library of Congress. Washington, D.C.

Root, Elihu. Papers. Library of Congress. Washington, D.C.

Shufeldt, Robert W. Papers. U.S. Navy Department Archives. National Archives. Washington, D.C.

Sill, John M. B. Papers. Michigan Historical Collections. The University of Michigan. Ann Arbor, Mich.

Taft, William H. Papers. Library of Congress. Washington, D.C.

U.S. Department of State Archives. Microfilm. National Archives. Washington, D.C.

Published Documents

British and Foreign State Papers. Vols. 86–99. London: His Majesty's Stationery Office, 1899–1910.

Carnegie Endowment for International Peace, ed. Korea, Treaties and Agreements. Washington: Carnegie Endowment for International Press, 1921.

Chung (Chŏng), Henry, ed. Korean Treaties. New York: Nicholas, 1919.

Dugdale, E. T. S., ed. and trans. German Diplomatic Documents, 1871–1914. 4 vols. London: Methuen, 1928–1931.

Gooch, George P., and Harold Temperley, eds. British Documents on the

Origin of the War, 1898-1914. 10 vols. London: His Majesty's Stationery Office, 1926-1936.

Ilsŏngnok (Daily records of the office of royal historians). Seoul: Kochŏn kanhaenghoe, Seoul National University, 1967-1972.

Itō Hirobumi, ed. *Chōsen kaiko siryo* (Documents on Korean diplomatic history). 3 vols. Tokyo: Hisho ruisan kankokai, 1936.

Kojong sidaesa (A history of the Kojong era). 6 vols. Seoul: Kuksa p'yŏnch'an wiwŏnhoe, 1970-1972.

Kojong silnok (The records of Kojong). Tokyo: Haksupwŏntaehak tongyang munhwa yŏn'guso, 1967.

Kojong-Sunjong silnok (The annals of Kojong and Sunjong). 4 vols. Seoul: T'amkutang, 1970-1977.

Koryŏ taehakkyo asea munche yŏn'guso, ed. *Kuhan'guk oekyomunsŏ* (Diplomatic documents of old Korea). 22 vols. Seoul: Koryo taehakkyo ch'ulp'anpu, 1965-1973.

Krasnyi Archiv (Red Archives). Vols. 2, 50-52. Moskba, Gosporitijdat, 1923, 1932. Translation: *The Chinese Social and Political Science Review* 17 (1933-1934): 80-515, 632-670; 18 (1934-1935): 572-594; 19 (1935-1936): 125-145, 234-267.

Ministère des Affaires Étrangères. *Documents Diplomatique Français, 1871-1911.* Paris: Imprimerie Nationale, 1930-1959.

Nihon gaiko bunsho (Japanese diplomatic documents). Vols. 13, 27-28. Tokyo: Kokusai rengyokai, 1950-1958.

Pipyŏnsa tamnok (The records of Pipyŏnsa). Seoul: Kuksa p'yŏnch'an wiwŏnhoe, 1959-1960.

Richardson, James D., ed. *A Compilation of the Messages and Papers of the Presidents.* Vols. 11-16. New York: Bureau of National Literature, 1897-1917.

Rockhill, William W., ed. *Treaties and Conventions with or Concerning China and Korea, 1894-1904, together with Various State Papers and Documents Affecting Foreign Interests.* Washington: Government Printing Office, 1904.

Sŭngjŏn'gwŏn ilki, Kojongp'yŏn (The diary of Sŭn'gjŏngwŏn, Kojong section). 15 vols. Seoul: Kuksa p'yŏnch'an wiwŏnhoe, 1967-1968.

Tonghakran kirok (The records of the tonghak rebellion), 2 pts. Han'guk saryo ch'ongsŏ, vol. 10. Seoul: Kuksa p'yŏnch'an wiwŏnhoe, 1959.

Tongmun ŭkio (Selected diplomatic documents, 1650-1811). 4 vols. Seoul: Kuksa p'yŏnch'an wiwŏnhoe, 1978.

U.S. Congress. House. *Extension of American Commerce: Proposed Mission to Japan and Korea.* H. Exec. Doc. 138, 28th Cong., 2nd sess., 1845.

U.S. Congress. Senate. *Senate Executive Documents.* S. Exec. Doc. 34, 33rd Cong., 2nd sess., 1855.

U.S. Department of State. *Commercial Relations of the United States,* 1895/1896-1902. Washington: Government Printing Office, 1897-1903.

———. [Department of Commerce and Labor from vol. 72]. *Consular Reports.* Vols. 54-77. Washington, D.C.: Government Printing Office, 1894-1905.

———. *Papers Relating to the Foreign Relations of the United States*, 1871–1906. Washington: Government Printing Office, 1872–1909.

U.S. Statutes at Large. Vols. 8, 11, 12, 23. Washington: Government Printing Office, 1844, 1857, 1863, 1885.

U.S. Treasury Department [Department of Commerce and Labor from 1904]. *The Foreign Commerce and Navigation of the United States*, 1894–1905. Washington: Government Printing Office, 1895–1906.

Memoirs, Letters, Diaries, and Speeches

Jongjŏng yŏnp'yo-Ŭmch'ŏngsa (Diary of Ŏ Yun-chung and Kim Yun-sik). Han'guk saryo ch'ongsŏ, vol. 6. Seoul: Kuksa p'yŏngchan wiwŏnhoe, 1958.

McKinley, William E. *Speeches and Addresses of William McKinley.* New York: Doubleday and McClure, 1900.

Maech'ŏn yarok (Unofficial record of Maechŏn). Han'guk saryo ch'ongsŏ, vol. 1. Seoul: Kuksa p'yŏnch'an wiwŏnhoe, 1956.

Meyendorf, A., ed. *Correspondence Diplomatique de M. Staal.* 2 vols. Paris: Rivere, 1929.

Morison, Elting E., et al., eds. *The Letters of Theodore Roosevelt.* 8 vols. Cambridge: Harvard University Press, 1951–1954.

Mutsu Munemitsu. *Hakushaku Mutsu Munemitsu iko* (Posthumous manuscripts of Count Mutsu Munemitsu). Tokyo: Iwanami, 1929.

Nevins, Allan, ed. *Letters of Grover Cleveland.* Boston: Houghton Mifflin, 1933.

Roosevelt, Theodore, *An Autobiography.* New York: Macmillan, 1913.

Rosen, Roman R. *Forty Years of Diplomacy.* 2 vols. New York: Knopf, 1922.

Sands, William F. *Undiplomatic Memoirs.* New York: McGraw-Hill, 1930.

Sokŭmch'ŏngsa (The diary of Kim Yun-sik, continuation). Han'guk saryo ch'ongsŏ, vol. 2. Seoul: Kuksa p'yŏnch'an wiwŏnhoe, 1960.

Swartout, Robert R., Jr., ed. *An American Advisor in Late Yi Korea: The Letters of Owen Nickerson Denny.* University, Ala.: University of Alabama Press, 1984.

Ŭmch'ŏngsa. See *Jongjŏng yŏnp'yo-Ŭmch'ongsa.*

Yarmolinsky, Abraham, ed. *The Memoirs of Count Witt.* Garden City, N.Y.: Doubleday and Page, 1921.

Yun Ch'i-ho. *Yun Ch'i-ho ilki* (The diary of Yun Ch'i-ho). Trans. Song p'yŏng-ki. 2 vols. Seoul: T'amkudang, 1975.

Yun Ch'iho's Diary 1890–1906. Vols. 2–6. Seoul: National History Compilation Committee, 1974–1976.

Newspapers and Periodicals

Independent, 1897–1899. Seoul.

Korean Repository. 5 vols. Seoul: Triangle Press, 1892, 1895–1898.

Korean Review. 6 vols. Seoul: Methodist Publishing House, 1901–1906.

SECONDARY SOURCES

Books

Akagi, Hidemichi. *Japan's Foreign Relations, 1542-1936: A Short History.* Tokyo: Hokuseido, 1936.

Allen, Horace N. *Korea: Facts and Fancy.* Seoul: Methodist Publishing House, 1904.

————. *Things Korean: A Collection of Sketches Missionary and Diplomatic.* New York: Revell, 1908.

Almond, Gabriel A. *The American People and Foreign Policy.* New York: Harcourt Brace, 1950.

Asakawa, Kanichi. *The Russo-Japanese Conflict: Its Causes and Issues.* Boston: Houghton Mifflin, 1908.

Battistini, Lawrence H. *The United States and Asia.* New York: Praeger, 1955.

Beale, Howard K. *Theodore Roosevelt and the Rise of America to World Power.* Baltimore, Md: The Johns Hopkins University Press, 1956.

Beasley, W. G. *The Modern History of Japan.* New York: Praeger, 1963.

Bemis, Samuel F., ed. *The American Secretaries of State and Their Diplomacy.* Vols. 7-9. New York: Pageant, 1958.

Bishop, Isabella L. *Korea and Her Neighbors: A Narrative of Travel with an Account of the Recent Vicissitudes and Present Conditions of the Country.* 2 vols. London: Murray, 1905.

Braistead, William R. *The United States Navy in the Pacific, 1909-1922.* Austin, Tex.: University of Texas Press, 1971.

Brown, Arthur J. *The Foreign Missionary: An Incarnation of a World Movement.* 2 vols. London: Murray, 1905.

————. *The Mastery of the Far East: The Story of Korea's Transformation and Japan's Supremacy in the Orient.* New York: Scribner's Sons, 1919.

Burton, Theodore E. *John Sherman.* Boston: Houghton Mifflin, 1904.

Cable, E. M. *United States-Korean Relations 1866-1871.* Seoul: Young Men's Christian Association Press, 1937.

Campbell, Charles S. *Special Business Interests and the Open Door Policy.* New Haven, Conn.: Yale University Press, 1951.

Challener, Richard D. *Admirals, Generals, and American Foreign Policy 1898-1914.* Princeton, N.J.: Princeton University Press, 1973.

Chang, Chung-fu. *The Anglo-Japanese Alliance.* Baltimore, Md.: The Johns Hopkins University Press, 1931.

Chien, Frederick Foo. *The Opening of Korea: A Study of Chinese Diplomacy 1876-1885.* New York: Shoe String, 1967.

Ch'oe Ching Young (Ch'oe Ch'ing-yong). *The Roles of the Taewŏn'gun, 1864-1873: Restoration in Yi Korea.* Harvard East Asian Monographs 45. Cambridge: Harvard East Asian Research Center, Harvard University, 1972.

Chung, Henry. *The Case of Korea.* New York: Revell, 1921.

————. *The Oriental Policy of the United States.* New York: Revell, 1919.

Clark, Allen DeGray. *Avison of Korea: The Life of Oliver R. Avison, M. D.* Seoul: Yonsei University Press, 1979.

Conroy, F. Hilary. *The Japanese Seizure of Korea, 1868-1910: A Study of Realism in International Relations.* Philadelphia: University of Pennsylvania Press, 1960.

Cook, Harold F. *Korea's 1884 Incident: Its Background and Kim Ok-kyun's Elusive Dream.* Seoul: Royal Asiatic Society, Korea Branch, 1972.

———. *Pioneer American Businessman in Korea: The Life and Times of Walter Davis Townsend.* Seoul: Royal Asiatic Society, Korea Branch, 1981.

Croly, Herbert D. *Willard Straight.* New York: Macmillan, 1925.

Curzon, George N. *Problems of the Far East: Japan-Korea-China.* London: Longmans, Green, 1896.

Dawes, Charles G. *A Journal of the McKinley Years.* Chicago: Donnelly (Lakeside) Press, 1950.

Dennett, Tyler. *Americans in Eastern Asia: A Critical Study of the Policy of the United States with Reference to China, Japan and Korea in the Nineteenth Century.* New York: Macmillan, 1922.

———. *John Hay: From Poetry to Politics.* New York: Dodd and Mead, 1934.

———. *Roosevelt and the Russo-Japanese War.* New York: Doubleday, 1925.

Dennis, Alfred L. P. *Adventure in American Foreign Policy, 1896-1906.* New York: Dutton, 1928.

Deuchler, Martina. *Confucian Gentlemen and Barbarian Envoys: The Opening of Korea, 1875-1885.* Seattle, Wash.: University of Washington Press. 1977.

Drake, Frederick. *The Empire of the Seas: A Biography of Rear Admiral Robert Wilson Shufeldt, USN.* Honolulu: University of Hawaii Press, 1984.

Dulebohn, George R. *Principles of Foreign Policy under the Cleveland Administration.* Philadelphia: University of Pennsylvania Press, 1941.

Dulles, Foster R. *America's Rise to World Power, 1898-1954.* The New American Nation Series. New York: Harper and Brothers, 1955.

———. *The Imperial Years.* New York: Crowell, 1956.

Esthus, Raymond A. *Theodore Roosevelt and Japan.* Seattle, Wash.: University of Washington Press, 1967.

Faulkner, Harold U. *The Decline of Laissez-Faire, 1897-1917.* The Economic History of the United States. Vol. 7. New York: Holt, Rinehart and Winston. 1951.

Foster, John W. *The Relation of Diplomacy to Foreign Mission.* Sewanee, Tenn.: University of Tennessee Press, 1906.

Gale, James S. *Korea in Transition.* New York: Eaton and Mains, 1909.

Gelber, Lionel L. *Rise of Anglo-American Friendship: A Study in World Politics, 1898-1906.* London: Oxford University Press, 1938.

Glad, Paul W. *McKinley, Bryan, and People.* New York: Lippincott, 1964.

Gresham, Matilda M. *Life of Walter Quintin Gresham, 1832-1895.* 2 vols. Chicago: Rand McNally, 1919.

Griffis, William E. *Corea, the Hermit Nation.* 7th ed. London: Harper and Brothers, 1904.

Griswold, A. Whitney. *The Far Eastern Policy of the United States.* New Haven, Conn.: Yale University Press, 1938.

Hagan, Kenneth. *American Gunboat Diplomacy and the Old Navy, 1877–89.* Greenwood, Conn.: Greenwood Press, 1973.

Hagedorn, Herman, ed. *The Works of Theodore Roosevelt.* Vols. 17–18, 20–21. New York: Scribner's Sons, 1925.

Han'guk chŏngsinmunhwa yŏn'guwŏn and The Wilson Center, eds. *Reflections on a Century of Korean–United States Relations.* Seoul: Han'guk chŏngsinmunhwa yŏn'guwŏn, 1983.

Harbaugh, William H. *Power and Responsibility: The Life and Times of Theodore Roosevelt.* New York: Farrar, Straus and Cudahy, 1961.

Harrington, Fred Harvey. *God, Mammon and the Japanese: Dr. Horace N. Allen and Korean-American Relations, 1884–1905.* Madison, Wisc.: University of Wisconsin Press, 1944.

Hishida, Seiji. *Japan among the Great Powers: a Survey of Her International Relations.* London: Longmans, 1940.

Hulbert, Homer B. *The Passing of Korea.* New York: Doubleday and Page, 1906.

Hunt, Michael H. *The Making of a Special Relationship: The United States and China to 1914.* New York: Columbia University Press, 1983.

Iriye, Akira. *Pacific Estrangement: Japanese and American Expansion, 1897–1911.* Harvard Studies in American–East Asian Relations 2. Cambridge: Harvard University Press, 1972.

Jessup, Philip C. *Elihu Root.* 2 vols. New York: Dodd and Mead, 1938.

Johnson, Robert Erwin. *Far China Station: The United States Navy in China Waters 1800–1898.* Annapolis, Md.: Naval Institute Press, 1979.

———. *Rear Admiral Rogers, 1812–1882.* Annapolis, Md.: Naval Institute Press, 1967.

Kaneko Kentaro, et al. *Itō Hirobumi den* [Itō Hirobumi: A biography]. 3 vols. Tokyo: Toseisha, 1942.

Kaplan, Morton A. *System and Process in International Politics.* New York: John Wiley and Sons, 1957.

Kelman, Herbert C., ed. *International Behavior: A Social and Psychological Analysis.* New York: Holt, Rinehart and Winston, 1966.

Kersten, Peter. *Naval Aristocracy: The Golden Age of Annapolis and the Emergence of Modern American Navalism.* New York: Free Press, 1972.

Kim, C. I. Eugene (Kim Ch'ong-ik), and Han-kyo Kim. *Korea and the Politics of Imperialism 1876–1910.* Berkeley and Los Angeles: University of California Press, 1967.

Kim, Key-hiuk (Kim Ky-hyŏk). *The Last Phase of the East Asian World Order: Korea, Japan, and the Chinese Empire, 1860–1882.* Berkeley and Los Angeles: University of California Press, 1980.

Kim, Kiusic (Kyu-sik). *The Far Eastern Situation.* n. p. 1933.

Kim Ok-kyun. *Kapsin ilki* [Kapsin diary]. Seoul: T'amkutang, 1975.

Kim Wŏn-mo. *Han-Mi sukyo paeknyŏnsa* (One-hundred-year history of Korean-American relations). KBS TV Open University Series, 8. Seoul: Han'guk bangsong saŏptan, 1982.

————. *Kŭndae Han-Mi kyosŏpsa* (The modern history of Korean–United States relations). Seoul: Hongsŏngsa, 1979.

Kirkland, Edward C. *Industry Comes of Age: Business, Labor, and Public Policy, 1860-1897.* The Economic History of the United States. Vol. 6. New York: Holt, Rinehart and Winston, 1961.

Koo, Youngnok (Ku Yŏng-nok), and Dae-sook Suh (Sŏh Dae-suk), eds. *Korea and the United States: A Century of Cooperation.* Honolulu: University of Hawaii Press, 1984.

Ku Yŏng-nok, et al. *Han'gukkwa Mikuk: kwakŏ, hyŏnchae, mirae* (Korea and the United States: the past, the present and the future). Seoul: Pakyŏngsa, 1983.

Ladd, George T. *In Korea with Marquis Itō.* London: Longmans, Green, 1908.

Langer, William L. *The Diplomacy of Imperialism, 1890-1902.* 2 vols. New York: Knopf, 1935.

Latourette, Kenneth S. *The Century in North Africa and Asia, A.D. 1800–A.D. 1914.* A History of the Expansion of Christianity. Vol. 6. New York: Harper and Brothers, 1944.

Lee, Chong-sik (Yi Ch'ŏng-sik). *The Politics of Korean Nationalism.* Berkeley and Los Angeles: University of California Press, 1963.

Lee, Yur-Bok (Yi Yur-bok). *Diplomatic Relations between the United States and Korea, 1866-1887.* New York: Humanities Press, 1970.

————. *Establishment of a Korean Legation in the United States, 1887-1890: A Study of Conflict between Confucian World Order and Modern International Relations.* Illinois Papers in Asian Studies, vol. 3, Urbana, Ill.: University of Illinois Center for Asian Studies, 1983.

————, and Wayne Patterson, eds. *One Hundred Years of Korean-American Relations 1882-1982.* University, Ala.: University of Alabama Press, 1986.

Leech, Margaret, *In the Days of McKinley.* New York: Harper and Brothers, 1959.

Lensen, George Alexander. *Balance of Intrigue: International Rivalries in Korea and Manchuria 1884-1899.* 2 vols. Tallahassee, Fla.: Florida State University Press, 1982.

Leopold, Richard W. *Elihu Root and the Conservative Tradition.* Boston: Little, Brown, 1954.

Liska, George. *International Equilibrium.* Cambridge: Harvard University Press, 1957.

McCordock, Robert S. *British Far Eastern Policy, 1894-1900.* New York: Columbia University Press, 1931.

McKenzie, Frederick A. *Korea's Fight for Freedom.* New York: Revell, 1920.

McLean, Joseph E. *William Rufus Day, Supreme Court Justice from Ohio.* Johns Hopkins Studies in History and Political Science. Baltimore, Md.: The Johns Hopkins University Press, 1946.

Mahan, Alfred Thayer. *The Influence of Sea Power upon History, 1660–1783.* Boston: Little Brown, 1890.

Maki, John M. *Japanese Imperialism: Its Cause and Cure.* New York: Knopf, 1945.

Malozemoff, Andrew. *Russian Far Eastern Policy, 1881–1904; with Special Emphasis on the Causes of the Russo-Japanese War.* Berkeley and Los Angeles: University of California Press, 1958.

May, Ernest R. *Imperial Diplomacy: The Emergence of Great Powers.* New York: Harcourt, Brace and World, 1961.

Millard, Thomas F. F. *America and the Far Eastern Question.* New York: Moffat, Yard, 1909.

———. *New Far East.* New York: Scribner's Sons, 1906.

———. *Our Eastern Question: American Contact with the Orient and the Trend of Relations with China and Japan.* New York: Century, 1916.

Morgan, H. Wayne. *William McKinley and His America.* Syracuse, N.Y.: Syracuse University Press, 1963.

Morgenthau, Hans J. *Politics among Nations: The Struggle for Power and Peace.* 4th ed. New York: Knopf, 1967.

Morse, Hosea B. *International Relations of the Chinese Empire. 3 vols.* London: Longmans, Green, 1910–1918.

Mott, Frank L. *A History of American Magazines. 6 vols.* Cambridge: Harvard University Press, 1957–1968.

Nahm (Nam), Andrew C., ed. *The United States and Korea: American-Korean Relations, 1866–1976.* Kalamazoo, Mich.: Center for Korean Studies, Western Michigan University, 1979.

Nash, Ian. *The Origins of the Russo-Japanese War.* London: Longman, 1985.

Nelson, Melvin Frederick. *Korea and the Old Order in Eastern Asia.* Baton Rouge, La.: Louisiana University Press, 1945.

Nevins, Allan. *Grover Cleveland: A Study of Courage.* New York: Dodd and Mead, 1932.

Okuhira Takehiko. *Chōsen kaikoku kosho shimatsu* (The process of negotiations for the opening of Korea). Tokyo: Kanae shoin, 1969.

Osgood, Robert E. *Ideals and Self-interest in America's Foreign Relations: The Great Transformation of the Twentieth Century.* Chicago: Chicago University Press, 1953.

Paik, L. George (Paek Nak-chun). *The History of Protestant Missions in Korea, 1832–1910.* P'yŏngyang: Union Christian College Press, 1929.

Pak Il-kŭn. *Kŭndae Han-Mi oekyosa* (The modern diplomatic history of Korea and the United States). Seoul: Pakusa, 1968.

———. *Mikukŭi kaekuk chŏngch'aekkwa Han-Mi oekyo kwanke* (The open-nation policy of the United States and Korean-American relations). Seoul: Ilchokak, 1981.

Palais, James B. *Politics and Policy in Traditional Korea.* Harvard East Asian Studies 82. Cambridge: Harvard University Press, 1975.

Paullin, Charles Oscar. *Diplomatic Negotiations of American Naval Officers 1778–1883.* Baltimore, Md.: The Johns Hopkins University Press, 1912. Reprint. Gloucester, Mass.: Peter Smith, 1967.

Pooley, Andrew, ed. *The Secret Memoirs of Count Tadasu Hayashi.* London: Nash, 1915.

Pringle, Henry F. *Theodore Roosevelt: A Biography.* New York: Harcourt, Brace and World, 1956.

Rhodes, Harry A., ed. *History of Korean Mission, Presbyterian Church, U. S. A., 1884–1934.* Seoul: Chōsen Mission Presbyterian Church, U.S.A., 1934.

Rockhill, William W. *China's Intercourse with Korea from the 15th Century to 1895.* London: Luzac, 1905.

Romanov, Boris A. *Russia in Manchuria, 1892–1906.* Ann Arbor, Mich.: Edwards, 1952.

Rosenau, James N. *National Leadership and Foreign Policy: A Case Study in the Mobilization of Public Support.* Princeton, N.J.: Princeton University Press, 1963.

————. *Public Opinion and Foreign Policy.* New York: Random House, 1961.

Sakamoto Kizan. *Gensui koshaku Yamagata Aritomo* (Prince general of the army Yamagata Aritomo). Tokyo: Siseido, 1922.

Savage-Landor, A. Henry. *Corea or Cho-sen: The Land of Morning Calm.* New York: Macmillan, 1895.

Schley, Winfield S. *Forty-five Years Under the Flag.* New York: Appleton, 1904.

Smith, Frederick E., and N. W. Sibley. *International Law as Interpreted during the Russo-Japanese War.* London: Unwin, 1905.

Sŏ Chung-sŏk. *Kŭktong kukche chŏngch'isa* (A history of international politics in the Far East), vol. 1. Seoul: Sinasa, 1960.

Swartout, Robert R., Jr. *Mandarins, Gunboats, and Power Politics: Owen Nickerson Denny and the International Rivalries in Korea.* Asian Studies at Hawaii, no. 25. Honolulu: University of Hawaii Press, 1980.

Tabohasi Kiyosi. *Kindai Nissen kankei no kenkyu* (A study of modern Japanese-Korean relations). 2 vols. Seoul: Chōsen shotokufu chushuin, 1940.

Tanin, O., and E. Yohan. *Militarism and Fascism in Japan.* London: Martin Lawrence, 1934. Reprint. Westport, Conn.: Greenwood, 1975.

Tansill, Charles C. *The Foreign Policy of Thomas F. Bayard.* New York: Fordham University Press, 1940.

Thayer, William R. *The Life and Letters of John Hay.* 2 vols. Boston: Houghton Mifflin, 1908.

Treat, Payson J. *Diplomatic Relations between the United States and Japan, 1895–1905.* Stanford, Calif.: Stanford University Press, 1939.

Underwood, Lillias H. *Fifteen Years among the Top-Knots.* Boston: American Tract, 1904.

————. *Underwood of Korea.* New York: Revell, 1918.

Varg, Paul A. *The Open Door Diplomat: The Life of W. W. Rockhill.* Illinois Studies in the Social Sciences, vol. 33. Urbana, Ill.: University of Illinois Press, 1952.

Weems, Clarence N., Jr., ed. *Hulbert's History of Korea.* 2 vols. New York: Hilary House, 1962.

Williams, Jesse L. *Mr. Cleveland: A Personal Impression.* New York: Dodd and Mead, 1909.

White, John Albert. *The Diplomacy of the Russo-Japan War.* Princeton, N.J.: Princeton University Press, 1964.

Yakontoff, Victor A. *Russia and the Soviet Union in the Far East.* New York: Coward-McCann, 1931.

Yanaga, Chitoshi, *Japan since Perry.* Westport, Conn.: Greenwood, 1949.

Yi Ki-paek. *Han'guksa sinron* (A new history of Korea). Rev. ed. Seoul: Ilchokak, 1983.

Yi Kwang-nin. *Han'guk kaehwasa yŏn'gu* (A study of the history of enlightenment in Korea). Seoul: Ilchokak, 1969.

Yi Sŏn-kŭn. *Han'guksa: ch'oekŭnsep'yŏn* (Korean history: most recent period). Seoul: Ŭlyu munhwasa, 1961.

Zabriskie, Edward H. *American-Russian Rivalry in the Far East.* Philadelphia: University of Pennsylvania Press, 1946.

Articles

Almond, Gabriel. "Public Opinion and National Security." *Public Opinion Quarterly* 20 (1956): 371–378.

Chay, John (Ch'oe Chong-sŏk). "The American Image of Korea to 1945." In *Korea and the United States: A Century of Cooperation,* edited by Youngnok Koo and Dae-sook Suh. Honolulu: University of Hawaii Press, 1984.

———. "The Dynamics of American-Korean Relations and Prospects for the Future." In *Problems and Prospects of American-East Asian Relations,* edited by John Chay. Boulder, Colo.: Westview Press, 1977.

———. "The First Three Decades of American-Korean Relations, 1882–1910: Reassessments and Reflections." In *U. S.-Korean Relations 1882–1982,* edited by Tae-hwan Kwak, et al. Seoul: Institute for Far Eastern Studies, Kyongnam University, 1982.

———. "Taft-Katsura Memorandum Reconsidered." *Pacific Historical Review* 37 (1968): 321–326.

Dennett, Tyler. "American Choice in the Far East in 1882." *American Historical Review* 30 (1924): 84–108.

———. "American 'Good Offices' in Asia." *American Journal of International Law* 16 (1922): 1–24.

———. "Early American Policy in Korea, 1883–1887: The Services of Lieutenant George C. Foulk." *Political Science Quarterly* 38 (1923): 82–103.

———. "President Roosevelt's Secret Pact with Japan." *Current History* 21 (1924): 15–21.

Deutsch, Karl W., and Richard L. Merritt. "Effects of Events on National and International Image." In *International Behavior: A Social and Psychological Analysis,* edited by Herbert C. Kelman. New York: Holt, Rinehart and Winston, 1951.

Esthus, Raymond A. "The Taft-Katsura Agreement—Reality or Myth?" *Journal of Modern History* 31 (1959): 46–51.

Gale, James S. "New Places of the Far East." *Outlook* 88 (1908): 275–277.

Heard, Augustine, et al. "China and Japan in Korea." *North American Review* 159 (1894): 307–308.

Hisa, Michitaro. "The Significance of the Japanese-China War." *Forum* 17 (1894): 316–327.

Kennan, George. "The Capital of Korea." *Outlook* 78 (1904): 464–472.

———. "Japanese in Korea." *Outlook* 81 (1905): 609–619.

———. "Korea: A Degenerate State." *Outlook* 81 (1905): 307–315.

———. "The Korean People: The Product of Decayed Civilization." *Outlook* 81 (1905): 407–416.

———. "The Land of the Morning Calm." *Outlook* 78 (1904): 363–369.

———. "Prince Itō and Korea." *Outlook* 93 (1909): 665–669.

———. "What Japan Has Done in Korea." *Outlook* 81 (1905): 669–673.

Lazarsfeld, Paul F. "Public Opinion and the Classical Tradition." *Public Opinion Quarterly* 21 (1957): 39–53.

Martin, Howard. "China and Japan in Korea." *North American Review* 19 (1894): 316–320.

Minger, Ralph E. "Taft's Mission to Japan: A Study in Personal Diplomacy." *Pacific Historical Review*, 30 (1961): 279–294.

———. "The Korean Mission to the United States in 1883." *Transactions of the Korean Branch of the Royal Asiatic Society* 18 (1929): 1–21.

Nevins, Allan. "United States and Sino-Korean Relations, 1885–1887." *Pacific Historical Review* 2 (1933): 292–304.

Norman, Henry. "The Question of Korea." *Contemporary Review* 66 (1894): 305–317.

Pak Kwŏn-sang. "Hankukŭi Mikuk insik" (The Korean perception of the United States). In *Reflections on a Century of Korean-United States Relations*, edited by Han'guk chŏngsinmunhwa yŏn'guwŏn and the Wilson Center, pp. 283–302. Seoul: Han'guk chŏngsinmunhwa yŏn'guwŏn, 1983.

Pollard, Robert T. "American Relations with Korea, 1882–1895." *Chinese Social and Political Science Review* 16 (1932): 435–471.

Rhodes, Henry F., and Robert T. Smith. "Theodore Roosevelt and the Korean Intervention Question: An Analysis of a President's Defense." *Koreana Quarterly* 11 (1969): 84–92.

Sands, William F. "Korea and Her Emperor." *Century Magazine* 47 (1905): 577–584.

Scott, James B. "The Government of the United States and American Missionaries." *American Journal of International Law* 6 (1911): 70–85.

Scott, William A. "Psychological and Social Correlates of International Image." In *International Behavior: A Social and Psychological Analysis*, edited by Herbert C. Kelman. New York: Holt, Rinehart and Winston, 1951.

Swartout, Robert R., Jr. "Cultural Conflict and Gunboat Diplomacy: The Development of the 1871 Korean-American Incident." *Journal of Social Sciences and Humanities* 43 (June 1976): 117–169.

———. "United States Ministers to Korea 1882–1905: The Loss of American Innocence." *Transactions of the Royal Asiatic Society* 57 (1982): 29–40.

Tsiang, T. F. "Sino-Japanese Diplomatic Relations, 1870–1894." *Chinese Social and Political Science Review* 17 (1933): 1–106.

Wright, Mary C. "The Adaptation of Ch'ing Diplomacy: The Case of Korea." *Journal of Asian Studies* 17 (1958): 373–381.

Yi Hyŏn-chong. "Kuhanmal Sŏkue chongkyoŭi p'okyo sanghang" (Distribution of the Christian churches in Korea at the end of the Yi Dynasty). *Idae sawŏn* 9 (1970): 18–49.

Unpublished Materials

Bridgham, Philip L. "American Policy toward Korean Independence, 1866–1910." Ph.D. diss., Fletcher School of Law and Diplomacy, 1951.

Jones, Frances A. "Foreign Diplomacy in Korea." Ph.D. diss., Harvard University, 1935.

Kim, Han-kyo. "The Demise of Korea, 1882–1910." Ph.D. diss., University of Chicago, 1962.

Noble, Harold J. "Korea and Her Relations with the United States before 1896." Ph.D. diss., Harvard University, 1931.

Reordan, Robert E. "The Role of George Clayton Foulk in United States–Korean Relations, 1884–1887." Ph.D. diss., Fordham University, 1959.

Ro, Kwang Hai (Ro Kwang-hae). "Power Politics in Korea and Its Impact on Korean Foreign and Domestic Affairs, 1882–1907." Ph.D. diss., University of Oklahoma, 1966.

Weems, Clarence N., Jr., "Japan's Acquisition of Korea, from the Annexation of Korea by Japan." M.A. thesis, Vanderbilt University, 1933.

———. "The Korean Reform and Independence Movement, 1881–1898." Ph.D. diss., University of California, Berkeley, 1954.

Yoo, Hong Sup (Yu Hong-sŏp). "Korea in International Far Eastern Relations." Ph.D. diss., American University, 1935.

INDEX

ABOUT THE AUTHOR

Jongsuk Chay received his doctorate in history from the University of Michigan, where he specialized in American diplomatic history. He has published a number of articles on Korean-American relations and is editor or coeditor of several books, including *The Problems and Prospects of American–East Asian Relations, U.S.–Korean Relations, 1881–1982,* and *Culture and International Relations.* He is currently professor of history at Pembroke State University.

STUDIES FROM
THE CENTER FOR
KOREAN STUDIES

Studies on Korea: A Scholar's Guide, edited by Han-Kyo Kim. 1980

Korean Communism, 1945–1980: A Reference Guide to the Political System, by Dae-Sook Suh. 1981

Korea and the United States: A Century of Cooperation, edited by Youngnok Koo and Dae-Sook Suh. 1984

The Reluctant Crusade: American Foreign Policy in Korea, 1941–1950, by James I. Matray. 1985

The Korean Frontier in America: Immigration to Hawaii, 1896–1910, by Wayne Patterson. 1988

Korean-American Relations: Documents Pertaining to the Far Eastern Diplomacy of the United States. Volume III. *The Period of Diminishing Influence, 1896–1905,* edited and with an introduction by Scott S. Burnett. 1989

Diplomacy of Asymmetry: Korean-American Relations to 1910, by Jongsuk Chay. 1990.

Production Notes

This book was designed by Roger Eggers. Composition and paging were done on the Quadex Composing System and typesetting on the Compugraphic 8400 by the design and production staff of University of Hawaii Press.

The text typeface is Trump and the display typeface is Gill Sans.

Offset presswork and binding were done by Vail-Ballou Press, Inc. Text paper is Writers RR Offset, basis 50.